ALL THE TALES FROM THE ARK

'Why should God choose to speak to Noah about important matters like building an ark and saving the animals?' said Mrs Noah. 'He's a good man, but he's not all that special. His carpentry's a nightmare and as for the animals… he runs a mile at the sight of a spider.'

The story of Noah, who built an ark to save all the animals, insects and birds from a great flood, is very well known. But have you ever wondered what happened next? Here are forty funny, imaginative and original stories telling what *might* have happened on board Noah's ark.

AVRIL ROWLANDS is the author of many books for children. When she is not writing, her hobbies include swimming, walking, theatre and steam railways.

Also by Avril Rowlands

The Animals' Christmas

The Animals' Easter

The Christmas Sheep and Other Stories

Animals to the Rescue

All the Tales
from the
ARK

Avril Rowlands
Illustrations by Rosslyn Moran

LION
Children's Books

Text copyright © 1993, 1995 and 1999 Avril Rowlands
Illustrations copyright © 1993, 1995 and 1999 Rosslyn Moran
This edition copyright © 2003 Lion Publishing

The moral rights of the author and illustrator
have been asserted

Published by
Lion Publishing plc
Mayfield House, 256 Banbury Road
Oxford OX2 7DH, England
www.lion-publishing.co.uk
ISBN 0 7459 4835 9

First published as individual volumes:
Tales from the Ark (1993)
More Tales from the Ark (1995)
The Rainbow's End & Other Tales from the Ark (1999)

First edition 2003
10 9 8 7 6 5 4 3 2 1 0

A catalogue record for this book is available
from the British Library

Typeset in 11.5/15 Zapf Calligraphic BT
Printed and bound in Great Britain
by Cox & Wyman Ltd, Reading

CONTENTS

All the Tales from the Ark is dedicated
to the memory of my dear friend, Leslie Guest,
for all his love, encouragement and support.

FOREWORD

I wrote the adventures in this book because
the familiar Bible story of the flood sparked
my imagination. I wondered what it might
have been like for all the people and animals
living together on the ark and, especially, how
Noah himself would have coped with life on
the ark.

You will find different approaches in the
stories because when I wrote the first book
I had no idea that a second and third book
would follow. I was surprised to discover that
in many ways the animals, insects and birds
who travelled with Noah and his family are
just like you and me!

I hope you enjoy this bumper book.

Avril Rowlands

Tales from the Ark

CONTENTS

1

NOAH'S TALE

Mr Noah was six hundred years old when God had a serious talk with him.

'It makes me very sad to have to say it, Mr Noah, but of all the people who live in this world I created, you are the only good one. I have been very patient, but there is so much wickedness and evil that I must do something about it. I shall make a fresh start.'

Mr Noah was upset when he heard this, but he had to admit that God was right.

'What are you going to do, God?' he asked.

God sighed. 'I am afraid that I shall have to destroy every living creature,' he said sadly. 'But I shall save you, Mr Noah, and your wife. I shall also save your three sons, Shem, Ham and Japheth and their wives. And I shall save two of all the living creatures in the world for they are all important. I shall be relying on you, Mr Noah, to look after them for me and keep them alive. This is what I want you to do ...'

Then God told Mr Noah how to build a wooden ark, which was like a large boat, so that when God sent a great flood to cover the earth, Mr Noah, his family and the animals could be saved.

Mr Noah was not much good at carpentry but his sons and daughters-in-law helped and the ark was built on time. They filled it with food of every kind and, on the great day, Mr Noah, a worried frown on his face and a long, long list in his hand, ticked off the animals as they entered the ark.

There were wild animals, tame animals, reptiles and insects, beasts and birds. There were large animals and small animals, ugly and good-looking ones. There were animals with nice natures and animals with nasty natures.

Two of each kind went into the ark: not one more and not one less. There were, however, no fish, because fish do not need saving from a flood.

Once everyone was safely inside, God shut the door

behind them.

'Will the ark be watertight?' asked Mr Noah anxiously.

'Of course it will,' said God. 'Now stop worrying, Noah, and look after everyone well, for in seven days I shall send the rain.'

So Mr Noah went into the great hall inside the ark, and if he was worried before, now he was terrified.

For there were lions and tigers, llamas and giraffes, leopards and lizards, sheep and cows, horses and goats, donkeys, elephants, camels, monkeys, snakes, birds . . . in fact every animal you can think of, plus all the ones you cannot think of. And not just one, but *two* of each, and they were all milling around the great hall, arguing, fighting, squawking, screeching and making the most terrible noise that had ever been heard.

Mrs Noah and her three daughters-in-law locked themselves in an empty cabin and Mr Noah's three sons cowered in a corner, trapped by two fierce-looking anteaters.

Mr Noah closed his eyes for a moment.

'Why me, God?' he asked. 'I don't even like animals!'

But God was busy preparing for the mighty storm that he would send on the world and did not answer. Besides, he had every confidence in Mr Noah.

Mr Noah opened his eyes.

'Silence!' he cried in a loud voice, sounding much

braver than he felt.

To his surprise, the animals quietened down.

'Now then,' said Mr Noah. 'We're stuck in here for at least forty days and forty nights—for God said it would rain for all that time—and we must live together in a friendly fashion, sharing our food, with give and take on all sides.'

'Yeah,' muttered one of the ant-eaters. 'Give me some ants and I'll take them all right.'

'Now,' said Mr Noah, ignoring this, 'I suggest the following rules...'

The larger of the two lions shook his magnificent mane and stepped forward.

'Pardon me,' he said, looking down his great nose. 'Pardon me, Mr Noah, but *I* am King of the Jungle, Lord of all Beasts, and if there's any rules to be made *I* make them.'

One of the tigers stood up and stretched lazily. His great claws scraped along the floor of the ark.

'Excuse me,' said the tiger in a gentle voice. 'Excuse me, but we tigers have always considered *ourselves* to be the most important of the animals, and if there's any decision-making going on round here, *we* are going to do it!'

'Fight you for it!' snapped the lion.

'As you please,' said the tiger sweetly.

Both animals bared their teeth and a minute later they

would have been at each other's throats if it had not been for Mr Noah.

'Behave yourselves!' he shouted.

Much to his surprise, the lion and tiger slunk away to opposite corners of the hall.

Feeling bolder because of his success, Mr Noah continued, 'You should be ashamed of yourselves,' he said severely. 'It's up to you both to set a good example to the other animals!'

'Now,' he said hurriedly, before the lion or tiger could answer back. 'Rule One, no fighting. Write that down, Shem. For some good reason only known to himself, God wanted two of each of you, alive, well and unharmed at the end of this voyage. And God has given me the job of looking after you. I didn't want the job, I didn't ask for it and in fact I'm beginning to think it might have been better to have drowned with everyone else than be shut up here with all of you. So if you've got any complaints, I don't want to hear them.'

There was a lot of mumbling and grumbling, squeaking and squawking, but only the tiger spoke. 'I think,' he said gravely, 'I think we should have a committee, composed of a small number of us more intelligent animals. Mr Noah can preside if he wishes.'

'What did he say?' asked one of the snakes, who was hard of hearing.

'A committee,' the tiger repeated in a louder voice, 'of

the most intelligent animals.'

'Fancies himself,' one of the geese cackled to the other. 'Those big cats are all the same.'

'Who's to say who should go on the committee?' squeaked a dormouse. 'You might be bigger than me, but are you cleverer?'

'We should *all* be on the committee,' said a giraffe, waving its long neck. 'We're all equal, aren't we? Didn't God say we're all equal?'

'*Important* was the word God used,' said Mr Noah. 'There is a difference.'

The giraffe looked as if he would disagree so Mr Noah went on hurriedly. 'But no. No committees, no discussions. We're here because God decided we should be saved.'

The mumblings and grumblings grew louder.

'Don't you *want* to be saved?' Mr Noah asked desperately.

The noise grew worse and Mr Noah and his sons escaped to the peace of their cabins and settled down to sleep.

But Mr Noah could not sleep. He lay in bed, listening to the wind howling round outside, and the snuffles and grunts of the animals inside, and he talked to God.

'Listen, God,' he said. 'It's not too late. You need a lion-tamer for this job, or a big game hunter, or at least a zoo keeper. I'm very grateful, of course, that you want to save me and my family, but honestly, I'm not cut out for the job.'

God listened to Mr Noah, but did not speak.

'And I'll tell you something, God,' Mr Noah went on. 'It's something I've never told anyone, not even my wife... I'm scared of spiders and we've got two on board.'

God laughed, for the first time since he realized that he would have to destroy the world.

'I chose the right man for the job, Noah,' he said. 'Go to sleep now and let me worry about the animals. Oh... and I knew about the spiders.'

And, strangely enough, Mr Noah felt comforted and fell fast asleep.

2
THE LION'S TALE

Mr Noah and his family, and two of every animal, insect and bird spent the first night safe inside the wooden ark, which God had told Mr Noah to make to save them from the flood.

But although they were safe, none of them slept well.

Mr Noah tossed and turned and had bad dreams about being drowned in the flood or eaten by an animal. Some of the animals were very noisy sleepers and kept waking him up. All night there was hissing, sighing, rumbling, muttering, squawking, squeaking, trumpeting and bellowing. It was all very disturbing.

The lion did not sleep well either. He paced angrily up and down his stall, his great tail thumping the floor behind him.

'I protest,' he said to his wife. 'I protest most strongly.'

'Mmm . . .?' said his wife, who was trying to sleep.

'I should have been put in charge of this whole operation. God should have given *me* the job. I can

21

control the animals better than Mr Noah. Aren't I the most powerful of all the beasts? Aren't I King of the Jungle?'

'Yes, dear,' said his wife sleepily. 'But we're not in the jungle now.'

The lion stopped. 'Of course we are,' he said. 'Everywhere's a jungle and only the strongest and toughest survive.' He started pacing once more, swishing his great tail from side to side. 'Only the strongest and toughest *deserve* to survive,' he added.

'Oh do be quiet and go to sleep,' his wife said. 'And

stop pacing up and down. You're making me dizzy.'

The following morning Mr Noah was just getting out of bed when there was a tap on the door of his cabin.

'Yes?' he called out sharply, in rather a bad temper because of the sleepless night. 'Who is it?'

The lion stuck his head round the door.

'I thought I ought to advise you,' he said in a majestic sort of voice, 'as you are *supposed* to be in charge here—that some of the animals are attempting to eat each other. Whether or not you can stop them is another matter. *I* could, of course, but then I'm not in charge . . .'

He found himself speaking to an empty room, for Mr Noah had run straight out of the cabin. The lion sniffed in disgust.

'Well really,' he said. 'Some people have no manners, no manners at all.' He sniffed again. 'Anyway, I'm only the messenger, a creature of no importance.'

His eye fell on the key that was in the lock of Mr Noah's cabin door and a cunning smile spread across his face.

'No importance at all,' he said in quite a different voice and padded off after Mr Noah.

In the big hall Mr Noah was horrified by what he saw.

'Stop!' he shouted. 'Stop it at once, do you hear?'

'Why should we?' asked one of the leopards.

'We always hunt for our food,' added the other.

'But you don't need to,' said Mr Noah. 'The food's all

23

provided.'

'What else are we meant to do to pass the time?' said one of the foxes.

'Well, I don't know, do I?' Mr Noah replied irritably, feeling tired, cross and rather silly when he realized he was dressed only in his nightshirt.

'Don't be such a spoilsport,' said the other fox, who was trying to coax a dormouse from its hiding place. 'It's all good fun and they *like* being hunted.'

'No, we don't,' said the dormouse, who was shivering with fright.

Mr Noah banged on the floor.

'This,' said Mr Noah loudly, 'has gone far enough! I shall make another rule: "Animals are strictly forbidden to eat one another while on this voyage." I'll get Shem to write it out and pin it up so that everyone can see.'

'But how many of us can read?' asked the monkey in a bored voice.

Mr Noah ignored this. 'I don't care what you do when we get back on dry land, but while we're in the ark you will all do as I say,' he said severely. 'Now behave yourselves while I go and get dressed.'

After he had gone the animals started muttering.

'Just who does he think he is?' asked the fox.

'God, most likely,' said the lion. He made his way through the teeming animals to the centre of the big hall. A window was set high up in the roof of the ark, and through it a shaft of sunlight shone on the deep gold of the lion's mane. He looked quite magnificent.

He called in a deep voice, 'Animals—fellow travellers—friends ...!'

'You're no friend of mine,' said the dormouse quietly.

'As I see it,' the lion went on, 'we are stuck in this ark for an unknown length of time. One of us has to be in charge and that one should be the strongest amongst us. That is the law of the jungle, as I'm sure you'll all agree.'

Some of the animals thumped their tails on the floor.

'Now this Mr Noah,' the lion continued, 'he's a good enough human, as humans go, but he isn't the strongest. So why should he be in charge?'

'Perhaps he's clever,' said one of the giraffes, frowning in concentration. 'You've got to be clever to be in charge.'

'Very true,' agreed the lion. 'And perhaps Mr Noah is clever. But it's hardly clever of him to order us about, laying down the law, making up rules as and when he chooses—now is it?'

More animals thumped their tails and there were murmurs of agreement. The lion beamed his approval.

'But,' said the dormouse timidly. 'God put Mr Noah in charge.'

The lion looked annoyed.

'*If* God did that,' he said in his grandest manner. 'Then God made a mistake.'

The tiger pricked up his ears. 'What are you up to?' he asked suspiciously.

'You'll see,' said the lion and turned and walked away.

While all this was going on in the big hall, Mr Noah was hurriedly getting dressed. As he did so, he talked to God.

'I'm not making a very good job of it, am I?' he asked humbly.

God smiled but said nothing.

'I thought,' Mr Noah went on, tying his belt round his waist, 'that if I showed them I was firm and not frightened—if I shouted a bit and laid down the law—then they'd behave properly. But I'm not sure they'll take any notice of me.'

Mr Noah put on his shoes. 'You put me in charge, God, so can't *you* do something about it? Can't you *make* them do what I say? It's for their own good.'

God sighed. 'I'm sorry, Noah. I don't rule by force.'

Noah was thinking about this when he heard a noise at the door of his cabin. He turned the handle, but the door would not open. He rattled it loudly, but the door remained firmly shut. It had been locked from the outside.

Mr Noah sat on his bed. 'What do I do, God?' he asked.

'Just wait,' said God. 'And think.'

The lion, well pleased with himself, walked back to the big hall. *That* took care of Mr Noah!

He stood in front of the crowd of animals. 'It's all sorted out,' he said. 'I'm in charge now.'

The tiger looked up. 'Who says?'

'I do,' said the lion, 'by virtue of being King of the Jungle, Lord of all Beasts, strongest...' he stopped and smiled modestly, '... and cleverest...'

'And biggest-headed,' added the monkey sourly.

'Where's Mr Noah?' asked the tiger.

'Quite safe,' said the lion. 'No need to worry—I've dealt with him.'

He smiled again and the dormouse shuddered. 'You haven't ... *eaten* him ... have you?' he asked faintly.

'Of course not,' said the lion.

'Yet,' he added.

The animals were silent.

'Now,' the lion went on briskly. 'As ruler here ...'

The tiger snarled. 'Ruler?' he said. 'You? We'll soon see about that.'

He sprang at the lion and everyone scattered as the fight began. It was a fierce fight which raged up and down and round and round the big hall, bumping off walls and flattening the smaller animals who could not get out of the way in time. The ark groaned and shook.

Mr Noah, locked in his cabin, put his head in his hands, while Mrs Noah, Shem, Ham, Japheth and their wives, who were not locked in, were all far too frightened to come out.

The other animals were frightened too, and one by one they slipped out of the big hall and made their way to Mr Noah's cabin. Eventually they were all squashed in the corridor outside.

'I don't think I want to be ruled by the lion,' said the dormouse.

'Or the tiger,' bleated one of the goats.

'Can't we ask Mr Noah to take charge again?'

suggested the dormouse.

The goat put his face to the keyhole.

'Mr Noah, we've been thinking. We'd like you to be in charge, so will you please come and stop the lion and tiger fighting.'

Mr Noah jumped off the bed and went to the door. 'Well yes,' he said. 'Of course. But I'm locked in.'

A minute later he heard the key being turned in the lock, the door opened and he was free.

Mr Noah led the procession back to the big hall. As they drew nearer the animals grew silent, listening anxiously for the sounds of fighting, but everything was quiet. Too quiet.

'Perhaps they've killed each other,' said the goat hopefully.

'Oh, I do hope not,' said Mr Noah and quickened his pace. He marched into the hall, then stopped abruptly, staring in amazement. The animals crowded round.

In front of them, side by side, lay the lion and the tiger. Worn out with fighting, they were both fast asleep and snoring gently.

The goat started to snigger, then the dormouse began squeaking and soon all the animals, insects and birds were laughing. Their laughter woke the lion and tiger.

'Wha—what happened?' asked the lion, hurriedly getting to his feet and snarling at the tiger.

'I think,' said the tiger with dignity, 'that the fight

was a draw.'

Just then the lion caught sight of Mr Noah. 'What are you doing here?' he asked. 'You should be locked in your cabin.'

The monkey pushed his way to the front, the key dangling from his long fingers. 'You might be strong,' he said, 'but you're not so clever. You left the key on the floor.'

The animals began laughing again.

'The animals came and asked me to take charge.' Mr Noah said mildly.

'Oh,' said the lion uncomfortably. 'I see.'

Mr Noah felt sorry for him. 'Look, I have an apology to make. I thought I could rule you all by shouting and laying down the law. But God doesn't rule like that and I shouldn't have tried.'

He looked at the lion. 'I'm not as strong as you, or the tiger, and I'm not very clever, but I'm very glad you locked me in because it made me talk to God and do some thinking. If we're going to survive this trip we've got to work together. So can we start again?' He put out his hand. 'Will you be my assistant, lion—and tiger, will you be my other assistant?'

There was a moment's pause before the lion said graciously. 'All right. I agree.'

'Me too,' said the tiger hurriedly.

The lion raised its great head and looked round at the

animals, who were all pressing eagerly against Mr Noah in order not to miss anything.

'Come along now,' said the lion in a grand voice. 'Give Mr Noah some room. Show some respect for the man God put in charge.'

The animals moved back and the lion left the hall in a stately fashion. Mr Noah sighed and followed. The tiger gave a crooked smile and went to his stall, while the animals, insects and birds all went to their various perching, nesting and sleeping places, and peace fell on the ark.

3

THE SHEEP'S TALE

According to God's instructions, Mr Noah, his family, and two of every animal, insect and bird were safely inside the ark well before the rain started. The rain began slowly, just a shower at first, but then the skies grew black and it began to pour. Everyone inside the ark went quiet as they listened to the sound of the rain drumming on the wooden roof. Suddenly a desperate bleating was heard above the noise.

'Mr Noah, Mr Noah...!'

One of the sheep ran across the big hall, its four black feet skittering this way and that on the floor, its woolly tail flopping from side to side.

'Mr Noah, something *terrible's* happened!'

'What?' asked Mr Noah.

'My wife is missing!'

'That's impossible,' said Mr Noah. 'God himself closed the door of the ark once we were all inside. And I counted you all as you came on board and there were two sheep, one ewe and one ram, just as there were two of every animal, insect and bird.'

'I know,' said the ram. 'But she isn't in the ark now, I've looked everywhere.'

Mr Noah thought for a moment, then he turned to the lion and tiger. 'She can't have gone far because the ark isn't *that* large,' he said. 'Will you help me search?'

'Of course,' said the lion graciously. 'Although,' he added in a low voice, 'why anyone would want to bother with a sheep is beyond me.'

'Unless you were hungry,' muttered the tiger, with a flash of his gleaming teeth.

The animals searched the ark from end to end and from top to bottom but there was no sign of the missing sheep.

'Oh dear,' said Mr Noah. 'I must talk to God about this.'

So he went to his cabin and shut the door.

While Mr Noah was talking to God, the missing sheep was outside, standing under a tree on the top of a rocky mountain, trying, unsuccessfully, to shelter from the rain. As the rain splashed through the branches, she though that perhaps she should not have been in such a hurry to leave the ark in the first place, and that perhaps the ark was not so bad after all. At least it was dry.

When all the animals had arrived at the ark, she had followed the ram up the ramp and waited patiently while

Mr Noah hunted through his long list.

'Sheep. Now let me see ... seagulls ... snails—no, before snails—ah yes, "Sheep, two, one ewe, one ram".' He ticked them off his list and they had entered the ark.

The ewe had looked in amazement at the massive wooden building. She had wandered from deck to deck, searching for something familiar, a patch of fresh green grass, a tree. But there was no green grass in the ark and there were no trees. There was food, yes, stored in great wooden containers, enough for all the animals, but nothing comfortable to lie on except some dry straw, nothing comfortable to chew on, and nothing at all to look at.

'Why have we come?' she asked the ram.

'Because Mr Noah told us to,' he replied. 'So that we could be saved from the flood.'

'I'm not sure I believe in this flood,' she said. 'I can't really believe that *all* the earth will be covered with

water, can you?'

It was one of the great eagles who answered her. He was sitting on a wooden beam high above the big hall.

'I'm afraid, madam, I do believe in it,' he said sadly. 'And although I wouldn't say this in Mr Noah's hearing, for he's a good man, between you and me I think it's a bit hard on all the animals and birds who have been left behind to drown in the flood. It's not our fault that the earth needs destroying—it's the fault of humans, not us.'

He flew off to the upper deck—for eagles like to be as high as possible—leaving the ewe and the ram in the hall.

'It still seems a lot of nonsense to me,' said the ewe. 'After all, we've only Mr Noah's word that this flood is going to happen.'

She left her partner and returned to the entrance to watch as more and more animals, insects and birds arrived.

'Hmm,' she thought to herself. 'It's going to be very crowded in here when everyone's aboard.'

There was already a terrible noise in the ark as the new arrivals chattered, squeaked, grunted and howled as they made themselves at home.

She looked past Mr Noah to the clearing in the forest where the ark had been built. Beyond the trees lay the gentle curve of a hill, thick with green grass and dappled with sunlight.

As Mr Noah was busy welcoming more animals, the sheep slipped quietly away from the ark and no one saw her go. She scampered through the forest until she reached the hill, then she wandered along, grazing contentedly. The grass, deep and thick and delicious, seemed to go on for ever. It was springy beneath her feet. The sky was blue, birds flashed and darted overhead and insects hummed and buzzed drowsily.

For six days she wandered, scarcely noticing the clouds that drifted across the sky, small wisps at first, then growing and thickening until at last the sun was blotted out.

When the first drops of rain fell, the sheep did not mind too much because she had a fine coat of wool to protect her. It was only when her coat was wet through that she began to shiver. She ran to a tree for shelter.

'I can stay here until the rain stops and then dry my coat in the sun,' she thought.

But the rain did not stop and the sun did not come out. The great round drops fell faster and faster and the clouds grew so thick and black they seemed to reach right down to the earth.

'Perhaps it was true what the eagle said,' the sheep

thought. 'Perhaps I should have stayed in the ark, but how was I to know that Mr Noah would be right?' She sighed. 'I'll just have to find my own way back and hope they'll take me in.'

But by now everything was hidden in a great blanket of mist. The sheep had no idea where the ark was or even where she was and she was suddenly very, very frightened. She walked round and round and up and down. The path began to climb, growing steeper and steeper, and as she struggled along it, the sheep knew that she was completely lost. And still it rained, and rained, and rained.

Inside the ark, Mr Noah was talking to God.

'These animals in the ark are my responsibility, God, so I must go and rescue her. But how?' He paused. 'I can't

swim, you see. At least, not very well.'

God smiled. 'Why don't you ask the animals?' he said.

Mr Noah nodded. 'Yes. I will.' He got up to go. 'Oh, and until we can rescue the sheep, will you look after her?'

'Of course,' said God.

'Yes,' said Mr Noah. 'Silly of me to have asked.'

He left his cabin, went to the big hall and called all the animals together.

'One of the sheep is missing,' he said, 'and I must go and find her.'

'How?' asked the monkey bluntly.

'Well,' said Mr Noah. 'I shall leave the ark and look for her.' He went to the big door and gave it a push. But it would not open from the inside for God had shut it tight.

'Trapped!' screeched the emu. 'We're trapped!'

The animals were silent. Suddenly the ark creaked and shuddered from end to end.

'We're afloat,' said the monkey.

'I don't like it,' said the ostrich, trying, unsuccessfully, to bury his head in the wooden planks of the floor.

'I never was good on boats,' said the dog, turning pale. 'Suffer from seasickness something horrid.'

'Please,' said Mr Noah. 'Let me think.'

'Let's *all* think,' said the lion.

'Couldn't we build a boat?' asked the beaver.

'*This* is a boat,' said the monkey scornfully.

'Yes, but if we made a small boat, we could row it and

steer it where we wanted. We can't steer the ark.'

'And what do you suggest we make it with?' asked the monkey sarcastically. 'Chop up the ark for wood?'

The beaver was silent.

'I think we should leave that silly sheep behind,' hissed the snake.

'So do I,' agreed the emu. 'She had no right to go and leave the ark. It's her own fault.'

Several of the animals agreed.

'It's not right to put the rest of us in danger,' added the snake. 'You must think of us, Mr Noah.'

The ram stood up. 'Look, I understand what you are all feeling and I know my wife was silly to go off like that, but she *is* my wife and I love her and I don't want to stay on this ark without her.' He turned to Mr Noah. 'If no one is prepared to rescue her then please let me go and be with her. She must be so frightened.'

'Of course we'll rescue her,' said Mr Noah. 'Each one of you is important, God said so. He also put me in charge, so it's my duty to go and find her. If I can't get out by the door, I shall have to jump from the roof. If I don't come back, Shem, you will take over charge here under God.'

He walked to the ladder leading to the trapdoor in the roof of the ark. 'Pity I never learnt to swim properly,' he muttered to himself under his breath. The eagle, who had very good hearing, called down to him.

'Mr Noah! Wait!' He flew to the ground. 'If it was left to me, I'd say we should leave the sheep behind, but if you say she's got to be rescued then I'll do it. You'll only drown.'

Mr Noah looked at the eagle with its fierce eyes and cruel beak. 'Are you sure?' he asked doubtfully.

'Of course I am,' said the eagle. He looked at Mr Noah. 'And don't worry. I promise I won't hurt her, although she deserves it.'

Mr Noah thanked the great eagle and pushed open the trapdoor. The eagle flew up and perched on the edge. He looked round at the driving rain, the grey swirling waters and the white mist.

'How very sad,' he said.

'What can you see?' Mr Noah asked anxiously.

'Very little,' said the eagle. 'The water is rising fast and the mist is thick. But wait ...'

He stretched his great wings and soared off into the sky. With his keen eyesight he had seen the topmost peak of a mountain which jutted out of the waters of the flood, looking like a tiny island in a swelling and fast-rising sea. At the very top, clinging forlornly to a rock, under a tree, was the missing sheep, wet, trembling and very scared.

The eagle swooped down out of the mist. He caught hold of her woolly coat in his great talons, lifted her up and flew back with her across the angry waters. His wings hurt with the effort, his eyes were almost blinded by the rain, but at last he reached the ark.

Mr Noah opened the trapdoor from inside, caught the sheep in his arms and brought her to safety inside the ark.

'I'm sorry,' said the sheep.

'That's all right,' said Mr Noah. 'I'm just glad you're home.'

He looked at the wet, shivering eagle. 'Thank you,' he said.

'Think nothing of it,' said the eagle, and promptly went to sleep.

4

THE TERMITE'S TALE

The rain, once started, did not stop, and soon the ark, containing Mr Noah, his family, and two of every kind of animal, insect and bird, was floating on top of the water which covered the earth.

Outside it was wet, but inside the ark was dry and snug and warm, if not entirely comfortable. It was not very comfortable to be living inside a wooden ark containing two of every living creature made by God—apart, of course, from fish.

'But it's better than being drowned in the flood,' Mr Noah told his wife, and she agreed.

There was a scratching at the door of Mr Noah's cabin and the lion came in.

'Excuse me, Mr Noah, but I think you ought to come. We've a slight problem,' he said. 'Well, a number of problems, in fact,' he added.

Mr Noah, who had been enjoying a quiet rest before feeding the animals, got wearily to his feet and followed

the lion to the upper deck.

As he climbed the steps he could hear a faint plopping noise which grew louder as he reached the top. When he turned the corner he could see drops of water falling onto the floor.

'It's not the only leak,' said the lion gloomily. 'The tiger and I have counted four already.'

'Oh dear,' said Mr Noah. He stared at the puddle on the floor. 'What are we going to do?'

One or two of the animals had followed them.

'*We* aren't going to do anything,' said the monkey in a smug voice. '*You* built the ark—*you* solve the problem.'

Mr Noah looked worried. 'I know my carpentry isn't very good, but God told me that the ark was watertight when we set off.' He called his sons. 'Shem, Ham, Japheth—do we have any bits of wood left over—anything we can use to fill the gaps?'

His sons shook their heads. 'We used it all on the building,' Shem said.

'And we didn't bring anything for repairs,' added Ham.

'Stupid of me not to think of that,' said Mr Noah. 'Right,' he went on in a brisk voice. 'The first thing is to catch the drips.'

Soon a bowl was placed under each hole. When they were full of water, they were emptied out of the trapdoor at the top of the ark.

But after a day or two *more* holes began to appear.

Mr Noah called a meeting of all the animals and asked for their help.

The elephants obligingly placed their long trunks up against two of the holes and sucked in as much water as they could before blowing it out of the trapdoor.

The giraffes stretched their long necks and stopped two more of the holes by wedging their heads against them. But they soon developed headaches and neckaches and had to stop.

The peacock, after much grumbling, spread his beautiful tail over one of the holes like an umbrella. The beavers offered to dam the holes if any mud and stones could be found. But nothing worked for long.

The ark began to feel decidedly damp and the only animals happy with the situation were the two hippopotami, who had missed the lakes of their home and stood for hours under the holes, wallowing under the steady drops of water.

Mr Noah had a talk with God.

'I'm sorry to trouble you, God, especially with all the problems you have with the flood and everything, but we've got problems here and I don't know what to do about it.'

'Tell me,' said God, although of course he already knew.

'You did say that the ark was watertight, and of

course I believe you, but it's not watertight now. It's sprung a leak—well, a lot of leaks actually—and some of them are more than leaks, they're downright holes and we're finding it very difficult to catch all the water. Perhaps my carpentry was worse than I thought,' Mr Noah added miserably.

'There was nothing wrong with your work, Noah,' God assured him. 'The ark was quite watertight when you set out. Keep your eyes and ears open and you will soon find the cause of the trouble.'

That night, when all the animals were asleep, Mr Noah was woken by a strange noise. He had grown used to the grunts and snores, the whistles and murmurings of the animals and could sleep through them, but this was different. He lay in his cabin and listened.

'Tap . . . tap, tap . . . tap . . .'

It stopped but soon started again further away. Mr Noah got up and left his cabin. Walking on bare feet he silently made his way towards the sound, pausing now and again to listen. The tapping grew louder. Mr Noah climbed the steps, from the bottom deck, to the middle, to the top. He crept along the corridor and the tapping grew louder still. He turned a corner . . .

. . . and stumbled across two woodpeckers, who were busy tapping into the wood with their long beaks and hard heads.

'Just a minute!' said Mr Noah, in a loud voice.

The woodpeckers turned and a fine spray of water began to dribble in through the holes they had just made.

'Hello, Mr Noah,' said one of the woodpeckers.

'What do you think you're doing?' Mr Noah asked sternly.

'It's obvious,' said the other woodpecker. 'We're pecking wood.'

'It's what we always do,' said the first woodpecker kindly. 'Peck wood.'

'That's why we're called...'

'WOODPECKERS!' they both shouted together and flew about laughing.

'But don't you know what will happen if you keep pecking?' Mr Noah asked. 'If you go on this way, we could sink.'

'No, we won't,' said the second woodpecker cheerfully.

'God'll save us, you'll see,' said the first with confidence.

'I'm sorry, but you can't go on doing it,' Mr Noah said in a decided voice. The woodpeckers looked upset.

'But we've got to peck something,' the first one said.

'It's in our nature, see,' the second one added.

'We make these holes to live in,' explained the first. 'But we can't live in any of the holes we've made here.'

'They're too wet,' the second one added disapprovingly.

'But we've provided holes for you to live in,' said Mr Noah.

The second woodpecker sniffed. 'It's not the same.'

The first woodpecker flapped his wings. 'And anyway, we *like* pecking wood. That's why we're called...'

'All right, all right,' said Mr Noah hastily. 'Just give me time to think about it.' He could not think properly with wet, cold feet. 'Just promise to stop for now.'

'Okay,' said the first woodpecker. 'We were going to pack it in for tonight anyway.'

Mr Noah spent the rest of the night deep in thought

and in the morning he had an answer. He went to the woodpeckers.

'How would you feel if I let you peck at a harmless piece of wood, perhaps the door to a cabin? Would that keep you happy?'

The woodpeckers considered.

'Well—so long as it's good wood,' said the first warily.

'All the wood on this ark is good,' said Mr Noah with dignity. 'God chose it himself.'

The woodpeckers pondered.

'All right,' said the first. 'It's a deal.'

So everyone was happy, apart from Shem, whose cabin door was chosen by the woodpeckers and whose days and nights were, from then on, rather noisy.

But there still remained the problem of the leaks in the ark. It was raining harder than ever now and more and more water was coming in.

'What are we going to do, God?' Mr Noah asked, quite worn out with baling out the water.

'Have you asked the animals for their ideas?' God said.

'Of course,' said Mr Noah. 'Everyone's helping. The elephants are holding their trunks ...'

'Yes,' said God. 'I know that. But have you asked *everyone*?'

'Yes,' said Mr Noah confidently. 'Everyone. At least,' he added doubtfully. 'I think I have.'

So Mr Noah walked round the ark, speaking to large animals and small, to wild animals and tame, to insects and birds—but no one had any suggestions on how to fill the holes. Just as he was about to give up he caught sight of a strange black mound in a dark corner of the ark. He stopped, looked, then tapped politely. Two white, wriggling ant-like creatures came out.

'Yes?' one of them asked.

'Excuse me, but who are you?' asked Mr Noah.

'Well, really!' said the other. 'You should know, Mr Noah—you ticked us off your list!'

'Did I?' said Mr Noah. 'I'm terribly sorry but there were so many, I've forgotten. Are you ants?'

'Ants indeed!' said the first huffily. 'We're *termites*! Quite different!'

'We are distantly related,' said the other termite mildly. 'Somewhere along the family tree.'

'*Very* distantly,' said the first.

'Well, I'm sorry,' Mr Noah said again. He touched the hard black mound. 'Would you mind telling me what this is?'

'It's our home,' said the first termite.

'You made it?' Mr Noah asked.

'Yes, of course!'

'What of?'

'Wood.'

Mr Noah was puzzled. 'But you haven't used any of

the wood on the ark—have you?' he asked.

'No. We've used our own.'

Mr Noah was even more puzzled. 'Your *own*?'

'It's quite simple really,' said the second termite. 'We feed on wood and store it inside our bodies. When we want to build a home, we just use it as we want. When we knew we were coming on this trip we stored a lot of wood as we didn't know what the living conditions would be like on the ark.'

'Besides,' added the first, 'we like to live in our own nest.'

Mr Noah tapped the termite house. 'And is it strong?' he asked.

'Strong!' echoed the first termite. 'I'll tell you something, Mr Noah. This nest is a lot stronger than your ark.'

'Would you—could you—please—give us some help then?' Mr Noah asked anxiously. 'We're in a dreadful pickle and I think you are the only ones who can get us out.'

The termites agreed so Mr Noah went away to organize the animals. The woodpeckers pecked away at Shem's cabin door and the beavers collected the wood shavings and took them to the termites. The termites ate the wood and produced the hard black substance they used in making their homes. The elephants, using their trunks, plastered the holes with the mixture and the peacock waved his tail to help dry it quickly.

One by one the holes were sealed and the bowls returned to their proper uses. Everyone on the ark was soon dry and comfortable again—as comfortable as it was possible to be with two of every animal, insect and bird living so close to one another, not to mention Mr Noah, Mrs Noah, their three sons and their wives.

And the ark did not sink but continued to float on the troubled waters of the world as the rain fell without stopping, day after day after day.

5

THE SKUNK'S TALE

Mr Noah, his family and two of every insect, animal and bird began to settle into their new life inside the ark, while the rain which God had sent flooded the earth.

Mr Noah was kept very busy each day settling arguments, looking after sick animals and generally trying to keep his little world as happy and content as possible. Each evening he went round the ark to make sure that everyone was comfortable for the night.

One evening, as he climbed to the second deck, he heard angry voices.

'Animals like you shouldn't be allowed!'

Mr Noah hurried up the steps.

'Disgraceful!'

'Anti-social!'

'Throw them overboard, I say!'

Mr Noah sniffed, then sniffed again, wrinkling his nose at the nasty smell which drifted down the corridor. He saw a group of animals huddled together and, as their voices grew louder, the smell grew stronger.

'Just who do you think you are, going round stinking the place out?' bleated the goat.

'This ark is becoming unfit for decent self-respecting animals,' said the emu primly.

'And insects,' added the ant.

'And birds,' said the vulture. 'We vultures have very sensitive noses.'

A burst of really smelly air made the animals fall back and Mr Noah could see two black and white spotted skunks, their backs to the wall.

The emu, overcome by the smell, fell flat on the floor, right on top of the hedgehog. 'Ow...! The pain! The smell!'

'Sorry, I'm sure,' said the hedgehog politely, struggling to get out from under her.

The skunks said nothing. They stood on their front legs, bared their sharp teeth and stamped up and down on the ground. Then they fell on all fours, lifted their tails and squirted some more smell at the animals, who began to creep away.

The goat trotted over to Mr Noah.

'Did you see that?' he asked.

'Yes,' said Mr Noah. 'And smelt it.'

'It's not right,' said the emu feebly. 'It shouldn't be allowed.'

The goose waved its long thin neck at Mr Noah.

'What are you going to do about it?' she asked.

'I think,' said Mr Noah, 'we'd better have a talk.'

They met, a short time later, in the big hall. All the animals were there—apart from the two skunks—and feelings ran high. The goat stopped Mr Noah as soon as he entered.

'That smell is making this place extremely unpleasant,' he complained.

'I didn't know it was going to be like this,' said the snail, 'or I wouldn't have come.'

'Please, everyone,' said Mr Noah. 'Can't we solve this in a friendly way? We all have habits that others don't like, but we've got to get along together. Can't you learn to live with the smell?'

'No,' said the fox bluntly.

'In my opinion, for what it's worth,' said the camel in a slow, deliberate voice, 'I think the skunks should be told in no uncertain terms that we are not prepared to tolerate their anti-social behaviour and if they don't immediately cease fouling the air we shall have no alternative but to remove them straightaway from this ... from this ...' he peered around ' ... edifice.'

'What's he talking about?' asked the giraffe.

'If they don't stop smelling we'll throw them out,' said the fox bluntly.

The lion looked at Mr Noah. 'If you want my advice—speaking as your assistant of course—unless something is done soon there'll be a riot.'

'Very well,' said Mr Noah, 'I'll see what I can do.'

Mr Noah returned to the skunks. But as he approached, they stood up and glared.

Mr Noah spoke very quickly. 'Look,' he said. 'Friends. I'm sorry to have to say this, but you've upset all the animals—to say nothing of the insects and birds—and they are not at all happy.'

The skunks rose on their front legs. Mr Noah, his own legs feeling weak and trembly, took a step backwards.

'In the interests of good relations you'll have to stop smelling the place out, otherwise we shall have to take stern action.'

The skunks stamped vigorously on the floor, stared him straight in the face and shot out a horrible smell. Mr Noah fell to the ground and banged his head with such force that he was knocked unconscious.

He came round to find himself in his cabin. He felt his sore head gently.

'What should I do, God?' he asked.

'You could try talking to them,' said God.

'I've just tried,' Mr Noah said indignantly, 'and look where it got me!'

'You didn't talk *to* them, you talked *at* them,' said God patiently.

'*You* talk to them then,' Mr Noah said grumpily. 'They might listen to you. At least *you* won't end up with a sore head.'

God laughed.

'It's no laughing matter,' said Mr Noah severely. 'I've a crisis on my hands and you're supposed to help.'

He really was feeling rather ill, otherwise he would not have spoken to God like that.

'I *am* helping, Noah,' God said gently. 'I'm giving you advice. Talk *to* the skunks and find out what is wrong.'

But Mr Noah did not want to take God's advice. He lay in his bed and nursed his sore head while the smell continued to spread right through the ark. One by one the animals, insects and birds came to his cabin to complain. Mr Noah pretended that his head was worse than it really was and refused to get up. But at last the smell grew so bad that Mr Noah had to do something. He sent for the lion and the tiger.

'Lion,' he said in a weak voice. 'And tiger. My

57

assistants. You know I'm laid up here with a broken head and so I can't do anything about the smell. But something must be done.'

'The animals are very angry,' said the lion. 'They might even take matters into their own hands.'

'You mean...?'

'Wring their smelly necks,' said the tiger.

Mr Noah was shocked. 'Lion... tiger... would you... could you... talk to the skunks on my behalf?'

'No,' said the tiger bluntly.

'They'd listen to you,' pleaded Mr Noah, 'animals like themselves.'

'But *you* have the authority,' said the lion gently. 'Authority from God. Far be it from me, a mere lion, to take over that authority.' He looked at Mr Noah and opened his eyes wide. 'Who knows where it could end? Why—the animals might even want me—us,' he added hastily as the tiger growled, 'to take over command here.'

'Yes,' said Mr Noah, 'Well—of course—I fully intend to deal with this, just as soon as I've recovered.'

The lion smiled sweetly. 'I wouldn't leave it too long,' he said, and he and the tiger left.

Mr Noah then sent for his eldest son.

'Shem,' he said. 'I've an important job for you.'

'Yes, Father?'

'I want you to try to find out why the skunks give off that terrible smell and persuade them, if you can, to stop.'

Shem turned pale. 'Me, Father?'

'Yes, you.'

'Very well, Father.'

Shem went out of the cabin but returned after only a few moments, looking dazed and sick.

'I did try, Father, I really did, but I just couldn't get near them.'

'All right, all right,' said Mr Noah testily. 'Send Ham to me.'

When Ham came Mr Noah gave him the same instructions. Ham turned green.

'Me, Father? You want me to go?'

'Yes,' said Mr Noah.

'But I suffer from sea-sickness. That smell will make me very, very ill.'

'Just do as I say,' said Mr Noah.

So Ham went out of the cabin but he was back even faster than his brother.

'Sorry, Dad.'

'You didn't even try,' grumbled Mr Noah. 'Send Japheth to me. He's a good, obedient lad.'

But Japheth was so frightened at the thought of having to deal with the skunks that he sent a note saying that he was too unwell even to leave his cabin. Mr Noah lay back in bed.

'Noah.'

It was God.

'Noah, I did not save you and your family from the flood or put you in charge of all the animals, insects and birds left in the world for you to disobey me.'

'Me, Lord?'

'Yes. I told *you* to talk to the skunks, not the lion or the tiger or your sons.'

'I thought I was just dealing with the matter as best I could,' said Mr Noah weakly. 'While I'm not well.'

'You thought nothing of the sort,' said God. 'Come on, Noah. Get up.'

'You're not ... angry ... with me?' Mr Noah asked anxiously.

'No,' said God. 'Just a little sad.'

Mr Noah felt ashamed. 'I'm sorry, God,' he said.

He got up, dressed, and went to see the skunks. The smell, by now, was frightful, and Mr Noah held his breath as he climbed the steps. The skunks were in their usual place, surrounded, at a safe distance, by a circle of threatening animals.

'Going to throw them overboard?' asked the fox.

'If you don't, I'll gladly tear out their throats,' said the leopard, pacing up and down. 'That'll soon stop their smell.'

'Just give me a minute with them,' said Mr Noah. 'Alone.'

The animals were surprised but did as he said and moved away. Mr Noah held out his hand.

'Come,' he said, 'I'm not going to threaten or harm you.'

The skunks rose to their feet and Mr Noah swallowed nervously.

'I just want you to tell me why you are making such a smell,' he said in a quavering voice.

One of the skunks stamped.

'Please,' said Mr Noah. 'I'm sorry if I frightened you before. I was just scared. I'm scared now.'

'Scared?' said one of the skunks. 'You? That's a laugh!'

The other skunk hissed. 'Shut up, you fool, it's all a

plot.' She turned to Mr Noah and squirted the foul smell at him, but Mr Noah ducked and missed its full force.

'I don't care what you do,' he said, feeling quite sick. 'I don't care if you knock me unconscious again. I only want to help you.'

The skunk got ready to squirt Mr Noah again, but the first one stopped her.

'Hold on a moment.' He turned to Mr Noah. 'You want to know why we make this smell, right?'

'Right,' said Mr Noah.

'Wouldn't you make a smell if you were scared witless?' the skunk said bluntly.

'But why are you scared?' asked Mr Noah.

'Wouldn't you be, if you were threatened by a load of animals, most of them bigger than you?'

'Why *did* they threaten you?'

'It was that goose started it,' said the other skunk sulkily. 'Flapping around, accusing us of pushing her. And then it went from bad to worse with all of them shouting and saying they'd do all sorts of horrible things to us. No wonder we smelt.'

'We were scared, see, and when we're scared we give off a smell,' explained the first skunk. 'Works wonderfully most times.'

'I see,' said Mr Noah. 'Well, look, God put me in charge here, although I don't know why because I'm not making a very good job of it. If I told you that you've nothing at all to be frightened about, would you believe me?'

'So long as the rest of the animals stop scaring us,' said the skunk.

'Come with me,' said Mr Noah.

He led the skunks to the big hall and they stood, rather uncomfortably, beside him while he explained to the animals, insects and birds that the skunks had only given off the smell because they had been frightened. After some discussion, the animals agreed not to frighten the skunks any more so long as the skunks stopped smelling. In fact, some of the smaller animals, who knew what it was like to feel scared, went out of their way to make the skunks feel safe and at home.

So the skunks became part of the family of the ark and the little world of the ark floated on and on.

6

THE DONKEY'S TALE

When God sent a great flood to destroy the earth, he told Mr Noah to make a wooden ark and take inside it his own family and two of every living creature in order to keep them alive. Two of every animal, insect and bird were living in the ark and it was full to bursting.

As many of the animals, insects and birds had never even seen, let alone lived with, other animals, insects and birds, there was much fighting and arguing before they all settled down together reasonably happily.

When the donkey arrived on board he was amazed at all the different creatures. On that first day, while his wife went to the stall given to them for the journey, he walked slowly round the big hall, wondering at everything he saw.

'I've never seen anything like it,' he said to his wife when at last he joined her. 'Did you know, my dear, that there's an incredible beast—well, two of them, of course—with huge long noses, so long that they touch the ground? They are very big and very heavy and I believe that Mr Noah is worried about them sharing accommodation, in case they overbalance the ark.'

'I expect you mean the elephants, dear,' said his wife, who prided herself upon her general knowledge.

'I expect I do,' agreed the donkey. He went off again, but soon returned.

'There's another animal,' he said excitedly, 'a great tall thing, with a long, long neck and a small head at the top.'

'A giraffe,' said his wife.

'If you say so,' said the donkey. He went off once more, but was soon trotting back.

'Did you know that there's an animal that can run as fast as the wind?' he said in wonder. 'He's running round the big hall now to keep himself in training.'

'Oh, a cheetah,' said his wife, not really very interested.

'And there's another animal with the most powerful hind legs. I was told that he can jump huge distances. I've never seen such an odd-shaped creature before.'

'Well, dear,' said his wife, 'kangaroos live in a different part of the world from us, so it's not surprising that we've never seen them.'

The donkey left the cabin and did not return until it was dark.

'There's an animal,' he said, breathlessly, 'that gives off light. It glows. It's called a glow-worm,' he added hurriedly, before his wife could speak.

'That's not an animal, that's an insect,' his wife said.

'Yes, dear,' said the donkey humbly. He looked at her in astonishment. 'How do you know so much?' he asked.

'I've kept my eyes and my ears open,' she said placidly.

'Don't you want to come and look at all the wonderful creatures in the hall?' asked the donkey.

'Later, dear,' she said. 'Right now, it's nice not to be working and I'm enjoying the holiday.'

So the donkey wandered round the ark on his own and marvelled and wondered at the variety of all the creatures God had made. But as the days passed, his wonder turned to envy. He looked down at himself and sighed.

'There are some beautiful animals in the ark,' he said. 'They make my old grey coat look very dull and boring.'

'Never mind,' said his wife affectionately. 'I like you just as you are.'

But the donkey was not consoled.

'Why are we so drab?' he asked.

'That's how God made us,' she replied.

'Well, I don't think it's fair,' said the donkey. 'Our life is boring enough as it is. Why couldn't God have made us beautiful? Why couldn't we have had something to be proud of—a beautiful tail, perhaps, like the peacock?'

'The peacock's *wife* has a very boring tail,' said his wife dryly, but the donkey was not listening.

'What are we, anyway? Just beasts of burden, only fit to fetch and carry,' he said gloomily. 'Tied up when we're not working and beaten if we don't work hard enough.'

'Someone has to do the work,' said his wife practically. 'We can't all be beautiful or clever. Anyway, we can't change what we are so we'd better make the best of it.'

But the donkey could not do that. Perhaps, he thought to himself, he *could* change if he tried hard enough. But he did not tell this to his wife. So he watched the elephant with his long trunk and tried pulling his own nose in the hope that it would grow. All he got was a sore nose.

He tried craning his neck, hoping it would lengthen

and become interesting like the giraffe's, but all he got was a stiff neck.

He practised jumping and challenged the kangaroo to a jumping match. He lost.

He tried running, but could only manage a fast trot and was soon tired out.

The other animals soon realized what he was doing. Some of them laughed but others were more sympathetic.

'Poor old donkey, trying to change into something more interesting,' said the elephant.

'Like me,' said the peacock, spreading his lovely tail.

'Someone ought to tell him it's no use,' the elephant went on.

'I really don't know why he bothers,' said the goat.

'If I looked as dull as he does, I'd bother,' said the leopard, who was very proud of his spots.

'He's only making an ass of himself,' said the fox and doubled up with laughter at his joke. 'He'll probably start to jump off tables, thinking that he can fly,' he said when he had finished laughing.

After a few days the donkey began to despair of ever changing into something less dull and boring. But one day he saw an animal he had not seen before. It looked rather like him in its shape and size but its coat was very different, for it was striped all over with great black and white stripes. The donkey was entranced.

'Excuse me,' he asked timidly. 'But—who are you?'

'Me?' said the animal, tossing its head. 'A zebra. And you're a donkey.'

'Yes,' admitted the donkey, ashamed. 'Please... can you tell me... how did you get those amazing, those wonderful stripes?'

'I was born with them,' the zebra replied.

'Oh,' said the donkey sadly.

'Don't tell me,' said his wife when he returned to his stall. 'You've met the zebra.'

'How did you know?' asked the donkey.

'I guessed. It had to happen some time or other.'

The donkey sighed and wandered off, thinking hard. How to get stripes—how, *how* to get those wonderful, bold, black and white stripes? He spent the whole day thinking. He kept apart from the other animals and missed all his meals. When night fell and the animals had settled down to sleep the donkey had got no further in his thinking. Suddenly he realized that he was very, very hungry.

The donkey trotted off to find the food stores. He lost his way and ended up in the kitchen used by Mr and Mrs Noah to prepare food for themselves and their family. There was nobody around.

He was about to leave when he saw a large bowl filled to the brim with something that looked like food. The donkey trotted over to it and snuffed his nose over the

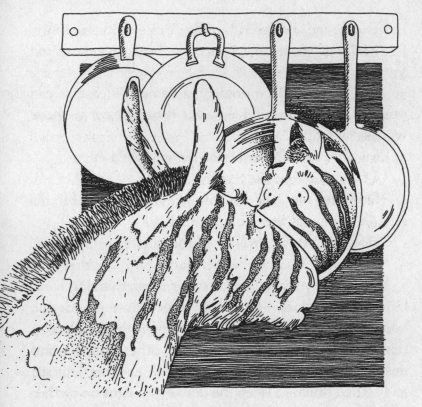

edge. The bowl spun off the table and on to the floor and the donkey was covered with a fine powdering of flour. He stepped back in alarm and his bottom collided with a pan of water, which splashed over him. Quite frightened by now, the donkey turned to go ... and there, facing him, was the zebra.

'I'm so sorry,' the donkey said apologetically. 'I didn't know this was your place. I'll get out right away.'

The zebra did not answer. It just looked at him with

big frightened eyes while water ran off its back and dripped slowly onto the floor. The donkey realized that he was staring at himself, his face reflected in the shiny surface of one of the pans.

He stared and stared and could not believe his eyes. 'It's me,' he said at last. 'And I'm striped.' He looked down at his legs. 'I've become a zebra. It's . . . it's a miracle.'

As if in a dream the donkey went out of the kitchen and into the big hall. The monkey, disturbed by the clatter, opened an eye as he passed.

'Oh, so it was you, was it, making that row just now?' he said sourly. 'Can't you let a poor animal sleep?' He opened the other eye and stared in amazement.

'Well, now I've seen everything,' he said.

The guinea-pig, who was a light sleeper, squinted up at the donkey and began to giggle. The owl swooped down to get a better look and in no time at all, all the animals, insects and birds were awake and staring at the donkey. They stared, then they laughed . . . and laughed . . . and laughed.

'That's the funniest thing I've ever seen,' said the crocodile, holding on to his scaly sides with his claws.

The donkey looked round, puzzled. Why were they all laughing? Why weren't they admiring him in his new zebra coat?

At last the noise woke his wife and she came into the big hall. When she saw him she shook her head. 'You silly old thing,' she said fondly.

'Why?' asked the donkey, bewildered. 'What have I done?'

The fresh wave of laughter brought Mr Noah hurrying into the hall. He stopped still in amazement when he saw the donkey, but he did not laugh. He was not even angry when he realized that the flour for the next day's bread was plastered all over the donkey's back.

'Come along, old thing,' he said. 'Let's clean you off, shall we?'

He led the bewildered donkey away and washed all traces of flour from his coat. It took a long time because the flour and water had mixed to form a hard paste. He spoke gently to the donkey, but the donkey just stood with his head bowed and did not say a word. As soon as he was clean he trotted slowly away.

'He'll soon get over it,' Mr Noah said to himself.

But the donkey did not get over it. He stopped talking to his wife, he stopped walking around the big hall, he stopped trying to change into something different, he even stopped eating. He just lay in the corner of his stall, growing weaker and weaker.

At last his wife went to see Mr Noah.

'Can't you do something, Mr Noah?' she asked. 'I've tried talking to him. Some of the animals have come to see him to say they are sorry they laughed, but nothing works. I'm really worried. If he doesn't eat, he'll die.'

When she had gone, Mr Noah talked to God.

'How can I help the donkey, God?' he asked. 'His wife and the animals have all tried.'

God thought for a moment, then said: 'Go to the donkey and tell him this. Tell him that ordinary, every-day creatures are very dear to me. Tell him that those who are beaten, mocked and laughed at by others have a place close to my heart. And so has he. Tell him that although others think he's a fool and he thinks he's dull and boring, he will prove wiser than many men. And tell him this—that one day a donkey, like himself, will bear my Son upon his back and ride proudly through a great city, and people will cheer him and throw fresh leaves and flowers in his path. Comfort him with my words—for he is very special to me.'

So Mr Noah went to the donkey and told him everything that God had said. At first the donkey would not listen. But in a little while he got to his feet and began to take some food. And when at last he was persuaded by Mr Noah and his wife to go into the big hall, he met with great kindness from the other animals, and nobody laughed at him, so that he soon felt quite well and happy.

'Perhaps it's not such a bad thing to be a donkey,' he said that night to his wife. 'Not if we're special to God.'

7

THE SON'S TALE

When God told Mr Noah to build the ark which was to save him and two of every animal, insect and bird in the world from the flood, God also told Mr Noah to take his wife, his three sons, Shem, Ham and Japheth and their wives into the ark so that they, too, would be saved.

The three sons helped their father build the ark, using wood specially chosen by God, and when the animals, insects and birds began to arrive, Shem, Ham and Japheth were there beside Mr Noah, sorting out problems, showing the animals where to sleep and looking after the hundred and one things that needed doing before everyone was safely inside.

They all took turns in cooking, cleaning and keeping the ark in good condition during the voyage. There was a lot of work to be done and, to begin with, no one grumbled. They were all much too grateful to be alive as the rain began to fall and the earth disappeared under the waters of the flood.

It was crowded on the ark and, after a while, tempers began to grow short. The rain fell steadily, day after day. Ham, especially, found life difficult.

'I'm bored,' he said one day to his elder brother.

Shem was surprised. 'I don't know how you can be bored with all this work,' he said.

'Well, I am,' said Ham. 'And I'm fed up. We shouldn't be doing work like this, cleaning up after the animals, feeding the animals, watering the animals, making sure they're kept happy.'

'Well, if we don't keep the animals happy, there's no hope for any of us,' Shem said.

'Nobody worries if *I'm* happy,' Ham said as he left the cabin.

Outside the cabin he stumbled over the hedgehog.

'Can't you look where you're going?' he asked angrily.

'I could say the same to you,' replied the hedgehog mildly, 'but I won't. Good day to you.'

Soon after that, the lion went to see Mr Noah.

'Acting on the instructions of the animals, insects and birds,' the lion began pompously, 'I have been sent to inform you that we are not happy about the behaviour of your second son, Ham. He's upset a good many of us.'

'Oh dear,' said Mr Noah.

'He kicked the rabbit yesterday,' the lion said.

'That's bad,' said Mr Noah.

'And he told the warthog he was surprised God had ever made such an ugly creature,' the lion went on. 'Quite upset his feelings, it did.'

'I'm not surprised,' said Mr Noah.

'I wouldn't let a cub of mine behave as your son does and we think it's high time you did something about it.'

'Yes indeed,' said Mr Noah. 'I'll speak to him at once.'

When Ham came to see him, Mr Noah was firm.

'You've been upsetting the animals and it's got to stop.'

'I haven't done anything,' Ham said.

'I've had the lion here with a list of complaints about your rude behaviour,' said Mr Noah.

'What a cheek! Anyway, who are they to complain? They ought to be grateful to us for saving them!'

'No, Ham,' said Mr Noah. 'Not grateful to *us*. Grateful to God. *He* saved them from the flood. He saved us too and don't you forget it.'

Ham left his father and went to the food store. It was his job that evening to give out the food and drink. But he was far too angry to keep his mind on his work and the animals received only a small amount of food that night and no water at all.

'The service on this voyage really is slipping,' said the emu, poking in her trough.

'Hey, lion, you're the assistant—is there any reason

why our food rations have been cut?' asked the bear bluntly.

'And our water,' called the otter. 'I must have water and my container is quite dry!'

'Here!' said the weasel, angrily pushing the polecat to one side. 'Get your filthy snout out of my feeding trough!'

The polecat pushed him back and in no more than a minute they were fighting round and round the big hall.

'Now then, what's all this?' said Mr Noah, hurrying on to the scene.

'It's him, he started it,' said the weasel.

'No I didn't, he did,' retorted the polecat.

'That's quite enough,' said Mr Noah sternly. 'Lion,

what happened?'

'It's our food,' said the lion. 'Mr Noah, are we running short of food?'

Mr Noah was astonished. 'No, of course not,' he said.

'Or water?' asked the otter anxiously.

'We've plenty of water. God told me exactly how much to take.'

'In that case, why have we all been given small helpings of food and no water this evening?' asked the bear.

'I knew it,' said the monkey in a 'told-you-so' voice. 'I knew it all along. We'll die of starvation and thirst.' He swung himself down from a beam in the roof. 'If we don't all drown first, that is.'

'Nonsense,' said Mr Noah. He looked in their food troughs and water containers. 'How very odd. Leave it with me.'

He went out of the hall and called his three sons.

'Shem, Ham, Japheth, which one of you filled the animals' food troughs and water containers just now?'

'I did, Father,' said Ham.

'Why did you give them short measure and no water?'

'I didn't!' said Ham.

Mr Noah sighed. 'I'm getting tired of all this,' he said. 'Go and give them the right amount of food and water and then come back here to me. And I think you should apologize for letting them go hungry and thirsty,' he added.

Ham was furious. 'Apologize? Me? To *them*? To a load of dirty, smelly animals? You must be joking!'

'I was never more serious,' said Mr Noah.

'Well *you* apologize to them then!' Ham shouted. 'Because I'm not!'

He went out of the cabin, slamming the door behind him. Mr Noah sighed while Shem and Japheth looked at each other.

'We'll do the work, Father,' Shem said.

'If you would help, I'd be grateful,' said Mr Noah. 'But Ham's right in a way. *I* should apologize to the animals, because God put me in charge.'

So Mr Noah went to the big hall and called the animals, insects and birds together.

'I'm very sorry that you have had short rations of food and no water,' he said. 'It won't happen again, I can assure you.'

'Why did it happen at all?' asked the monkey grumpily.

'Because my second son was not thinking about what he was doing,' Mr Noah explained.

'No need to make excuses for him,' called the bear, 'we all know he doesn't like us.'

'If he wasn't *your* son I'd soon make short work of him,' growled the tiger.

Mr Noah was very unhappy when he heard this. He

went to his cabin and talked his problem over with God.

'You see, God, I know it's difficult for him—it is for all of us—cooped up here day after day. And there's nothing more depressing than constant rain, is there? But he really must behave better towards the animals, otherwise we'll have no end of trouble.'

While Mr Noah was talking to God, Ham was talking to his wife.

'... and when he said he expected me to *apologize* to the animals ... Well, that was it. I refuse to do another stroke of work on behalf of that lazy, good-for-nothing bunch of creatures out there.'

'But your father ...' began his wife.

Ham interrupted. 'Father! You know what I think? I think he's gone off his head. Let's face it, he's six hundred years old. All this worry—building the ark and everything. He's gone round the bend. What those animals need is a strong hand and no nonsense.' He paced up and down the cabin.

'But God ...' began his wife.

'I know what you're going to say,' Ham said. 'God put my dad in charge, so we've just got to put up with it. Well, you know what I think? I think it was pretty unfair of God to burden the old man with this voyage. A sick old fellow like that ...'

'He's not sick ...' protested his wife.

'Whose side are you on?' Ham asked, but did not give

80

her time to reply. 'God should have chosen a younger man, a fitter man—my brother Shem for example... although he's a bit soft like dad. No—God should have chosen *me* to be in charge here.'

There was a knock on the door and Japheth put his head in.

'Father says you're to go and see him in his cabin.'

'Oh, he does, does he...' Ham began.

'Yes,' said Japheth. 'Now.'

A short while later Ham knocked on Mr Noah's cabin door and went inside.

'Now, Father,' he started to say, 'I've been thinking...'

'I've been thinking too,' said his father, cutting him short. 'And, what's more to the point, I've been talking to God. Have *you* talked to God lately?'

'No, but I really don't see...' Ham began.

'That's the problem,' said his father. 'You don't see beyond the end of your nose.'

Ham tried again. 'Look, Dad. I'm sorry if I was rude, but I was upset when you believed a bunch of wild animals rather than me.'

'I believed my own eyes,' said Mr Noah. 'The animals were hungry and thirsty.'

'Yes, but, well... does it matter that much?' Ham said. 'If you ask me, you take far too much trouble over those animals and it's not good for them—or for you for that

matter. You're not as young as you were.'

His father was silent.

'Look,' Ham went on. 'God chose us to survive. Our family. So he must think that we're a bit special. He put us in charge of the animals. He gave us power over them.'

'He didn't give us power over all the other creatures on this ark to destroy them,' Mr Noah retorted. 'God wants us to work *with* him to keep all of us alive on this ark and that's a big responsibility. I don't know why God chose us to survive, but I do know that it wasn't because we're cleverer or wiser than anyone else, and we're

Shop Name: CHRISTIAN BOOKCENTRE   A/c No. : 088524   18

Title: ALL THE TALES FROM THE ARK PB   2004

Author: ROWLANDS AVRIL

Publisher: LION   Supplier: STL

Retail Price: £6.99   Vat Rate: 0.00%   ISBN: 0-7459.4835-9

Subject: J10 CHILDREN'S FICTION

Order No.: 858636 (2)

Date: 01/07/04

Qty Required: Your Ref: 01/07/2004

certainly not cleverer or wiser than God.'

Ham was silent.

Mr Noah looked at him. 'Go away now—and let's have no more talk about my age either. You're as old as you feel and at the moment I don't feel a day older than two hundred and fifty. If God thinks I'm fit to do the job, who am I to argue? He'll give me all the strength I need.'

So Ham went away to his cabin and thought about what his father had said. Then he went to the big hall and told the animals, insects and birds that he was sorry he had been rude to them and sorry that he had not given them enough to eat or drink.

'Quite right too,' growled the bear.

'Let's hope it doesn't happen again,' the emu sniffed.

'But I expect it will,' said the monkey.

'Oh come on now,' said the hedgehog peaceably. 'He said he's sorry, so let's leave it at that.'

So they did leave it at that. Ham no longer grumbled about the animals or shirked his jobs and the animals no longer went short of food or water. And, for a time, there was peace in the ark.

8

THE PIG'S TALE

The ant-eater and the goose both said afterwards that it was all the pigs' own fault for being greedy. The two pigs said that the monkey started it. The monkey said nothing.

The ark had been afloat for a long time as the rain, which God had sent, had flooded the land. God told Mr Noah that the rain would continue for forty days and forty nights. Mr Noah's son, Shem, had made a calendar which hung in the big hall and every morning Mr Noah crossed through the previous day. The chart now had twenty crosses.

'Which means,' said the owl, who liked doing sums, 'that we have had twenty days of rain. In other words,' he paused while he worked out the figures, 'there are twenty days of rain left.'

'You could say,' said the camel slowly, after thinking the matter over, 'that the voyage is half over.'

'Or there's half still to come,' the monkey added gloomily.

'That depends how you look at it.' The eagle spoke from a rafter high up in the big hall. 'To those who look on the bright side of life, we're half-way through this trip. But to those who look on the gloomy side, we've still half of it left.'

'And the second half is bound to be worse,' said the monkey.

'Why's that?' asked the hedgehog.

'Because that's life,' the monkey said.

'I've enjoyed the first half of this trip,' said the dormouse. 'And I expect the second half will be even better.'

'I'm so glad you're happy,' said the monkey sourly. 'Personally I can think of better things to do than being stuck here. Especially with some of our less well-mannered fellow-travellers,' he added, glancing at the two pigs who were busy swilling down their food with many grunts and snuffles of pleasure.

The emu giggled, then sniffed disapprovingly. 'Not very nice,' she said, 'to those of us who were brought up with *manners*.'

'Lowers the tone of the place,' agreed the ant-eater.

The animals all turned to watch the pigs who, having completely cleaned out their own feeding troughs, were now wandering round the other animals' troughs, hungrily eating all the left-overs.

'If you ask *my* opinion,' said one of the geese loudly,

'God shouldn't have allowed greedy animals like them on board.'

'Hush,' said the other goose. 'They'll hear.'

'Serves them right if they do.'

The pigs *had* heard, not just what the goose had said but what everyone else had said as well, and they were very hurt, because pigs are sensitive animals and get upset easily.

'The thing is, they're right,' said the sow that evening to her husband. 'We *are* greedy.'

'No, we're not,' the boar replied. 'I wouldn't call it greedy to have healthy appetites.'

'I'm just so *hungry* all the time,' the sow said unhappily. 'I think we should ask Mr Noah for bigger rations.'

The boar shook his head. 'We can't do that, honey. The other animals wouldn't like it.'

'They don't like us anyway,' said the sow. 'You heard what they said just because we ate their left-overs. And I do hate waste.'

So the pigs continued to eat the animals' left-over food and, before long, some of the animals began to lie in wait for them at mealtimes in order to poke fun.

'Old greedy-guts are on their way,' cawed the jackdaw in a shrill voice.

'They'll burst if they get any fatter,' said the scorpion, staring at the pigs' waddling walk.

The pigs tried to ignore what was being said, but it was hard, especially when the comments became more and more unkind. It was harder still when the animals began to push and jostle them when they were eating.

The crocodile who knocked over their feeding trough said that it was an accident and that he was very sorry— but there was a particularly nasty grin on his face when he said it and he sniggered loudly when he saw the pigs rooting round on the floor for their meal.

That evening the sow was in tears and her husband very angry.

'*Can't* we go to Mr Noah?' sniffed the sow.

'No,' said her husband. 'It would be telling tales, and besides, Mr Noah has enough problems.'

'Well, I can't take much more of this,' the sow wailed.

Not all the animals joined in the teasing.

'Can't you leave them alone?' asked the kangaroo. 'They're only eating what we don't want.'

'It's stealing,' said the goose in a self-righteous voice.

'Aw, come on,' said the kangaroo. 'They're not doing any harm. It's not right to bully them.'

'It's not bullying, it's only teasing,' said the scorpion.

The kangaroo shrugged. 'Same difference,' he said as he hopped away.

'And it's only a bit of fun,' the jackdaw called out.

'Not much fun for the pigs,' muttered the hedgehog, but he was afraid to speak out loud in case the animals turned on him instead.

That evening the cheetah had the idea of hiding the pigs' food. The animals watched in delight as the pigs arrived for their meal, only to stop in dismay when they saw their empty feeding troughs.

'Come on, where have you put it?' demanded the boar.

'Put what?' asked the cheetah, innocently.

'Our food.'

'What food?' asked the ant-eater.

'Why would we want to put your food anywhere?' asked the scorpion.

'Food? Food? I see no food,' called the jackdaw, flapping his wings wildly and laughing so much that he nearly fell off his perch.

'I'm so hungry!' wailed the sow, in tears.

'Serves you right for being so greedy,' said the ant-eater.

It was too all much for the boar. With a squeal of rage he hurled himself at the ant-eater and soon the big hall was filled with fighting animals. Food was thrown everywhere. It plastered the walls and was trodden underfoot as everyone joined in the fight.

'Just *what* is going on here?'

It was Mr Noah.

The fighting stopped and the lion put on his most dignified air. 'There was a small disagreement,' he said loftily. 'And a minor scuffle broke out. It's nothing really.'

'It looks a great deal more than nothing,' said Mr Noah. He looked around at the animals. None of them spoke.

Mr Noah sighed. 'We haven't any food to spare, I'm afraid, so you'd better clean up and if there's anything left worth eating, that will have to do for your supper.'

When he had gone the animals turned on the pigs.

'Thanks to *you* we haven't anything to eat,' said the emu angrily.

The pigs backed away.

'Don't think we'll forget it,' hissed the goose, waving his long neck.

The pigs turned and fled. That night they talked together in whispers.

'What do you think they'll *do*?' asked the sow.

'I don't know, honey.'

'Will they ever let us eat again?'

The boar was silent.

'I'm so hungry my stomach's rumbling,' said the sow.

'Keep quiet a moment,' said the boar. 'I'm thinking.'

'It's so unfair!'

The boar got to his feet. 'Come on,' he said. 'But quietly.'

They set off, tiptoeing along the dark corridors of the ark. The sow followed the boar nervously. Suddenly the boar stopped and the sow bumped into him.

'There!'

'Where?' asked the sow, nursing a sore nose.

'I guessed as much,' said the boar, very pleased with himself.

He nudged open a door and the two pigs walked into the vast store room that held all the food on the ark. The pigs looked around in wonder.

'I guess we'd better eat fast,' said the boar practically. 'We mustn't be caught here.'

So the two pigs ate as fast as they could. They ate and

ate and when they simply could not squeeze in another mouthful, they staggered back to their sty and fell into a deep and contented sleep.

The following evening the pigs faced the same sneering crowd of animals. Once again their food had been hidden. The sow began to cry.

'Come on, honey,' said the boar. 'We're not stopping to be treated like this,' and he led her out of the big hall.

That night, when everyone was asleep, they returned to the store and stuffed themselves full.

When Mr Noah entered the food store the following day he could not believe his eyes.

'Shem, Ham, Japheth!' he called. 'You haven't been giving the animals extra food, have you?'

'No, Father.'

'Then why have the food supplies gone down so much?'

'Some of the animals have probably been helping themselves,' said Ham. 'I told you to put a lock on the door.'

'I thought I could trust them,' Mr Noah said sadly.

'Shall I call the animals together, Father?' asked Shem. 'You'll want to find the culprit.'

Mr Noah thought for a moment, then he remembered the fight. He shook his head. 'I think this could be a bit complicated. I'd better talk it over with God.'

That night, when the pigs returned to the store-room, they found Mr Noah waiting for them, a grim expression on his face. The pigs squealed in fright.

'Oh—oh!' said the sow. 'My heart—I'm sure I'm having a heart attack!'

'Just sit down, honey,' said the boar, 'and take it easy.' He turned to Mr Noah. 'I can explain everything,' he said. 'We were just getting our rations.'

'But you are given your rations with the other animals,' Mr Noah said, puzzled.

'Well—not exactly, sir.'

'I think you'd better tell me all about it,' said Mr Noah.

He listened quietly as they spoke and did not interrupt.

'Didn't you realize that you were stealing?' he asked

92

when they had finished.

The pigs looked at each other. 'I guess we didn't think of it like that,' said the boar.

'Because the animals hid our food, we just thought we were getting what we were entitled to,' said the sow.

Mr Noah looked round the store-room. 'Well, you've eaten your way through a lot more than your fair share. We'll all have to eat a bit less from now on.'

'I'm very sorry,' said the boar. 'It was my idea to come here.'

'I'm sorry too,' said the sow. 'But we were frightened, you see.'

'Why didn't you come and tell me that the animals were bullying you?' Mr Noah asked gently.

There was silence for a moment, then the boar spoke. '*I* said we shouldn't. I was wrong about that too. I'm really sorry.'

The following morning Mr Noah called all the animals, insects and birds together and told them what had happened. He also told them that their food rations would have to be cut for the rest of the journey.

'Those pigs!' muttered the crocodile. 'Just wait 'til I get my teeth into them!'

'You'll leave the pigs alone,' said Mr Noah sternly. 'And it's not all their fault by any means. You're all to blame. The pigs were wrong to steal, but you were cruel to make fun of them and bully and frighten them.'

'Not all of us bullied the pigs,' said the lion with dignity.

'Maybe not,' said Mr Noah. 'But those of you who knew what was going on and did nothing to stop it are almost as bad.'

The animals were silent.

'I've never locked the store-room because I preferred to trust you,' Mr Noah said. 'Do you want me to lock it now?'

'No,' said the hedgehog. 'I'll come and guard it if you like.'

The cheetah laughed. 'Some guard,' he said. He turned to Mr Noah. 'I'm sorry for my part in bullying the pigs. You're right. We're all to blame. I'll make sure it doesn't happen again and I'm sure you don't need to lock the store-room.'

The rest of the animals agreed, and at feeding time there was peace in the ark.

'But I'm still hungry,' wailed the sow.

'Here,' said the hedgehog, going up to her. 'You can have some of my food. I don't need as much as you.'

'Thank you,' said the sow quietly.

And she dried her eyes and was content.

9

THE SPIDER'S TALE

When all the animals, insects and birds were queueing to enter the ark, Mr Noah looked at them and was amazed at the variety of creatures that existed in the world.

First there were the animals. Big ones and small ones, wild ones and tame, nice ones and nasty ones, tall and short, ugly and beautiful, clever and stupid. The animals walked, jumped, hopped, ran and slithered up the ramp and into the ark.

Then there were the birds. Chirping and cheeping, squawking and squeaking, fluttering and cooing. Large birds and small. Fierce and gentle. The air was alive with the beat of their wings and the chatter of their voices as they flew into the ark.

And lastly came the insects. Creeping and crawling, wriggling and squirming, flying and jumping, the insects came in all shapes and sizes and the look of some of them sent shivers down Mr Noah's back.

But of all the creatures that came into the ark, none

upset Mr Noah as much as the two
black, hairy, long-legged spiders.

'You see, God,' Mr Noah said, once he
was safe in his cabin. 'I'm scared of spiders.'

But God already knew.

Once the door of the ark was closed and Mr
Noah was busy with his daily jobs, he tried not to
think too much about the spiders.

'After all,' said his wife, 'they're God's creatures
just like you and me and perhaps they're scared of
us.'

Which was all very true, but it did not help Mr
Noah.

To make matters worse, the spiders liked exploring. They explored all over the ark, and especially—
or so it seemed to Mr Noah—inside his cabin.

'Please,' Mr Noah said after he had found them
scuttling across the floor. 'Would you mind not
coming in here without knocking?'

'Why?' asked one of the spiders.

'Because it's private. All the other animals knock
if they want to see me.'

'But we don't want to see you particularly,' said
the other spider. 'We just like exploring.'

'Besides,' said the first spider. 'We
can't knock. Our legs wouldn't be strong
enough for you to hear.'

Mr Noah looked at the large number of black legs around the body of the spider and tried not to shudder.

'You don't like us, do you?' said the second spider suddenly.

'Whatever makes you say that?' Mr Noah asked. 'Of course I like you.'

'No, you don't,' the spider persisted. 'Don't think we haven't noticed.'

'If God hadn't told you to look after us, you'd probably squash us,' added the first spider. 'Lots of humans do.'

'No, I wouldn't,' said Mr Noah, but he did not sound convincing.

'It's all right,' the first spider said kindly. 'We understand.'

'I don't know why people don't like us,' the second spider said thoughtfully. 'We're really useful and there are lots of uglier animals and insects than us.'

'I'm sorry,' said Mr Noah. 'I don't know why it is, but I can't help it.'

'We can't help what we look like,' said the first spider. 'I might not have wanted to be born with all these hairy legs.' She waved them around. 'I might have wanted to be like you . . .' she looked at him for a moment, ' . . . or perhaps something rather nicer-looking.'

'And let's face it, we don't harm anyone,' said the second. 'Apart from insects, of course.'

'Come on,' said his wife. 'It's no use staying here. I know when we're not wanted.'

So the two spiders scuttled away and Mr Noah watched them go, glad that they were leaving his cabin, but feeling rather guilty all the same.

'Why am I frightened of them, God?' Mr Noah asked. 'I mean, they're quite right, there are lots of uglier creatures on board but they don't make me shudder and want to run away.'

Just then there was an almighty crash and the whole ark shook.

'Speak to you later, God,' said Mr Noah, and he rushed out of his cabin. The corridor was full of animals and everyone was talking at once.

'He's dead, he's dead, I know he is!' shrieked the emu.

'I just can't stand the sight of blood!' quavered the peacock.

'Stand back,' called the tiger, 'give him some room!'

'I always did say those stairs were a death trap,' said the monkey to anyone who would listen. 'Knew it soon as I came on board.'

Mr Noah knelt over the body of the horse.

'He's not dead, is he?' asked the mare, his wife.

'No,' said Mr Noah, after a quick examination. 'He's not dead. But he's knocked himself out and cut one of his legs rather badly. Shem, go and fetch some water, will you, and tell your mother. She's good at nursing. We'll clean him up and then carry him to his stable.' He turned to the animals. 'How did it happen?'

'I don't know,' said the tiger.

'He slipped,' said the bear. 'Silly thing to do, but it could have happened to anyone.'

'It's those stairs,' said the goose. 'I agree with the monkey. I've always thought they were dangerous. I'm just surprised it hasn't happened before.'

The horse did not come round until late in the evening. When he did, he had a bad headache, which was not surprising. Over the next few days a constant stream of animals, insects and birds came to visit the patient and cheer him up.

Some of the birds sang to soothe his sore head; the squirrel brought him nuts from his private store; the giraffe told long and not very funny stories (which brought back the horse's headache), and the koala bear and the guinea-pig, finding his straw warm and comfortable, moved into his stable. The horse began to feel better, but the cuts on his leg would not heal.

Mrs Noah tried all the ointments she had brought with her but nothing seemed to work. After a while the cuts became infected and the horse grew very ill.

'Good fresh air and sunshine is what he needs,' Mrs Noah said, shaking her head. 'There's nothing more I can do.'

Mr Noah went to see the sick horse who lay sweating

in his stable. His eyes were glazed and his coat was matted and rough to the touch.

'I'm not going to die, am I?' asked the horse in a weak voice.

'No, of course not,' Mr Noah said reassuringly. 'I shall go and talk to God.'

But Mr Noah was very worried.

'What shall I do, God?' he asked. 'How can I save the horse? If he dies there'll be no more horses in the world once the rain stops and the flood goes down. You can't mean that to happen, God. Can't you work a miracle?'

Suddenly Mr Noah felt something tickling the back of his hand. He looked down and jumped in fright. One of the spiders was walking across his hand and up his arm! He shook his arm vigorously and the spider gracefully spun itself to the floor.

'I told you not to come in here without knocking,' Mr Noah said, angry because he had been frightened.

'We did knock, but you didn't hear us,' said the spider.

'So we had to come in, because it's all rather urgent,' explained his wife.

'What do you mean?' asked Mr Noah.

'The horse, of course,' she said patiently. 'You want to save the horse, don't you?'

'I was just talking to God about it when you interrupted me,' Mr Noah replied.

'Exactly,' said the first spider. 'So let's go.'

'Go?' asked Mr Noah. 'Where?'

'To see the horse. Come on, we're wasting time.'

Mr Noah looked at the spiders' black, hairy bodies. 'But what can you do?' he asked in astonishment.

'Nothing if we don't hurry,' said the first spider, already at the door.

The horse was tossing and turning, making small sounds. His wife lay beside him and licked him gently from time to time. Mrs Noah kept the straw piled high around him and many of the animals, insects and birds in the ark were assembled outside, silently watching.

The spiders scuttled through the crowd and crawled onto the horse's leg. The horse twitched a little.

'Now then, dear, it's all right,' said the first spider in a comfortable voice. 'We're not going to hurt you. We're just going to weave a web of the finest silk threads to cover your bad leg and that will make it comfortable.' She turned to her husband. 'You start that end and I'll start this.'

'Hmmph,' said the monkey. '*That* won't do any good!'

'Have you got a better idea?' asked the dormouse.

'Well ...'

'Keep quiet then,' growled the tiger.

The monkey and all the animals kept quiet as the two spiders spun their silken web over and around the cuts on the horse's leg. They made a gentle buzzing sound and the horse lay still. Soon the horse's leg was covered in a

shimmering web of silver strands. The spiders made
silken ladders for themselves, climbed down, and settled
on the straw beside the horse.

'What happens next?' asked the tiger in a loud
whisper.

'Nothing,' said the spider. 'This isn't a circus. The
horse needs peace and quiet. I suggest you all go away.'

Some of the animals did go, but most of them stayed,
falling asleep one by one. The horse fell asleep too. His
breathing was noisy and harsh-sounding. By the middle

of the night the only ones awake were the guinea-pig, who only ever slept for a minute or two at a time, the two spiders, and Mr and Mrs Noah, who spent the night talking to God.

Just before dawn the horse's breathing changed to a deep, peaceful sound and his coat began to regain its rich brown colour. Mrs Noah touched it gently.

'His skin feels warm and smooth,' she said quietly. 'The fever's gone and he's getting better.'

Mr Noah looked at the two spiders and, for once, he

did not shudder when he saw their black, hairy bodies and he was not frightened by their long furry legs.

He held out his hands and the spiders crawled onto them.

'Thank you,' said Mr Noah. 'I'll never be frightened of you again.'

10
THE MONKEY'S TALE

The ark, which Mr Noah had built to God's instructions, had been afloat for over twenty days. The small ship was wrapped in swirling grey mist as it drifted around an endless sea. The rain continued to fall, day after day after day.

Inside the ark, the animals, insects and birds began to wonder whether the rain would ever stop and whether the flood would go down so that they could live on dry land again.

'I'd just like to see a bit of sun and blue sky,' sighed the lark. 'This rain gets me down.'

'Give us a song to cheer us up,' said the camel, but the lark shook her head and went to perch high in the rafters where she could stare out of the window at the slanting rain.

Some of the animals hibernated, tucking themselves into corners and sleeping through the long days and nights. Everyone found life on board the ark more and more difficult.

'We'll be stuck on this ark for ever,' the monkey said gloomily. 'You mark my words.'

'Do you really think so?' the goat asked anxiously.

The camel sniffed. 'Don't take any notice of him. He always looks on the black side of things.'

'*Is* there another side?' the monkey asked sarcastically.

'If we're stuck on this ark, what about food?' asked the pig. 'What happens when we come to the end of the food?'

'We starve,' said the monkey.

'Oh dear,' said the pig, turning pale.

The monkey hunched himself into his corner. 'This whole trip was doomed from the start,' he said. 'It was just a crazy idea of Mr Noah's.'

'But it wasn't Mr Noah's idea, it was God's idea,' said the dog. 'And anyway, it's only going to rain for forty days. That what Mr Noah says and he got that straight from God.'

The monkey gave a secret little smile. 'Suppose Mr Noah got it wrong?'

'He couldn't have,' said the dog.

'He might have,' the monkey persisted. 'He's only a human after all, and they're not anything like as clever as they make out.'

'They're a great deal cleverer than you,' said the dog, bristling.

'Oh, we all know how well *you* get on with them,' sneered the monkey.

'Mr Noah is a good man,' said the dormouse who was lying half-asleep on some straw.

'I never said he wasn't. But, good or not, he could still have got it wrong.' The monkey looked round the circle of doubtful faces. 'That's why I'm saying we'll be on this ark for ever.'

There was a dismayed silence.

Then the bear said bluntly, 'You like upsetting things and making mischief, don't you?'

'Me?' said the monkey, raising his eyebrows. 'We have to look at the facts, don't we?' And he looked round at the crowd of gloomy faces.

The giant tortoise, who seldom spoke, slowly lifted his great head and looked at the monkey.

'I have lived longer than you, monkey,' he said in his deep voice. 'In fact, I have lived longer than you all. I can remember times when the rain came and the rivers rose and flooded the land. They were terrible times. But in the end the rain stopped and the waters went down. And I can remember times of drought, dreadful times when everything was dry and all living creatures cried out for water. But the rain came in the end. And this flood will pass also. Everything passes in time.'

'But this time it might be different,' said the monkey.

The giant tortoise stared at the monkey. His wise old

eyes in his lined and wrinkled face were stern. 'I think not,' he said.

'Well, all we can do is trust in Mr Noah and hope that we survive,' said the dog.

The monkey turned on him. 'I've no hope at all that we'll survive, and I don't trust Mr Noah or anyone else,' he said. 'Anyway, I'm tired of all this talking. You believe what you want. I don't believe in what I can't see and I can't see any sign of the rain stopping.'

The days passed and the rain showed no sign of stopping. The atmosphere in the ark grew more and more gloomy. Everyone was affected. Arguments and fights broke out among the animals, the birds refused to sing and Mr Noah's sons and their wives rushed through their jobs and spent as much time as they could shut up in their cabins. Meanwhile the monkey went around with an 'I told you so' expression on his face. This made even the gentlest animals want to bite him.

Even Mr Noah became gloomy and began to have doubts. He wondered whether he *had* got it wrong after all. Maybe he had not understood God. Perhaps the rain would not stop after forty days and then where would they be? A small, frail ark sailing for ever without food, without water and with a cargo of increasingly hungry animals. Mr Noah shuddered at the thought.

Perhaps, Mr Noah thought at last, *God* might have got it wrong. He tried talking to God, but God must have been busy because he did not answer.

Mr Noah stopped trying to cheer up the animals, he felt so miserable himself. He spent more and more time in his cabin thinking about the life he used to have before the flood. He remembered the house he had lived in with his wife and sons and thought longingly of his fine vineyards. His wine had been the best in the neighbourhood. Mr Noah wondered whether he would ever make wine again and whether life would ever be the same again.

There was a knock on his door. It was the lion.

'I'm sorry to trouble you, Mr Noah, but you must

come quickly.'

'Why? What's happened?'

'It's the frogs.'

Mr Noah left his cabin and hurried down the corridor, the lion at his heels.

'They've hopped on to the roof and they're threatening to jump off.'

'Why?'

'Because the monkey says it'll never stop raining and we're stuck on this ark for ever and the frogs said that if that's the case they'd rather die now and get it over with.'

'Oh dear.'

'Yes, and the monkey says perhaps we should all do that. But *he* doesn't seem too anxious to jump off himself. Personally I think it's all a trick to get more space and more food for himself—I wouldn't trust that monkey an inch. But anyway, some of the animals are already

climbing onto the roof.'

When Mr Noah and the lion reached the top of the ark they found not only the frogs, but also the ostrich perched on the roof while a host of animals, insects and birds crowded the corridor. Mr Noah put his head through the trapdoor and peered out.

'Whatever are you doing?' he asked.

'We think the monkey's right,' croaked the frog. 'It'll never stop raining and there's no point going on and on hoping that everything will come right. So we've decided to end it now.'

'Please come down,' Mr Noah pleaded. 'Why listen to what the monkey says?'

'Because it makes sense,' said the other frog.

'But God makes sense too,' said Mr Noah. 'And we have his promise that the rain will stop.'

'How do we know that?' sneered the monkey, who was down in the corridor. 'We only have *your* word for it. And we haven't seen much of you lately, have we? Perhaps you've been doubting God as well?'

Mr Noah turned red, for that was exactly what he had been doing. But he answered stoutly.

'Look, I know it's difficult. But we have to trust God. That's the only hope we have.'

Suddenly the ostrich shrieked. 'Help! I don't like heights!'

'Then why did you climb up there in the first place,

you silly creature?' asked the lion crossly.

'Save me, Mr Noah!' screeched the ostrich. 'I don't want to die!'

The frog gulped. 'Neither do I,' he said suddenly.

Mr Noah held out his arms and caught the ostrich, who wriggled and squirmed. Eventually he managed to get the bird back into the ark. Slowly the frogs followed and the trapdoor was shut. The animals returned to the big hall and Mr Noah went to his cabin.

'God, are you there?' he asked.

'I'm always here,' God said.

'They're saying that this rain is never going to end,' said Mr Noah unhappily.

'I know what they are saying,' said God.

'What can I do about it?'

'Trust me,' God replied.

'I do.'

'Do you? What about your doubts? What about your vineyard, Noah, and your worries about the future?'

Mr Noah was silent.

'The animals will never believe you unless you yourself believe what I say.'

Mr Noah looked down.

'Noah,' said God. 'It all depends on you. I can't make you trust me.'

There was a long silence. At last Mr Noah spoke in a small voice.

'If I hadn't trusted you, Lord, I wouldn't be here now. I'd have drowned long ago.' He looked up. 'I'm sorry for doubting you.'

'There's nothing wrong in having doubts, Noah, so don't apologize,' said God.

Mr Noah went to the big hall and called everyone together. He cleared his throat and held up his hand for silence.

'God has promised that we'll be saved, and God does not break his promises,' he said firmly. 'Just be patient a little longer and don't lose hope.'

'All very fine words,' the monkey sneered. 'But it hasn't stopped the rain.'

The eagle suddenly swept down into the hall.

'The rain *has* stopped,' he called out.

He flew up to the trapdoor and pushed it wide open. And for the first time for forty days and forty nights, the animals, insects and birds felt cold fresh *dry* air stream down on their upturned faces.

'Look!' cried the skylark, her face uplifted to catch the breeze. 'There's blue sky!'

The clouds that had wrapped the earth in a grey mist were blowing away, driven by winds that sent them scudding across the sky. One patch of blue appeared, then another and soon the whole sky was radiant with colour, blue and red and gold, as the setting sun sank towards the horizon.

One after another the birds flew up and out of the ark, singing for joy. The light of the sun shone on their faces, and their wings seemed tipped with gold.

Some animals and insects clambered on to the roof, holding on to each other tightly to make sure they did not fall off. The ones left inside began to dance and sing and Mr and Mrs Noah and their family thanked God for ending the rain.

And the monkey?

The monkey went quietly to his sleeping place and no one missed him at all.

11

THE ELEPHANT'S TALE

The morning after the rain had stopped, the lion woke Mr Noah early.

'Excuse me, Mr Noah, but we've had a check and everyone's present and correct.'

Mr Noah blinked. 'Pleasant and...?'

'*Present*, Mr Noah. Ready and waiting.'

Mr Noah shook his head and tried to wake up.

'Waiting for what?'

'The door to open, of course.'

'What door?'

'The door to the ark. Will you open it yourself or will we have the pleasure of seeing God perform the grand opening ceremony?'

Mr Noah got out of bed and groped for his sandals. 'I think I'd better come,' he said.

The corridor outside his cabin was full of hurrying animals, crawling insects and flying birds. The babble of noise grew louder as Mr Noah approached the big hall.

Inside, he found a crowd of excited animals, insects and birds all milling around in front of the big closed door of the ark. Even his sons and their wives were waiting eagerly, clutching their few belongings in their hands.

A cheer went up as he appeared. Someone started to sing 'For he's a jolly good fellow' at the back of the hall.

'C'mon, Mr Noah, stir yourself!' called the fox.

'Open the door, Mr Noah!' cried the jackal. 'I want to go hunting again!'

Mr Noah blinked at all the excitement.

'I'm sorry,' he said, 'but there's been some mistake.'

'Mistake?'

The singing stopped and the shouts died away.

'What sort of a mistake?' asked the leopard slowly.

'Didn't you tell us that God said it would rain for forty days and forty nights?' asked the jackal.

'Well, yes,' agreed Mr Noah.

'And during that time the earth would be flooded, but all of us here in this ark would be saved from the flood?'

'Of course.'

'And after forty days and forty nights the rain would stop?'

'Absolutely.'

The jackal thrust his face close to Mr Noah's.

'Well, the rain's stopped now, hasn't it? So what's to stop us from leaving, eh?'

Mr Noah took a step back. 'Just take a look outside.'

The eagle, who had been keeping to his perch high up in the rafters of the hall and close to the trapdoor, looked down on the assembled group.

'We can't leave,' he said. 'If we opened the door now, the ark would fill with water and sink. We're still floating on an endless sea and there is no land at all in sight.'

Everyone heard this in silence. The panther, who had been pacing up and down impatiently, turned to Mr Noah.

'Well?' he asked in a silky voice.

'Well what? What the eagle said is right. We can't leave the ark yet.'

'How long?' snapped the fox.

Mr Noah shook his head. 'I don't know.'

'Didn't God tell you how long it would be before we could leave?' asked the panther.

'No. I'm afraid he didn't.'

'Then I suggest you go and ask him,' said the jackal.

Mr Noah was worried as he spoke to God. 'Don't get me wrong, God. I'm not asking for myself, but there are some very angry animals out there and I'm not sure how I'll manage to keep them quiet unless you can give me a hint about how long it will be before the flood-waters subside.'

But God shook his head. 'I'm sorry, Noah, I can't tell you that. I can't tell you everything. You will just have to be patient and wait.'

'Wait?,' squeaked Mr Noah in a frightened voice. 'Wait? Well, that's all very well, God, and I'm happy enough to wait, as you know, but what do I tell the animals? I can't ask *them* to be patient. You don't know them like I do.'

God smiled. 'The animals will surprise you,' he said.

'That's what I'm afraid of,' Mr Noah said darkly, but God spoke no more.

When Mr Noah told the animals, insects and birds what God had said, there were angry faces and even

angrier voices.

'False pretences, that's what it is. You got us here under false pretences,' said the ant-eater.

'Forty days is what you said and forty days is what I understood,' the jackal complained.

'I think, Mr Noah, you have some explaining to do,' said the panther in a dangerously quiet voice and the animals murmured agreement. They began to close in on Mr Noah in a menacing way, but instead of being frightened, Mr Noah grew angry.

'Just a minute!' he said loudly. 'Just a minute! All I ever said was that God wanted to save two of each of you from the flood. He told me to build this ark and said that once the door was shut, it would rain for forty days and forty nights until the earth and all its wickedness was wiped out. God never gave a time limit as to how long we'd have to stay on the ark. If God *does* know he's not saying, and why should he? It's not my fault that you can't leave the ark.'

The animals were quiet now. Mr Noah went on. 'Look, I know it's a disappointment, but be sensible. Now that the rain's stopped, the flood-waters will go down eventually.'

'It's like a prison sentence without knowing when you'll be let out,' muttered the rat in a dejected voice.

The emu sniffed. 'Never having been in prison, I really couldn't say,' she said. She turned to Mr Noah. 'I still think it's your fault. It really is too bad of you.'

Mr Noah sighed. 'Just be thankful that you're alive and safe.'

There was some restless murmuring in the hall, then the elephant spoke. 'That's very true, Mr Noah. We *should* be grateful. And my wife and I thank you for saving us from the flood.'

The elephant's wife looked round the hall. 'I think, instead of sitting here complaining, we ought to do something with the time we still have together on the ark.'

'Like what?' asked the fox abruptly.

'Like ... um ... like ... having a party,' she said. 'And, if you all agree, we will organize it.'

The tiger brightened up. 'I'll help,' he said.

'And me,' said the giraffe.

'Count us in,' called the birds.

The tiger smiled happily. 'We'll form a committee.'

'Thank you, God,' said Mr Noah quietly. 'You said the animals would surprise me.'

Plans for the party were soon under way. Suggestions for entertainment poured in. The committee took lots of decisions and the elephants—who did most of the work—could be seen, and heard, thundering from one end of the ark to the other. The party was going to last for a whole day. It would include games and competitions, side-shows and displays.

'If you like,' said the peacock graciously, 'I'll display my beautiful tail once an hour for those who wish to admire it.'

'Thank you very much,' said the elephant.

The mandrill laughed. 'In that case I'll display my beautiful red and pink bottom,' he said rudely. 'I bet I get as many admirers as the peacock.'

It took both elephants and the entire committee a long time to soothe the peacock's ruffled feelings.

The next day, every corner of the ark was filled with animals, insects and birds practising for the party. The elephants went round with their long trunks in the air and worried expressions on their faces.

'Food,' said the elephant. 'I know food is rationed, but we do need something a bit special for the party.'

He went off in search of Mr Noah.

'Notices,' said the elephant's wife. 'We need notices about the party.'

'Why?' asked the tiger. 'Everyone knows about it.'

'Just in case they don't,' she said. 'Who can write?'

'Who can read?' asked the monkey, who had been keeping out of all the preparations.

'Mr Noah's sons can write,' said the tiger. 'I'll go and ask them.'

Then the elephant's wife had another thought. 'We must clean and decorate the big hall,' she said. 'Now let me think...'

The night before the party when most of the animals, insects and birds were safely asleep, the committee met in the big hall. They worked hard and by morning the place was transformed. The floor shone with wax provided by the bees and polished by the elephants and tigers. The walls had been hung with lacy webs made by the spiders. The eating place groaned with extra rations of food and everything shimmered in the glow worm's soft light.

As the animals, insects and birds entered the hall on the following day, they gasped in amazement.

Then Mr Noah and his family arrived.

'This is wonderful,' said Mr Noah, his face beaming with pleasure. 'Why didn't you tell us what you'd planned? We would have come and helped.'

'We wanted it to be a surprise for you and Mrs Noah as much as for everyone else,' said the elephant. 'It's our way of saying thank you for all you have done for us.'

Before long, everyone had settled down to the serious business of eating. Once the feast was over the competitions began. The polar bear challenged the tiger for the title 'Strongest Animal on the Ark'. They lifted the two hippopotami who were very heavy. The cheetah challenged any animal to a race round the hall for the title 'Fastest Animal on the Ark'. Not to be outdone, the sloth, the tortoise and the snail entered a competition for the title 'Slowest Animal on the Ark' and were still finishing the course two days after the party had ended!

The termites demonstrated their house-building skills, the woodpeckers pecked wood, the kangaroo beat his own record for the long jump, while the peacock graciously showed off his tail. The mandrill did not show off anything and the lion, with great dignity, acted as Master of Ceremonies.

Then came the entertainment. The chameleon, in a very dramatic performance, changed colour from green to red to brown. This was followed by the snake who shed his entire skin. The giraffe told long and not very funny stories and the penguins, neat and tidy in black and white, did a song and dance routine.

The donkey did a juggling act and was applauded every time he dropped a plate—which was very often—and everyone gasped at the magpie's amazing conjuring tricks as he made various objects disappear. The spiders performed a trapeze act on fine webs they had woven for the purpose and a mixed choir of birds, conducted by the blackbird, sang a medley of songs for the audience to join in.

At the end they all clapped loudly, for a long, long time. Even the crocodile—who was not the easiest of animals to please—said that he hadn't enjoyed himself so much for years.

After the entertainment came the dancing. The wolf asked the sheep to dance, the leopard could be seen with the cow, and the fox bent his head politely to listen to something the rabbit was saying as they danced together. The flamingo gave a solo performance and the only moment of panic came when the two elephants, flushed with success, danced too heavily at the far end of the hall, causing the ark to dip and wobble in the water. The animals dragged them back to the centre and the dancing continued until late into the night.

There was a magic about that party and no one wanted it to end. Afloat on a black sea, the small ark was filled with laughter and song and a feeling of goodwill among the humans, animals, insects and birds that had never been there before.

'It's been a lovely evening,' said the elephant's wife, and there were tears in her eyes.

'Yes it has,' said the dormouse. He sighed. 'If only it could always be like this.'

'Yes,' agreed Mr Noah. 'If only it could.'

12

THE DOVE'S TALE

'I do feel ill,' said the kangaroo, as the ark dipped and bobbed on the water.

'You shouldn't have jumped about so much last night,' said the hippopotamus. 'Made me quite dizzy watching you.'

It was the day after the party in which the animals, insects and birds on board the ark had celebrated the stopping of the rain.

'*I* didn't jump about and I feel ill too,' groaned the giraffe. 'What's happened to the floor? It's going up and down.'

'It's the after-effects of the party,' said the lion, who was slumped against the wall, looking quite pale and unlike himself. 'Why is it that one always feels unwell after a party?' He stopped suddenly. 'Oh dear,' he said in a quavering voice. 'I do feel sick.'

The eagle flew in through the trapdoor in the roof of the ark. 'It's wonderful out there,' he said. 'There's a fine, strong wind blowing. And there are some huge waves. The sea's very rough.'

But few of the animals heard him. They were feeling far too ill.

The wind blew for several days, tossing the little ark up and down on stormy waters. Almost all the animals were seasick, many of the insects felt off-colour and Mr Noah, Mrs Noah and their entire family kept to their cabins as much as they could.

'But just think,' said Mr Noah, trying to keep cheerful as he tottered around with a green face, 'this wind will soon dry up the flood.'

'Can't be soon enough for me,' groaned the dog, who did not like travelling on boats at the best of times.

But although the wind was strong, no land appeared, and the sea of flood-water on which the ark floated seemed as deep as ever.

Then the wind dropped. The scudding clouds cleared away and a hot sun shone out of a blue sky. Each day the birds streamed out of the ark and circled high in the air, searching for land. The animals began to feel better and those who could swim dived off the side of the ark and searched underwater. Those who could neither fly nor swim took it in turns to sit up on the roof and enjoy the fresh air.

'I do like lying in the sun,' said the tiger, stretching out on the roof of the ark.

'Be careful!' squeaked the hedgehog. 'You nearly knocked me off.'

'Sorry,' said the tiger. 'I wonder why Mr Noah didn't make the roof of the ark any bigger? There would have been room for more of us up here.'

The eagle, who was circling above them, laughed. 'I don't suppose Mr Noah was thinking about sunbathing when he built the ark,' he said.

'It's all right for you,' the tiger grumbled. 'You can fly.'

The giraffe poked his long neck through the trapdoor.

'Come on,' he said to the tiger. 'Shift yourself. You've been up here twice as long as anyone else. Get down and let someone else have a chance.'

The tiger stood and stretched. 'Oh, very w...e...ll!'

His voice ended in a shriek as the ark shuddered and jerked. The tiger lost his footing and slid to the very edge of the roof.

'Help ... !'

The hedgehog, the giraffe and the monkey grabbed at his tail while the birds circled low, uttering cries of distress.

Mr Noah jumped on to the roof and helped pull the tiger to safety.

'What happened?' the tiger asked, badly shaken.

'We must have hit something,' Mr Noah said.

'An iceberg,' called the polar bear, who was in the water enjoying a swim. 'Have we hit an iceberg, Mr Noah?'

'No, of course not,' said Mr Noah. 'It's far too warm for icebergs. I think it must be land of some sort. Perhaps the top of a mountain.'

'Is the ark all right?' asked the dormouse, anxiously poking his head through the trapdoor. 'It hasn't been damaged, has it?'

'I'll go and look,' said the polar bear. He dived out of sight but surfaced a moment later on the other side of the ark. 'No damage, but we're stuck on something,' he called.

'Isn't it exciting?' said the monkey sarcastically. 'I can't wait for the ark to capsize.'

'Oh shut up,' said the tiger irritably, and went down

to the big hall to recover.

That evening the birds met on the roof.

'It's wonderful to be flying again,' said the nightingale. 'I feel as if the whole world has just been born.'

'I didn't want to come back,' said the seagull. 'I wanted to fly on and on across the sea.'

'Well, why did you come back?' asked the raven. He looked round at the birds. 'Why did any of us come back? We've got wings, haven't we? We're not tied to this ark. There must be land somewhere and we can fly away to find it.'

'I don't think that's right,' said the dove in her soft voice. 'We can't just fly off and leave everyone behind. That would be selfish.'

'Why should we worry about everyone else?' asked the raven. 'When have they worried about us?'

'That's not the point,' said the dove gently. 'We're all in this together.'

'No, we're not,' said the raven. 'We're all in this because Mr Noah was told by God to save two of each of us from the flood. It was just chance that we were chosen.'

'Mr Noah has fed us and looked after us,' said the eagle.

'And kept us safe from being eaten,' said the sparrow.

'All right,' said the raven. 'Mr Noah has been good to us. But I don't see that staying here when we don't need to is going to help Mr Noah. Look at it this way. Aren't

we the ones who are selfish by staying and using the food and space that others need?'

The birds murmured as they thought about this. Then the eagle spoke harshly. 'You're just trying to find excuses for going off and doing what you want to do!'

'No, I'm not!' said the raven angrily.

Mr Noah put his head through the trapdoor.

'There you all are, I was looking for you. I need your help. I'd like one of you to fly away from the ark to see if there is any sight of land. Would anyone volunteer?

'As the bird with the keenest eyesight . . .' the eagle began.

'I'll go,' said the raven quickly.

The blackbird looked at him. 'You won't come back,' he said. 'You just told us so.'

'I will,' said the raven. He turned to Mr Noah. 'Honestly, Mr Noah, I will come back.'

Mr Noah looked round the circle of birds. No one

spoke.

He turned to the raven. 'Very well,' he said. 'I trust you.'

The following day the raven flew out of the ark, high into the blue sky. The ark grew smaller and smaller until it was just a tiny speck on the wide sea.

'I'm free!' called the raven, but no one heard him.

He flew higher still and the ark disappeared from sight.

'Oh, how good to get away!' the raven thought. 'How good to be flying in the silent air with the sun on my wings...'

He flew on and on.

'Just a little further...' he thought. 'There'll be land a little further. If I do find land, should I go back to the ark and tell them, or keep it to myself?' he wondered. 'I could be the first bird in the world. I could be the *only* bird in the world...'

The daylight faded and the raven grew tired and hungry.

'Perhaps I'll go back tonight and have a rest and some food and then try again tomorrow,' he thought.

He turned round, but the sky had grown very dark and the sea even darker. Where was the ark? The raven was afraid.

'I shouldn't have been so keen to go,' he said out loud, but no one heard him.

'I've been very selfish,' he said, but the wind carried his words away.

'I wish I could find my way home,' he called in despair.

Inside the ark, Mr Noah was growing more and more worried.

'I shouldn't have sent him, Lord,' he said. 'The other birds told me he wouldn't come back. I shouldn't have trusted him.'

'It would be a sad world without trust,' said God. 'You did what you thought right, Noah. Now go to bed and get some rest and leave the raven to my care.'

But although Mr Noah went to bed, he could not sleep, and the following morning he was up at dawn, standing on the roof of the ark, looking anxiously into the sky.

Suddenly he shouted out loud. There, in the distance, flying very, very slowly, was the raven. He landed with a thud on the roof of the ark.

'I'm sorry,' he gasped. 'I wasn't going to come back at all ... then I was hungry ... and tired ... lost my way ...'

'Did you see any land?' asked the eagle, who was circling above.

The raven slowly shook his head. 'No land ...'

'Never mind,' said Mr Noah. 'I'm just glad you did come back.'

He gave the raven food and put him to bed. It was some days before Mr Noah asked for another volunteer to fly off in search of land.

'Do you still trust us?' asked the eagle slowly. 'We feel that the raven let us all down.'

'I trust you,' said Mr Noah.

The birds were silent for a moment, then the dove stirred.

'If you and God think it right for one of us to go, then I volunteer,' she said in her gentle voice.

'Thank you,' said Mr Noah.

For a while longer they waited and watched, but the flood-waters seemed as high as ever and no land appeared, so at last the dove flew out of the ark. She circled once, twice, three times and her eyes were dazzled by the sun. She flew in great sweeping arcs, backwards and forwards across the sea but there was no sign of land. At last it began to grow dark and the dove returned to the ark. She was so tired that Mr Noah had to hold her in his hands and help her inside.

'There is no land as far as I can see,' she said wearily, 'and I travelled for miles.'

'We'll wait a bit longer,' said Mr Noah. 'As long as the sun shines the flood-waters will dry up.'

The sun carried on shining and the animals carried on taking turns to bask in the warm air on the roof of the ark. The insects did what insects usually do and the birds flew around, strengthening their wings for the return to the world.

Seven days later the dove set out again from the ark. She was stronger now and could fly further. She flew low, skimming the surface of the water as she watched for any sign of land. All day she flew but she could see nothing.

'Oh dear,' she thought. 'I did so want to take good news back to Mr Noah.'

The sun slipped lower and lower in the sky until it disappeared below the horizon. Disappointed, the dove turned to go. She flew slowly, still searching in the red afterglow of sunset.

Then she spotted it. There was something sticking up out of the water. She flew down to look. It was a branch, a branch of a tree and on it were some leaves. The dove plucked one and flew back in triumph to the ark.

There was enormous excitement at her return.

'What is it?' asked the polar bear, prodding it with a curious paw.

'It's a leaf, you fool,' said the goat.

'I can see it's a leaf, but what sort?' asked the polar

bear. 'I've never seen anything quite like it before.'

'It's from an olive tree,' said the donkey. 'There's a lot of them where I come from.'

'What does it mean?' asked the emu excitedly.

'It means land,' said Mr Noah. 'It means that the water on earth has gone down and the tree-tops are above the water.'

'So can we get off the ark?' asked the hedgehog.

'Soon, soon,' said Mr Noah.

He waited another seven days before doing anything more.

'Better be safe than sorry,' he said.

This time he sent both doves. 'I think you should both go,' he said. 'Because if you do find land, there's no point in your returning here.'

The two doves went round the ark saying goodbye to the other birds as well as the animals and insects.

'You know, I feel quite upset at the thought of leaving,' said one of the doves. 'In some ways I almost hope we don't find land, although I know that's silly.'

Last of all the doves went to Mr Noah.

'If we don't come back, Mr Noah, we'll never forget you,' they said.

'And I'll never forget you,' said Mr Noah. He took them gently in both his hands. 'I'll always think of you as messengers of peace, for you brought the news that God has kept his promise.'

The doves flew up through the trapdoor. They circled low over the ark, calling their goodbyes, then they soared up into the air and were gone.

They never came back.

A few days later Mr Noah looked out of the trapdoor in the roof of the ark and saw dry land all about him!

13
THE DORMOUSE'S TALE

After forty days and forty nights the rain—which God had sent to destroy the earth and all its wickedness—had stopped. The flood waters had gone down and the ark was grounded on the top of a mountain called Ararat.

The animals, insects and birds who had shared the ark with Mr Noah and his family for so long were all ready to leave. They crowded into the big hall, noisy and excited.

'Where's Mr Noah?' asked the goat irritably. 'Why doesn't he come and open the door?'

'Yes,' said the wolf licking his lips. 'I want to get out of here and go hunting again.'

The fox grinned and eyed the rabbits and the dormice thoughtfully.

'Mmm... tasty... very tasty... but which to eat first?'

'It's so hard to make decisions, isn't it?' said the panther softly as he paced up and down. The jackal laughed, showing sharp teeth.

The dormouse and his wife listened to this talk and shivered.

Mr Noah, in the meantime, was still in his cabin, slowly packing his things and talking to God.

'You know I didn't want to take the job on in the first place, God, and I must admit that at times I didn't think we'd make it, but now it's all over I feel quite sad.'

'It isn't all over yet, Noah,' God said.

'Isn't it?'

'Not quite.'

There was a knock and the lion entered. He had washed and brushed his mane and looked quite splendid..

'Ah, Mr Noah, forgive me for interrupting but everyone's waiting.'

'Waiting?'

'For you to open the door—unless of course God himself honours us with his presence.'

Mr Noah got to his feet.

'Of course,' he said. 'How stupid of me. I didn't think you'd all be quite so eager to go. I must come and say goodbye.'

The lion bowed himself out.

'I see what you mean, God, about it not being over,' Mr Noah said. 'I'm shirking my duties.'

God smiled, but said nothing.

Mr Noah left his cabin and closed the door behind

him. He was a short man with rounded shoulders bent with age. His beard had grown long during the voyage and his robe was shabby and much mended. He did not look at all important. He slowly made his way along the corridor and entered the big hall. When they saw him, all the animals and insects stood up and cheered. The birds flew down from the rafters and, at a signal from the blackbird, burst into song.

'Three cheers for Mr Noah!' quacked the duck, and the noise echoed through the ark. Mr Noah stopped still in

amazement. He looked round the hall and tears came to his eyes.

The cheers ended in a storm of clapping. Tails thumped on the floor, birds flapped their wings and the elephant did a short dance with the kangaroo. Mr Noah held up his hand for silence.

'My dear friends,' he began, but his voice was quite choked. He cleared his throat and started again. 'My *very* dear friends. This is altogether too kind of you. Much too kind. But you shouldn't cheer me, you know. I just did what God told me. He's the one who saved you from the flood.'

'But you made it possible,' said the lion. He stepped forwards in a dignified manner and coughed importantly. 'Hmph, her-umph... Mr Noah, on behalf of all the creatures of the world...'

'Cut the cackle and open the door,' called the fox rudely.

The lion ignored him. 'On this most important, indeed illustrious, occasion...'

'What's he talking about?' asked the giraffe.

'... I take it upon myself as your assistant and King of all the Animals...'

'Watch it,' said the tiger dangerously.

'... to offer our deepest thanks to Mr Noah, Mrs Noah, their sons Shem, Ham and Japheth and their sons' most charming wives...'

The crocodile yawned loudly.

'...for saving us from the flood. We animals...'

'He doesn't mean us, dear, we're not animals, I'm pleased to say,' said the cockroach to his wife.

'We animals...'

A chant began at the back of the hall.

'Open the door, *open the door*, OPEN THE DOOR...!'

It grew louder and the lion, looking rather put out, stopped speaking.

'Thank you, lion, for those kind thoughts,' said Mr Noah hurriedly. 'You and the tiger have both been very good and faithful assistants. Now,' he said in a louder voice. 'Before I open the door and we go our separate ways, I need to cross your names off my list.'

'Why do you need to do that?' asked the goose. 'We're all here, same as when we started, apart from the doves of course.'

'I like to keep things straight,' said Mr Noah.

So, with a certain amount of grumbling and pushing, the animals, insects and birds formed into a queue.

'All this red tape is very tiring,' grumbled the goose.

'Well, I think it's excellent,' said the magpie fussily. 'These things should be checked.'

'To make sure you haven't been stealing bits of the ark, I suppose,' the monkey said sourly.

'Well, really...!' The magpie bristled.

'Oh dear,' said the ostrich. 'I think I can feel one of my

142

headaches coming on.'

At last the checking was completed.

'Well,' said Mr Noah, putting a large cross beside a name. 'That seems to be that. I just want to say goodbye, good luck for the future and may God bless you all.' He made his way to the stout door. 'Now . . .'

'Wait a minute, Father.' Japheth came hurrying up, waving his list in his hand. 'Wait a minute. There's two animals missing.'

'Missing?'

'Yes. The dormice aren't here.'

'They're not animals, they're rodents,' said the fox.

Mr Noah turned and called out loudly, 'Are the dormice anywhere in the hall?'

There was silence.

He tried again. 'Has anybody seen the dormice?'

'No, but I'd like to,' said the fox, grinning and licking his lips.

'We'd better search the ark.'

The search lasted for some time. The animals, insects and birds went everywhere, calling the dormice by name and peering into the smallest of holes, but it was Mr Noah who found them cowering inside a cupboard in his cabin.

Mr Noah stared down at them.

'Whatever are you doing here? Don't you know we've been searching for you?'

'W-w-well . . .' stammered one of the dormice.

'It's like this . . .' the other began.

Mr Noah sighed. 'You can't stay there in the cupboard. Come along to the big hall. All the animals are anxious to get away.'

'Yes,' said the first dormouse. 'That's just it. They want to get away so they can begin hunting again and the first thing they'll hunt is us.'

'That's nonsense,' said Mr Noah.

'No, it isn't. We heard them talking in the hall just now, about how nice it would be to go hunting again. That fox had his eye on us and so did some of the other animals. I don't think we'll last two minutes once we're off this ark.'

The dormice were shaking with fright.

'I see,' said Mr Noah slowly. He sat on the bed. 'But surely it won't be like that, not now you've all got to know each other? I can't believe the other animals would want to eat you.'

'Not only the animals,' said the first dormouse. 'That eagle had a very nasty glint in his eye.'

'We've been dreading this day,' confessed the second dormouse. 'It's kept us awake at night, worrying.'

'Well, I'm very sorry . . .' began Mr Noah.

'You see, we've really enjoyed it here,' said the first dormouse. 'We've been cared for and looked after and you've no idea what a relief it's been not to have to worry

144

about finding food for ourselves...'

'... or being eaten by others,' chimed in the second dormouse.

'We've *mattered*. You've listened to us when we've talked and sometimes the bigger animals have listened too. It's been so safe here. Safe and friendly. We just don't want to go. Please, can't we stay?'

'Can't we?' added the second dormouse.

They looked up at him with pleading faces.

'I don't know what to say,' said Mr Noah. 'All I've thought about was keeping you safe during this trip. I never thought about the future.' He put his head in his hands. 'Perhaps that was what you meant, God, when you said it wasn't all over.' He looked at the dormice. 'Go back to the hall and wait for me there. I've got to think about this, and talk to God.'

The dormice looked at one another. 'I think we'd rather stay here in this cupboard, if you don't mind.'

'It's safer,' agreed the other dormouse.

'But none of the animals will harm you on the ark,' said Mr Noah.

'They'll be pretty angry with us for the delay,' the first dormouse said and shivered.

'All right,' said Mr Noah. 'But just be quiet a minute while I talk this over with God.'

'We'll be quiet as mice,' said the dormouse with an anxious smile.

'What shall I do, God?' Mr Noah asked. 'Have I kept the animals safe on the ark only for them to be eaten as soon as they go outside?'

'Your part is finished once they leave the ark, Noah,' God replied. 'I did not ask you to do anything else.'

'Yes, but I can't just let them go to their deaths,' argued Mr Noah. 'I mean, what would have been the point of keeping them safe all these weeks?'

'You are not responsible for them, Noah. I am. Can't you trust me?'

'I do, Lord,' said Mr Noah. He looked up. 'But I still feel responsible,' he added.

God smiled. 'You are a faithful servant, Noah, and I am very fond of you, but you cannot take the weight of the world and all its problems on your shoulders.'

'No, Lord. But surely I can do *something*.'

God considered for a moment. 'Very well. Go back to the hall and tell all the animals, insects and birds what has happened.'

Mr Noah stood up and went over to the cupboard.

'Come along,' he said. 'We're going to the big hall and I'm going to tell the animals, insects and birds what you told me.'

'Is that wise?' asked the dormouse.

'It's what God suggests,' said Mr Noah. He looked down at the two dormice who were still shivering with fright. 'And don't be frightened. We're all in God's hands and he will protect you.'

The dormice came out of the cupboard and went with Mr Noah to the big hall. And for the last time Mr Noah called together a meeting of all the creatures in the ark.

14
THE END OF THE VOYAGE

It was very quiet in the big hall as Mr Noah stepped forwards and told the animals, insects and birds that the two dormice were afraid to leave the ark for fear they would be eaten.

When he had finished speaking the fox said angrily, 'It's a load of rubbish!'

'No, it's not,' said the dormouse. 'We *are* frightened. Some of you would snap us up in an instant if it weren't for Mr Noah.'

'Hear, hear!' said the ant. 'You're not the only ones to be frightened about leaving. We're scared too.'

'So are we!' called the rabbits.

At this there was uproar in the hall. Some of the animals were shouting agreement and others were roaring them down.

'Quiet!' Mr Noah shouted.

The fox jumped on to a table. 'You don't want to be taken in, Mr Noah! Those dormice would tell you anything to get your sympathy!' He thumped his tail loudly. 'I tell you, they're not worth saving! Why, if they weren't kept down, they'd be over-running the world! Vermin, that's what they are!'

'There's no need to be rude!' squeaked the dormouse and the animals, insects and birds all began shouting once more.

'QUIET!' roared Mr Noah. 'QUIET!! Haven't you learned *anything* on this voyage? I had thought—I had *hoped*—that you would have learned to understand and respect each other a little during the time we've been together.'

'Very true,' said the donkey, nodding his head. 'I've learnt that there are an awful lot of animals in the world beside myself.'

'Shush, dear,' said his wife. 'I don't think Mr Noah meant that.'

'I think Mr Noah's got a point,' the beaver said slowly. 'While we've been on this ark we've all had to face the same danger. We've got on pretty well on the whole and it would be sad to think that everything we've learned would be lost when we go out into the world.'

'What do you suggest we do about it?' asked the camel.

'I don't know,' said the beaver.

'Well, I suggest we should stop all this chatter and get out of the ark,' said the jackal impatiently. 'Anyone would

think you *liked* being here.'

'That's just the point,' said the dormouse earnestly. 'Some of us *do* like it here. At least, I'm sure we'd all rather be in the fresh air again, but some of us like feeling safe, and we do feel safe on the ark.'

'Mr Noah, what do you think?' asked the hedgehog.

'I don't know,' said Mr Noah slowly. 'But if God found the world so wicked that he had to destroy it, then surely those of us he saved from the flood should try to make the new world a better place.'

'Impossible,' said the monkey sarcastically.

'Perhaps I should remind you that it wasn't *our* wickedness that caused God to flood the world,' said the eagle. 'You humans are to blame, not us.'

'I don't know,' said the dormouse. 'It's very easy to blame others, but nobody's perfect, whatever you say.'

The eagle glared at him. 'Just you wait,' he hissed.

'But what can we *do*?' asked the jackal impatiently.

There was silence in the hall. Then the donkey spoke. 'I've got an idea,' he said slowly. 'I know I'm a bit stupid, but I *have* got an idea. Please listen to it.'

'Do you think you should, dear?' asked his wife.

The donkey took a deep breath and began. 'It is right, isn't it, Mr Noah, that we are the only creatures left in the world?' he asked.

'Quite right.'

'So my wife and I are the only two donkeys left?'

'Yes.'

'And God saved us so that there will always be donkeys in the world?'

The jackal yawned loudly.

'That's true.'

'So it must be important to God that we survive, not just on the ark but when we're off it as well?'

'Well, yes,' said Mr Noah.

'In that case, why don't we all agree that none of us who have been on the ark will hunt or eat each other?'

The monkey scratched himself noisily. 'Now I've heard it all!' he said in a sarcastic voice.

The donkey looked round the big hall. 'We could form ourselves into a sort of league and agree that, as long as we are alive, we will not harm one another.'

There was silence. The animals, insects and birds looked at one another, suspiciously, doubtingly, warily... hopefully.

'Do you think it would work?' asked the hedgehog.

'I don't know,' said the donkey. He shrugged, rather embarrassed at the attention he was getting. 'It's only an idea and I know I'm not very good at ideas ...'

'I think it's a very good idea,' said Mr Noah.

'So do I,' said the dormouse.

'And I'll vote for it,' said the tiger loudly. 'All those in favour?'

There was a roar of agreement.

'Now,' said the tiger briskly, 'we need someone to be the first Head of our new United League of Animals, Insects and Birds ...'

'Do we?' asked the goose.

'Of course we do,' said the tiger. 'Every organization has to have someone in charge. Are there any suggestions?'

'Well,' said the lion. 'Ah, hmm ... well ...'

'The lion?' suggested the goose. 'After all, he is King of the Jungle.'

The lion smiled graciously at the goose.

'Personally I always thought the lion dreamed up that title for himself,' said the tiger huffily.

'Well, what about you?' suggested the panther.

'I don't mind,' said the tiger modestly.

'I suggest the bear,' snapped the lion. 'Brawn before brains and he's the strongest animal among us.'

'Why do we need a *Head* anyway?' murmured the

squirrel.' *Tails* are far more important.' He waved his fine one in the air.

'I think it should be the donkey,' said the dormouse. 'After all, he came up with the idea in the first place.'

'Oh no,' said the donkey, shaking his head. 'I couldn't do it. I'm much too stupid.'

'Why should it be an animal, anyway?' asked the cockroach. 'Why not an insect? Animals always like to push themselves forwards.'

'Why not a bird?' asked the seagull. 'The eagle would have my vote.'

'The owl is the wisest,' said the falcon.

The animals, insects and birds all began speaking at once.

'If we can't even agree on someone to be the Head of our new league, what *can* we agree on?' asked the donkey sadly.

The monkey smiled in a superior way. 'These things never work,' he said to no one in particular.

'Can I suggest Mr Noah?' said the dormouse. 'He is neither an animal, an insect or a bird and he's kept us safe during this voyage. I would rather have him than one of us.'

'But what do I have to do?' asked Mr Noah.

'Look after us in the world,' said the dormouse.

The animals, insects and birds quietened down and looked at Mr Noah expectantly.

'What shall I do, God?' Mr Noah asked. 'It's a big

responsibility.'

'It is indeed,' said God. 'But one that is right. I give all the creatures of the world into your hands. Look after them well.'

Mr Noah was silent for a moment.

'Very well,' he said at last. 'If that is what you want me to do, God.' He raised his voice. 'If that is what you all want, then I accept the charge and I and my sons will try to look after you and keep you from harm.'

'Well then,' said the fox brightly. 'Now we're all friends together I think Mr Noah should open the door and let us out.'

Mr Noah turned to the dormouse. 'Are you any happier?' he asked.

'Yes,' said the dormouse after a moment's thought.

'I think so.'

'Very well then.'

Mr Noah went to the big door that God himself had closed at the start of the journey. It opened at his touch and sunlight streamed into the hall.

And Mr Noah led the animals, insects and birds out of the ark. There were wild animals, tame animals, reptiles and insects, birds and beasts. There were large animals and small animals, ugly and good-looking ones. There were animals with nice natures and animals with nasty natures. Two of every kind had gone into the ark and two of every kind—apart from the doves—came out of the ark to stand with Mr Noah on the green grass and look with wonder at the fresh new world around them.

Then the birds rose into the air like a cloud, circling

Mr Noah and his family as they called their goodbyes. Mr Noah lifted his hands and blessed them and they flew away.

'Goodbye,' said the skunks and slunk off among the trees.

'Goodbye,' said the termites as they abandoned their home on the ark and wriggled away.

'Goodbye,' grunted the pigs as they set off in search of food.

'Goodbye, goodbye,' called all the animals and insects as they went their own ways out of the clearing and into the wood.

'It's been an experience,' said the lion grandly as he offered his paw for Mr Noah to shake.

'Thank you and goodbye,' said the spiders shyly and waved their long legs.

Mr Noah stood and watched them all go.

'Goodbye and God bless you,' he called.

'Well,' said the fox. 'Good hunting.' He winked and made a playful grab at the dormouse, laughing out loud as the dormouse squeaked in fright.

'Only teasing,' he said and swaggered off.

Mr Noah watched until the last of the animals had gone, then he and his family thanked God for having brought them all safely through the flood.

'Will they keep their promise to each other, God?' he asked.

'For a while,' God said.

'And will we keep our promise to care for them?'

'*You* will, Noah,' God replied.

The sunlit day grew overcast and a few drops of rain began to fall.

'Are you starting the flood again, Lord?' Mr Noah asked humbly.

'No,' said God. 'For whatever promises are made and broken, this *I* promise. I will never again destroy all living things by water and never again shall there be a flood to destroy the earth.'

The rain fell harder and Mr Noah stared miserably at the wet ground.

'Cheer up, Noah,' said God. 'Look up at the sky.'

Mr Noah looked up and there, high above him, he saw the perfect arc of a rainbow, its colours glowing as the sun burst through the clouds—red, orange, yellow, green, blue, indigo and violet.

'This rainbow is my promise to you and to all who live after you,' said God. 'Whenever you see a rainbow in the sky you will think of my promise and know that I will never again send a flood to destroy the earth. And, Noah . . .'

'Yes, Lord?'

'Remember that *I* do not break my promises.'

'No, Lord,' said Mr Noah.

Then, as the rain stopped and the sun shone warm on

his face, Mr Noah looked around at his wife, his three sons, Shem, Ham and Japheth and their wives.

'Funny,' he said, 'but it seems lonely without the animals. I shall miss them.' He sighed. 'I must admit I've grown rather fond of them.'

'Even the spiders?' asked God.

Mr Noah smiled. 'Especially the spiders,' he said.

More Tales from the Ark

CONTENTS

1
NOAH'S TALE

Mr Noah was a worried man. He had been ever since God had dropped his bombshell and turned Mr Noah's life upside down.

'I am afraid,' God had said to Mr Noah, 'that I shall have to destroy the world and every living creature, for it has become an evil place. But I shall save you, Mr Noah, and your wife and sons and their wives. And I shall save two of all the living creatures in the world.'

God told Mr Noah to build a wooden ark, which was like a large boat, so that when he sent a flood to cover the earth, Mr Noah, his family and the animals would be saved.

'And you, Mr Noah, will look after the animals for me, for they are all important. I'm relying on you to keep them alive.'

Mr Noah was sad at the thought of the world being destroyed and worried at the job God had given him to do. He pleaded with God.

'I'm very grateful, God, please believe me, but I don't think I'm the right person. I've never kept any animals apart from two cats, and I've only got them to keep the mice down. I don't even really like animals. I'm sure you could choose someone better than me.'

But God wanted Mr Noah.

Mr Noah tried again. 'I'm not a very good organizer, God, and you'll need a good organizer for this trip. I get muddled, you see.'

But God did not reply. Besides, he had every faith in Mr Noah.

'It's not as if I'm a young man,' Mr Noah told his wife that night. 'God should have chosen a younger, better man for the job.' (Mr Noah was six hundred years old at the time.)

'A younger one maybe,' said his wife, 'but there's not a better one. And God chose *you* for the job, so do try and get some sleep.'

But sleep would not come to Mr Noah that night. He tossed and turned and worried. At last he sat bolt upright.

'What on earth do aardvarks eat?' he demanded. But his wife was snoring gently by his side and did not reply.

Mr Noah had had little sleep since then. As the days passed, his worries grew.

'Ouch!' he cried, as he hit his thumb with a hammer for the third time.

'Look, Father,' said his eldest son Shem, 'why don't

you go and welcome the animals and leave building the ark to us?'

His other sons, Ham and Japheth, nodded in agreement.

'I'm sure you've plenty of other work to do,' Shem added tactfully.

'And you know you're not much good at carpentry,' Ham said bluntly.

Mr Noah looked stubborn. 'God told *me* to build the ark,' he said.

Shem, Ham and Japheth looked at each other, then carried on with the building. But after a few minutes . . .

'Owwh!' cried Mr Noah, as he hit his sore thumb for a fourth time.

'Please, Father . . .' said Shem.

Just then Mrs Noah called from the house.

'Noah, will you come? Two flamingos have arrived and say they must speak to you. They seem a bit upset.'

Mr Noah climbed down from the ark. He was really quite pleased to have an excuse to go, and his sons were equally pleased to be rid of him.

'Now we can get on faster,' said Ham.

Mr Noah did not return to the ark. After he had talked to the flamingos, the chimpanzees had to be chased off his grapevines. Then the beavers arrived and began building a dam across the stream which provided water for Mr Noah's farm. The emus turned their noses up at

the sleeping arrangements and one of the polar bears
fainted with the heat. Mr Noah was kept very busy.
There was so much to do and so little time.

'Can't you get some of the animals to give you a
hand?' his wife asked, as they ate their evening meal.
'Those nice elephants offered to help the boys with the
building, and even the monkeys said they'd swing down
and pick up the tools that got dropped—not that I trust
them that much. Very sarcastic they were.'

'The beavers want to help, too,' said Japheth.

'I can't have help,' Mr Noah replied. 'God gave *me* the job and I must do it by myself.'

'But you're not building the ark by yourself,' his wife pointed out. 'Our sons are helping.'

'Yes,' said Mr Noah, frowning. 'But perhaps I should have tried.'

'The ark would sink,' Ham said.

'Don't be so rude to your father!' said his mother sharply, but Mr Noah was not even listening.

How could he make sure that two of every animal, insect, and bird were on board at the right time? Say he missed one or two? God might never forgive him. Word must already have got around, for animals were beginning to arrive, turning up at Mr Noah's farmhouse at all hours of the day and night. It was a problem knowing where to put them and how to feed them, and the two chimpanzees could not be stopped from stripping the grapes from his vineyards.

Food was another problem. How was he to get all the food required for so many animals? Mr Noah spent hours making lists of what the animals, insects and birds ate. It made depressing reading, for many of them just ate each other.

Then there was the building of the ark itself, which kept being held up as Mr Noah was too busy to supervise the work.

Worries piled up along with the lists in Mr Noah's office. He grew short-tempered and his sons and their wives and even Mrs Noah began to avoid him. And as the day for boarding the ark drew nearer, Mr Noah began to panic.

'It'll never be ready on time,' he thought, and hit his thumbs and fingers as he tried to work faster.

'The food'll never arrive in time,' he thought, and sent out messages far and wide.

And one dreadful afternoon when the beavers successfully dammed his stream and all the water to his farm dried up, and his vineyards—long since stripped of grapes—were finally trampled down by the hippos and the elephants, Mr Noah despaired.

He stopped doing any work and sat in the wreckage of his once beautiful farm. Sadly he thought of his past life, remembering how he had enjoyed watching his grapes grow round and fat under the summer sun. Although he had complained about the hard work, he had been content with his life. His eyes misted over and two fat tears fell on the long list he held in his hand. He was too old for change and it was all very frightening.

'I can't do it,' he thought, as he caught sight of the chimpanzees scratching themselves for fleas. 'Should two fleas be taken on the ark?' he wondered. God had not said anything about fleas.

He put his head in his hands and groaned. 'I can't do it.'

Then he jumped to his feet and began to pace up and down.

'I can't, I *can't*, I CAN'T DO IT! God will have to find someone else. It's not too late.'

'Noah.'

It was God speaking, but Mr Noah did not hear him at first; he was too upset.

'Noah, listen to me.'

'Oh, God, is that you?' Mr Noah said, words falling over themselves in his panic. 'Where have you been? I've been so upset and so worried and got into such a state.

I don't want to leave, I can't leave, and I can't do the job you've given me. I don't want to die in the flood, but this is too much for an old man. Anyway, I don't like animals—you should see the way some of them behave! Please, God, find someone else.'

'Noah,' said God patiently. 'Stop talking, sit down and be quiet for a moment.'

Mr Noah did what God said and immediately began to feel a bit better.

'Now then, are you listening?'

'Yes, God,' said Mr Noah.

'Good. I've been wanting to help you for a long time, but you haven't given me the chance.'

'Haven't I?'

'No. You've been too busy trying to do everything yourself.'

'Have I?'

'Yes.'

'Oh,' said Mr Noah. 'I thought that was what you wanted.'

'You should have asked me, Noah,' said God.

'You haven't been around much lately,' Mr Noah grumbled. Then he felt ashamed. 'I expect you've been too busy.'

'I'm never too busy to help you,' said God. 'As long as you trust me, everything will turn out well.'

'Yes, God,' said Mr Noah.

172

'*Do* you trust me?' God asked, and it seemed to Mr Noah, as he sat in the sun among his ruined vineyards, that this was the most important question he had ever been asked. He thought back over his long life, remembering how, even as a child, he had always taken his problems to God. And God had never let him down, he thought. Not once. It was a long time before he spoke.

'Yes,' he said at last. 'Yes, God, I do trust you.'

'Well then,' said God. 'There's nothing for you to worry about.'

Mr Noah sat for a while longer, enjoying a sense of peace he had not known for a long time. Then he went back to his house and told his wife and sons that he was sorry for having been so bad-tempered. Everyone felt so much better that they worked even harder. Some of the animals helped, and soon the ark was ready.

And if Mr Noah still had worries, which he had—especially when he saw some of the more ferocious animals arrive on his farm—and if his stomach felt churned up at the thought of the future, which it did—many times a day—no one knew about it, except God. And God, Mr Noah knew, would help him with whatever lay ahead.

2

THE PEACOCK'S TALE

Once the ark had been built, Mr Noah and his sons filled it with food, water and everything that might possibly be needed for the long voyage ahead. For God had told Mr Noah that he would send a great flood to cover the earth, but that Mr Noah, his family, and two of every animal, insect and bird would be kept safe inside the ark.

Mr Noah packed some things for himself and put on his second-best robe.

'There's no point taking our *best* clothes,' he said to his wife, 'as there'll be plenty of dirty jobs to do on the ark. I don't think many of the animals will be house-trained.'

'Well, I'm not leaving my best robe to be ruined in the flood!' Mrs Noah retorted, and put it on.

Mr Noah walked slowly round his farm for the very last time before pinning a large notice to the front door:

**GONE AWAY. ENQUIRIES TO THE ARK.
ADDRESS UNKNOWN.**

'There's no point locking the place up,' he thought sadly.

But Mr Noah did not have time for any more sad thoughts. He was kept far too busy standing at the entrance to the ark, welcoming the animals, insects and birds and ticking them off on a great long list. Mrs Noah stood beside him dressed in her best robe, and very fine she looked too.

When everyone was safely inside, God himself shut the door behind them.

Some of the animals settled in quickly, grateful for shelter from the storm clouds gathering overhead. But one or two were full of complaints. The peacock was the worst.

'It really isn't good enough,' he said, strutting up and down the great hall, his beak turned up at the noise and smell of the other animals.

'Never mind, dear,' said his wife, a rather drab-looking little peahen.

'What isn't good enough?' asked the fox, who was eyeing the two dormice with mouth-watering interest.

'Any of this,' said the peacock, fanning out his beautiful tail. 'I never thought that my beloved wife and I would be required to *share* accommodation on this voyage. I shall have to complain.'

'Who to?' asked the fox. 'God? I think he's *far* too busy right now to attend to you.' He chuckled at the

thought, much to the relief of the dormice, who hurriedly scuttled away.

'To "The Management",' the peacock replied grandly.

'What's that?' asked the buffalo, blowing water out through his nose. The peacock looked at him in disgust.

'"The Management", I imagine, is that shabbily-dressed person who welcomed us on board. *If* it could be called a welcome,' he went on. 'I did not like having to wait in a queue with the rabble.'

'Who is the rabble?' asked the donkey. 'I don't think I've heard of an animal of that name, but then there are so many wonderful creatures here I've never heard of. It's been quite an eye-opener for me.'

'Huh!' snorted the peacock, and stalked off in search of Mr Noah. His wife hurried after him.

'Silly old thing,' said the buffalo. 'Just who does he think he is?'

'It's his wife I feel sorry for,' said the rabbit comfortably. 'I wouldn't like to be married to him.'

The peacock found Mr Noah in his cabin, putting the finishing touches to a large notice:

RULES OF THE ARK
1. PASSENGERS ARE REQUESTED NOT TO FIGHT
2. PASSENGERS ARE ABSOLUTELY FORBIDDEN
TO EAT EACH OTHER DURING THE VOYAGE
3. ANY COMPLAINTS ARE TO BE REFERRED TO ME
OR MY ASSISTANTS, LION AND TIGER
Mr Noah

Mr Noah looked up as the peacock and peahen entered. 'Hello. What can I do for you?'

'I've a complaint,' said the peacock.

'Oh dear,' said Mr Noah. He sat on his bed. 'How can I help?'

'I'm sure you'll agree that my tail is very beautiful,' the peacock began, unfurling it in the small cabin and smudging Mr Noah's notice in the process.

'Yes, indeed,' said Mr Noah.

'I would say,' said the peacock, 'that I have a more beautiful tail than any other creature in the world.'

'Very possibly,' said Mr Noah.

'It's a great responsibility,' the peacock went on, 'and I have to spend a lot of time looking after it.'

'I'm sure,' Mr Noah said in a respectful voice.

'I need peace, quiet and space for this,' the peacock went on. 'And there's neither peace, quiet or space in the great hall.'

'No,' said Mr Noah. 'I don't suppose there is.'

'Mr Noah, I am a sensitive and highly-strung bird. I don't ask for much. Just a cabin to myself—with my dear wife of course...' He looked disdainfully around Mr Noah's cabin. '... A little larger than this would suit me perfectly. And meals to be served in my room. I really *cannot* be expected to eat with the other animals.'

Mr Noah sighed. 'I'm very sorry but I can't do that. We haven't any spare cabins at all. There's an awful lot of animals, insects and birds to be accommodated.'

'But that's not good enough...' the peacock began, his voice getting louder.

'Well, God designed the ark,' said Mr Noah, 'and he's very economical. He never wastes anything he's created. I'm afraid that there's nothing at all I can do.'

'I see,' snapped the peacock, and he stormed out of the cabin.

'Now, dear, don't take on so,' said his wife as she

178

hurried after him. 'It'll only give you a funny turn. You know it will.'

Mr Noah sighed again. 'Oh dear, God,' he said. 'Whatever am I to do? As if I hadn't enough problems already.'

'This one will go away,' said God. 'You'll see.'

But the problem did not go away. In fact, it got worse. The peacock complained all day and every day and soon many of the other animals started complaining too. The giraffes demanded more headroom, the hippos more water, the penguins more ice, the bats more dark and the butterflies more light.

'There ought to have been different *classes* of accommodation,' said the emu self-righteously.

'Based on what?' asked the buffalo. 'The length of your tail?'

'I wouldn't stand a chance then,' said the guinea-pig cheerfully. ' 'Cause I haven't got one.'

'And I'd get chucked out of first class,' said the gecko. 'For mine's just dropped off.'

'What do you mean?' asked the donkey, quite mystified.

The gecko shrugged. 'My tail always drops off if I get a fright.'

'What gave you a fright?' asked the rhinoceros.

'Your ugly face for a start,' said the gecko, and slithered off, laughing.

'Those lizards,' sniffed the emu. '*Very* underbred.' And she went to find the peacock, who was holding forth at the far end of the hall.

'I feel that God should have been more selective,' the peacock was saying as the emu joined him. 'Why decide to save two of every animal, insect and bird in creation, when we all know there are plenty we could happily do without?'

'You for one,' the swallow called down from her perch.

'It would have been a wonderful opportunity for God to have tidied things up a bit,' the peacock went on. 'If some of the rougher, uglier animals had not been allowed on the ark, there would have been more room for the rest of us.' He pulled his tail away from the jackdaw who had just flown in and perched on it.

The animals began to grow tired of the peacock's grumbles and more and more of them complained to Mr Noah.

'I wouldn't mind if he'd only talk a little more quietly,' said the ostrich. 'But he's got such a loud, unpleasant voice it's given me quite a headache.'

There were so many complaints that Mr Noah locked himself in his cabin and refused to hear any more.

'What *am* I to do, God?' he asked.

'Don't worry,' said God, 'and do nothing.'

'I can't help but worry,' Mr Noah said crossly, but he

took God's advice and did nothing.

The next day the peacock did not appear in the great hall, much to the relief of many of the animals.

'Probably giving his boring old tail a spring-clean,' said the guinea-pig.

'I wish it would fall out,' said the otter. 'I'm that fed up with him going on about it.'

'But it's so beautiful,' sighed the donkey. 'I wish mine was half as beautiful.'

'If only he was as beautiful *inside* as he is *outside*,' said the buffalo. 'I know I'm ugly, but at least I'm not vain.'

The following day the peacock was still missing. The peahen was missing too. On the third day Mr Noah began a search, but it was some time before he discovered them, hidden away in the darkest corner of the ark. The peacock was sobbing.

'It's the most awful thing that's ever happened!'

'Now then, what's the trouble?' said Mr Noah.

The peahen turned to him. 'Oh dear, Mr Noah, he'll die from the shame of it.'

'Whatever's wrong?' asked Mr Noah.

The peacock came out from the corner in which he was hiding and Mr Noah gasped. For every one of his beautiful tail feathers had gone.

'Bald,' sobbed the peacock. 'Tail-less. I can't, I just can't face them!'

'How did it happen?' Mr Noah asked.

'All peacocks lose their tails,' said the peahen. 'I told him so, but he wouldn't listen. He never listens to me. Perhaps it'll teach the silly thing a lesson,' she added tartly, while the peacock sobbed even louder.

It look a lot of persuading before the peacock would agree to follow Mr Noah into the great hall. His arrival caused uproar.

The jackdaw fell off his perch laughing, while the buffalo spluttered so much that he nearly choked.

'Serves him right,' said the gecko, whose own tail was beginning to grow again.

'You don't rate even third-class accommodation,' said the rhinoceros bluntly. 'If God saw you now you wouldn't even get a place on the ark!'

'All right,' said the peacock in a tearful voice. 'I'm sorry. I thought I was better than all of you, because of my tail, but I'm not. I shouldn't have said the things I did. But it was a b-b-beautiful tail,' he added, beginning to sob again.

Just then the eagle called out in his great voice.

'Quiet, everyone!'

In the silence that followed they could all hear a heavy drumming noise on the roof of the ark.

'The rain has begun,' said the eagle. He spread his great wings.

'I think,' he said, 'that there should be no more complaints. There are more important things to worry about than the peacock's tail. If we had been left outside, we should all have perished.'

No one could disagree with that and the animals, insects and birds were unusually quiet as they went to their perches, nests and holes that night.

3

THE POLAR BEAR'S TALE

It had been raining for some days now and the ark was starting to float on a rising flood of water. It was very crowded on board, as two of every animal, insect and bird in creation take up a great deal of space, but gradually everyone began to settle down. Soon all the animals had, more or less, found a place for themselves and were, more or less, happy. Everyone, that is, apart from the polar bear.

For the polar bear, having come from a land where there were very few animals, was quite amazed by the number and variety he saw around him. He wanted to make friends with all of them, but did not know how to go about it. So he prowled around, making the smaller animals nervous and the larger ones puzzled.

'What's he after?' asked the rhinoceros suspiciously.

'I don't know that he's *after* anything,' said the brown bear.

The rhinoceros was not convinced. 'If he thinks he can wallow in my water, he's got another think coming.'

'I just want to be friends,' said the polar bear.

'Why?' asked the other rhinoceros.

The polar bear did not know how to answer that and ambled away. Making friends was not as easy as he had first thought. Then he had an idea. If he agreed with everything the animals said, they would be sure to like him.

'It's so cold here,' grumbled the camel. 'I feel it after the heat of the desert.'

'Yes, it is cold,' said the polar bear, who secretly thought the great hall was uncomfortably warm.

'It's not the cold,' said the cheetah, pacing restlessly up and down. 'It's the boredom. I want to feel the wind in my fur as I run through the wild country.'

'I'm bored too,' agreed the polar bear.

'Well I find all this rather restful,' said the tiger sleepily. 'Not having to find my food, not having any responsibilities. I could get used to this life.'

'So could I,' the polar bear agreed.

'I'll tell you what's *boring* around here,' snapped the rhinoceros crossly. 'Animals that agree with everything you say. That's what's *really* boring.'

'Yes,' said the polar bear. 'That's very true.'

The rhinoceros snorted and walked off, and one by one the other animals followed.

'Why do I always say the wrong thing?' the polar bear said later to his wife. 'I only want to be friends.'

'You try too hard,' his wife said. 'You should just be yourself.'

'But I want them to like me,' said the polar bear unhappily.

'You can't *make* people like you,' said his wife. 'You mustn't mind so much.'

But the polar bear did mind. He minded very much indeed. Every day he went into the great hall and tried to make friends with one or other of the animals. But the more he tried, the worse it became. The animals first made fun of him and then ignored him, so he took to sitting in the rain on the roof of the ark, quite alone and most unhappy.

'If I said I had two heads,' said the hippopotamus, 'you know what the polar bear would say?'

'What?' asked the giraffe.

'He'd say that he had two heads as well,' replied the hippo and burst into a gruff laugh.

'That's rather unkind,' said Mr Noah, who was passing at the time. 'He only wants to be friends.'

'I choose my friends,' said the camel haughtily. 'And I don't make friends with colourless animals who have no conversation and come from outlandish places.'

'He can't help his colour,' said Mr Noah mildly.

'Or lack of it,' said the lion, looking with pride at his great golden mane.

Mr Noah turned to the brown bear. 'Perhaps you'd be

his friend?' he said. 'After all, you are related.'

'Only distantly,' said the brown bear hurriedly. But the brown bear was a kind animal, so he padded off. He found the polar bear sitting in his usual place, hunched up on the roof of the ark.

'What are you doing all by yourself?' the brown bear asked, poking his head through the trap door. 'It's wet and miserable up here.'

'It's better by myself,' said the polar bear sadly. 'Then I don't upset the others. Oh, brown bear, you've got lots of friends. Tell me what I should do to make them like me.'

The brown bear thought about it for a while, then a slow smile began to spread across his face and he licked his lips.

'Just give them honey,' he said.

'Honey?' repeated the polar bear.

'Nothing like honey for making friends,' said the brown bear. 'Can't get enough of it myself.'

'Where do I get it from?' asked the polar bear.

'From bees, of course,' said the brown bear, shaking his head at such ignorance.

'Bees?'

The brown bear nodded. 'But don't tell them I told you. Funny things, bees. Temperamental. You want to be careful with bees.'

The polar bear took his advice and approached the bees very carefully.

'Excuse me,' he said politely.

The bees came out of their hive and buzzed round his head.

'Could I... is it possible...? Could I have some honey?' he asked.

'Honey?' they repeated.

'Please,' said the polar bear politely.

'You want honey?' asked the bees.

'If you don't mind,' said the polar bear.

'What do you want it for?' one of the bees asked suspiciously.

'To make friends,' said the polar bear. 'So that the other animals will like me.'

The bees buzzed together for some time. Then one of them turned to the polar bear.

'No,' she said. 'We don't give honey to polar bears.'

'Why not?' asked the polar bear, mystified.

'Because no polar bear has ever asked for any honey before,' said the other bee.

'But I'm asking you now,' said the polar bear.

'Sorry,' said the bee. And they both went into their hive and closed the door.

'Don't you worry,' said the brown bear when he heard about it later. 'I'll get it for you. Me and the bees are the best of friends.'

'Aren't you lucky,' said the polar bear enviously. 'I wish the bees would become *my* best friends.'

The brown bear went to the hive and knocked on the door, but the bees were out. He hesitated a moment, scratching his head.

'They won't miss a little honey if I take it,' he thought to himself. 'It's not really stealing as it's not for me.'

Reassured, he helped himself. But as he was carrying the honey away from the hive, the sweet smell of it made his nose twitch and his mouth water.

'What am I doing giving this honey to the polar bear?' he thought. 'He won't make any friends with it. Much better if *I* eat it. I can be his friend if he wants one.'

So he sat down and ate all the honey.

When the bees returned to their hive they were furious.

'It's that polar bear!' they said, buzzing furiously. 'Just wait till we get him!'

'It wasn't the polar bear,' said the skylark. 'He's still up on the roof. It was the brown bear.'

'Right,' said the bees, and they chased the brown bear round and round the ark until he grew quite dizzy.

'Leave me alone!' he squealed. 'I'm sorry . . . I won't do it again . . . !'

'That'll teach you to steal,' buzzed the bees angrily.

The animals thought it a very good joke and laughed at the brown bear. But it did not make them feel any more kindly towards the polar bear.

'Should have done his own dirty work,' sniffed the camel.

'As if *I* could be bribed by gifts of honey,' said the lion loftily.

The polar bear, even more lonely now, stayed on the roof of the ark and refused to come down. Mr Noah, quite upset, had a long talk to God.

'I don't know what to do about it,' he said. 'The polar bear can't stay up there for the whole of the voyage. Besides, I don't like the thought of him being unhappy.'

God thought for a moment. 'Go to the polar bear,' he said, 'and tell him that he won't make friends until he stops being so self-centred. If he wants friends, he must think of others rather than himself.'

'Well,' said Mr Noah doubtfully. 'I'll tell him, of course, but I don't think it will do any good.'

'Tell him that friendship cannot be bought,' said God. 'If it's not freely given then it's not real friendship.'

'All right,' said Mr Noah, getting up from his bed.

'And Noah,' said God, 'this is most important. Tell him that I am his friend—as I am the friend of *all* living creatures.'

Mr Noah climbed up to the roof of the ark and told the polar bear what God had said. He had to shout to make himself heard above the noise of the wind and rain. But the polar bear hardly listened. He just hunched his shoulders and turned away.

Sadly, Mr Noah began to leave. The rain was lashing down and the roof of the ark was very slippery. He took a step, then slipped on the wet surface. He slithered right down the steep slope and fell off, straight into the deep waters below.

'Help!' he shouted as he fell. 'Help, I can't swim! Please, someone—HELP!!'

The polar bear heard him. He turned, jumped up, dived into the water and caught Mr Noah in his strong teeth before he sank beneath the waves. The animals, hearing the commotion, streamed out of the great hall and crowded up to the roof.

They saw the polar bear swimming with powerful strokes back to the ark. The giraffe bent his long neck and took the dripping wet Mr Noah from the polar bear. Then the kangaroo kept him warm in her pouch while she took him down to his cabin, where Mrs Noah put him to bed.

Later that evening the lion and the tiger went on to the roof.

'Er . . . hmm . . .' said the lion. The polar bear turned around.

'We've come,' said the lion, 'on behalf of the other animals. They sent us to tell you that we are all sorry for treating you in the way we did. If you would care to come down to the great hall, we would be honoured to be your friends.'

The polar bear swallowed hard.

'Really?' he asked.

'Really,' the tiger assured him.

'All of you?' asked the polar bear, not quite believing him.

'All of us,' said the lion solemnly.

'You were very brave,' the tiger added.

'I wasn't brave at all,' said the polar bear humbly. 'I can't help being a good swimmer. But Mr Noah was the only one who seemed to care about me and I couldn't let him drown.'

Warmly tucked up in his bed, and none the worse for his ordeal, Mr Noah was talking to God.

'Did you make me fall off the roof of the ark deliberately, God, so that the polar bear would rescue me?'

'Would I do a thing like that?' said God reproachfully.

Mr Noah smiled, turned over and went to sleep.

4

THE BUTTERFLY'S TALE

The rain fell, day after day, and the world was flooded. Earth and sky disappeared in a thick grey fog and it grew very cold. The wind howled, there were rumblings of thunder and flashes of lightning, but the ark, which God had told Mr Noah to build, remained afloat. Mr Noah, Mrs Noah, their sons and wives and two of every animal, insect and bird were safe and dry inside.

The sky grew black and it was dark inside the ark. Mr Noah lit lamps, but did not light many for fear of running out of oil.

The butterflies were unhappy in the dark and their brilliantly coloured wings grew dull and lifeless.

'How long do you think it will go on for?' asked one butterfly.

'Mr Noah said that it would rain for forty days and forty nights,' her husband replied.

'And how long has it already been raining?'

'I don't know,' said her husband. 'I never thought to count.'

'What's the point in counting?' said the grasshopper gloomily. 'It won't make the time pass any faster.'

'That's true.' The butterfly turned to his wife. 'Try to sleep,' he said. He touched his wife's delicate blue wings. 'You're shivering.'

'I'm cold,' she said.

'Tuck yourself under my wings,' her husband said, 'and I'll keep you warm.'

Soon he was fast asleep, but his wife remained awake. She looked up at the window in the great hall and watched with fearful eyes as the storm clouds grew thicker and the rain thudded against the roof.

'It's like night out there,' she whispered, but her husband slept on and did not hear her.

'I'm scared of the dark,' she whispered, but her husband only sighed and fluttered his wings in his sleep.

Mr Noah, making his round of the animals, insects and birds, heard the butterfly and hurried to her side.

'There's nothing to be afraid of,' he said gently. 'We're here because God wants us to be saved from the flood. He'll protect us and keep us from harm.'

'Yes,' said the butterfly. 'I know. But I'm still scared of the dark. I need the light in order to live. My cousin, the moth, flies at night, but butterflies fly in the sunshine.'

Mr Noah thought for a moment. 'I know,' he said. 'I'll

bring you an oil lamp and you can look at its flame and think of the sun. Would you like that?'

'Yes, please,' said the butterfly.

So Mr Noah went to his cabin and picked up his own lamp.

'Do you think this will help, God?' he asked anxiously.

'It might,' said God. 'And it's a kind thought.'

'Well, I can do without it,' said Mr Noah stoutly. But he looked round a little fearfully as the dark shadows seemed to leap from the walls of his cabin when he carried the oil lamp away.

The butterfly was grateful.

'Thank you,' she said. 'It's warm as well as light.'

'Yes it is,' said Mr Noah. 'But be careful now that you don't go too close or else you'll burn your wings.'

'I won't,' said the butterfly, and for a time she was happy as she stared deep into the flame. She pretended that it was a summer's day and that she was in a bright garden, basking in the warmth of the sun. But all too soon the oil ran out, the flame flickered and died and the butterfly was frightened once more.

'Mr Noah,' she called. 'Mr Noah. Could I have some more oil, please?'

But Mr Noah shook his head. 'I'm very sorry,' he said, 'but there really isn't any to spare. God told me exactly how much to bring and we've got just enough.'

'Oh dear,' the butterfly said fearfully.

'I'll talk to God and see if he can think of anything,' promised Mr Noah.

So Mr Noah went to his cabin and sat in the darkness and talked to God. The rain thudded on the roof and the wind whistled mournfully. Mr Noah shivered.

'I'm not surprised the butterfly is frightened, God,' he said. 'I'm a bit scared myself. Ever since I got locked in the woodshed by mistake and had to stay there all night, I've not really liked the dark.'

'If you're frightened, Noah,' said God, 'just remember that I created night as well as day. I am God of the dark as well as the light. I will never leave you to face the fears of the night alone.'

'Yes, God,' said Mr Noah, feeling a bit happier. 'I'll remember that. I'll tell the butterfly that, too.'

He went to tell the butterfly straight away, but she just looked at him with her big scared eyes. Mr Noah did not know what to do.

'Why don't you ask one of the other animals to help?' said God.

'Like who?' asked Mr Noah.

'One who isn't afraid of the dark,' said God.

'I don't know of any,' said Mr Noah.

'Think, Noah,' God said.

So Mr Noah sat in his cabin and thought.

'I know,' he said. 'There are her cousins, the moths.

They might help.'

He found the moths flying round and round the flame of one of the oil lamps, darting in and away, each time flying closer.

'You want to be careful,' Mr Noah said. 'You could get burnt.'

'Pooh,' said one of the moths. 'We're not frightened.'

'It's a good game,' said the other moth.

'It's very dangerous,' said Mr Noah.

'Well, everyone needs a bit of danger in their lives,' said the first moth.

'There's danger you can avoid, and danger you can't,' said Mr Noah sternly. He picked up the lamp and blew it out. 'I'm sorry, but I'm responsible for you while you're on the ark and God wants both of you safe at the end of the voyage.'

'Spoilsport,' said the second moth.

'I came to see if you would help me,' said Mr Noah. 'The butterfly is very unhappy. She's afraid of the dark. I thought that perhaps you might talk to her and reassure her that the dark needn't be frightening.'

'Why should we help you when you wouldn't let us play our game?' asked the first moth crossly.

'Because she's your cousin,' said Mr Noah. 'And because we've all got to help each other during this voyage if we're to survive.'

'Oh, go away and ask someone else,' said the second moth disagreeably.

So Mr Noah went away and talked to God once more.

'That idea didn't work, did it?' he said.

'There are other night animals besides moths, Noah,' said God.

'I suppose so,' said Mr Noah wearily. 'But it's a bit difficult finding them in the dark.'

Just then Mr Noah felt, rather than heard, a faint rustling of wings and he saw a dark shape hanging upside down at the end of his bed.

'Did someone want me?' came a soft voice.

'Of course!' said Mr Noah. 'Yes please, bat. I think you

might be just what's needed!'

'Now,' said the bat to the butterfly. 'What's this Mr Noah tells me?'

'I'm afraid of the dark,' said the butterfly in a small voice.

'But the dark is beautiful,' said the bat. 'As I fly though the night, it's like flying through velvet.'

'How do you see where you're going?' asked the butterfly.

'I don't need to see,' said the bat. 'I hear instead. Come with me. I'll take you to the darkest places on the ark and you'll see that there's nothing to be frightened about.'

The butterfly climbed hesitantly onto the back of the bat.

'Where are you going?' asked the owl. He blinked at her solemnly.

'The bat's showing me that there's nothing to fear from the dark,' said the butterfly.

'Nothing to fear? Of course there's nothing to fear,' came the brisk voice of the badger, speaking from a corner of the great hall. 'The dark, when the world is quiet and still, is the best time of all. It's the time for thinking.'

'I didn't know you could think,' snuffled the aardvark. 'I find the night-time best because the ants and termites are asleep so I can creep up on them unawares. And very tasty they are too,' he said licking his lips.

'Well, I like the night-time because it's safer,' croaked

the frog.

'So do I,' agreed the hedgehog.

'And my skin doesn't dry out as it would do in the sun,' the frog continued.

'I like it because it's cooler,' said the gerbil. 'In the desert, I always burrow into the ground during the day.'

'So you see, lots of us prefer the night,' the badger told the butterfly.

The hedgehog came close to the butterfly. 'It's really very nice of you to come and see us,' she said shyly. 'We don't often see such beautiful creatures at night.'

The bat took the butterfly to all the darkest corners on the ark and, as she met more of the animals, insects and birds that are awake at night, she saw that there was nothing at all to fear. At last she met the two moths.

'Hello,' she said shyly. 'I don't think we've met before.'

'Hmm,' said the first moth. 'So you're the one that got us into trouble with Mr Noah.'

'Trouble?'

'Yes,' said the other moth. 'He blew out the oil lamp

we were playing with.'

'Oh, I am sorry,' said the butterfly.

'Don't be sorry for them,' said the bat. 'They're just stupid. If it wasn't for Mr Noah, they'd have been burnt by the flame.'

He flew off, leaving the moths staring after him in surprise.

The butterfly slipped back into her place beside her husband. 'Thank you for taking me,' she said to the bat. 'I feel a lot better now.'

'It's been a great pleasure,' said the bat and flew away. The butterfly folded her wings and prepared to go to sleep. But just then she saw the glow of two faint lights.

'Mr Noah said you were frightened, so we thought we'd come and give you some light,' said one of the glow-worms.

'How kind of you,' said the butterfly. 'How kind everyone has been.'

The glow-worms stationed themselves one on either side of her, and the butterfly watched their comforting light and thought about the friends she had made in the darkness until she fell fast asleep.

Outside, the darkness began to lift and the light of day flooded in, although the rain continued without ceasing.

5

THE PARROT'S TALE

When God decided that he would send a flood to destroy
the world, he told Mr Noah that it would rain for forty
days and forty nights. The first of the great storms turned
the sky black and it became as dark as night inside the
small ark which housed Mr Noah, Mrs Noah, their sons,
their wives and two of every animal, insect and bird.
Many slept during the darkest days, but woke up when
the sky grew lighter and the storm lifted.

'Is it over?' hissed the snake, slithering out of a hole.

'Is what over?' the elephant asked.

'The rain, of course.'

'Of course it's not over,' said the fox. 'Can't you hear
it pounding on the roof?'

The snake listened for a moment. 'I can't hear
anything.'

'That's because you're deaf,' said the fox.

'I'm not deaf,' said the snake, coiling himself neatly
into a pyramid.

The fox grinned, then whispered, 'You are.'

'What was that you said?' the snake asked suspiciously.

The animals burst out laughing.

'Quiet everyone!' came the voice of Mr Noah, speaking from the shadows at the far end of the great hall. The laughter stopped.

'If you don't behave, there won't be double rations of food.'

'Are there to be double rations of food?' asked one of the pigs anxiously. The pigs were always anxious about food.

'Only if you behave.'

For the rest of the day the snake and the fox and all the animals, insects and birds on the ark behaved very well indeed. Only the monkey, scratching himself for the fleas who had decided to make a temporary home in his fur, was scornful.

'Bribing you, that's what Mr Noah's doing,' he said sourly. He scratched a bit harder. 'And if you fleas don't hop it quick, there'll be some very bad behaviour from me, double rations or no double rations!'

'Misery-guts!' said one of the fleas and they jumped onto the hedgehog's back.

At feeding time, Mr Noah and his three sons Shem, Ham and Japheth, came round with the food.

'What's this?' asked the pig, rooting around in his sty.

'This isn't double rations.'

'Neither's this,' said the fox. 'Come on, Mr Noah. What about your promise?'

'What promise?'

'You promised double rations if we behaved.'

'When did I promise that?' Mr Noah asked.

'This morning,' said the fox.

'Everyone heard you,' added the pig.

'Well, I'm very sorry,' said Mr Noah. 'But you must have dreamed it, for I never said anything of the sort.' He turned to his sons. 'Did you?'

His sons shook their heads.

'Well!' said the emu, after Mr Noah and his sons had gone. 'Words fail me!'

'Me too,' said the pig gloomily.

'I needn't have wasted all day trying to be good,' hissed the snake sadly.

'I never thought Mr Noah would stoop to such low-down tricks,' said the fox.

The jackal shook his head. 'It's just what I've always said. Never trust a human.'

'Stop tickling!' said the hedgehog. But he was speaking to the fleas so no one took any notice.

There was much grumbling that evening as the animals, insects and birds ate their meal and settled down for the night. But high up in the rafters of the great hall the parrot was laughing. He laughed so much that he nearly fell off his perch.

'That's confused them,' he said to his wife. 'Did you ever hear such a fuss?'

'It's very naughty of you,' his wife replied. 'You really shouldn't do it.'

'It's only a bit of fun.'

'It's not fun at all. It's making mischief.'

'Oh, don't be so miserable,' the parrot said crossly. He cleared his throat, then spoke in Mr Noah's voice.

'Lion,' he said. 'Tiger. Would you both come to my cabin. I've some very important things to discuss with you.' He cackled with laughter and said in his own voice. 'That'll upset them all right. Silly old things.'

A very surprised Mr Noah opened the door of his cabin to the lion and the tiger.

'Hello,' he said. 'What can I do for you?'

'What can *we* do for *you*?' the lion asked.

'What do you mean?' said Mr Noah.

'You asked us to come,' said the tiger. 'So we came.'

'No, I didn't,' said Mr Noah, confused.

The lion and tiger looked at one another.

'You said you had important things to discuss with us,' said the lion.

'Well, I'm sorry,' said Mr Noah, a bit crossly. 'But I haven't anything, important or otherwise, to discuss with you.'

And he closed the door of his cabin.

'I knew it,' said the lion as he and the tiger trotted away. 'It had to come. The strain of it is beginning to tell. Mr Noah is going mad. I said all along that he wasn't strong enough. God really should have put me in charge.'

'Or me,' said the tiger.

The parrot continued to mimic Mr Noah's voice. He also mimicked some of the other animals' voices. Soon everyone grew very cross and there were all sorts of arguments and fights. The parrot watched from his perch high above the great hall and enjoyed the trouble he was causing.

'Just look at them,' he said, hooting with delight and flapping his wings up and down. 'Look at the fuss they're in. Mr Noah too. I'm cleverer than all of them.'

'You must stop this,' said his wife. 'It's very childish.'

'Don't be so silly,' the parrot retorted.

'It's also unkind,' said his wife.

'It's not unkind. It's a good laugh.'

'Only for you,' said his wife. But the parrot took no notice.

Mr Noah became most alarmed at what was happening and had a serious talk to God. 'What's going on, God?' he asked. 'And what can I do about it? I must do something or there'll be a riot on board. I thought at first it was the lion, but now I'm not so sure.'

The door to his cabin opened and the parrot's wife flew in.

'I'm so sorry to disturb you, Mr Noah,' she said. 'But I've tried talking to him and it does no good. I'm really ashamed of all the trouble he's causing ...'

After she had finished her story, Mr Noah went to the parrot and gave him a good telling-off. He was very cross, and so were the animals, insects and birds when they heard about it.

The parrot sulked on his perch.

'It was only meant as a bit of fun,' he said. 'I don't know why everyone's taken it so badly.'

'It wasn't a bit of fun and you know it,' his wife said severely.

The parrot glowered at her. 'If you hadn't gone and told Mr Noah, he'd never have known,' he said crossly.

'He would,' said his wife. 'When I went in, he was discussing it with God.'

'Why does God talk to Mr Noah and not to me?' the parrot asked.

'Because God's no fool and you *are*,' his wife said shortly.

The parrot was not listening. 'What makes Mr Noah so important that he can have a conversation with God?' he thought to himself. 'It can't be because he's clever for I'm sure I'm as clever as him. And it's not his voice,

because he's got rather a boring voice.' He sat on his perch and watched Mr Noah. 'I know,' he said out loud. 'It's because he wears clothes. *That's* why God talks to him. He wears clothes and we don't. Hmm . . .' and he grew very thoughtful.

'Just what are you plotting now?' his wife asked suspiciously, but the parrot flew away without replying.

It was some time before she saw him again. And when she did, she barely recognized him. For the parrot, waddling self-consciously into the great hall, was dressed. He was wearing a strange assortment of clothes taken from Mr and Mrs Noah's cabins. On his head was a long red and white scarf, tied like a turban, and round his body hung a shapeless brown gown. His clawed feet were thrust into sandals.

The parrot looked at his wife. 'Now I'll be able to talk to God,' he said with some satisfaction. But when he tried to fly up to his perch, the sandals fell off his feet with a thud and the animals, insects and birds in the great hall turned to stare. They stared, then they smiled, then they laughed. They laughed so much that they had to hold on to one another and some of them rolled around the great hall, shaking with mirth.

'What's so funny?' asked the parrot, but no one had the breath to tell him.

The noise brought Mr Noah running to the great hall. When he saw the parrot he had to smile, but tried not to laugh.

'So that's where my robe has gone,' he said mildly.

'I didn't mean to steal it,' the parrot said, hurriedly throwing off the borrowed clothes. 'I thought that if I wore clothes then I could talk to God like you and he would talk to me.'

Mr Noah looked round the grinning animals. 'Come with me,' he said to the parrot.

They went to his cabin and sat on the bed. 'I don't know why God speaks to me,' Mr Noah said once they were alone. 'But it's not because I wear clothes.'

'Oh,' said the parrot, surprised.

Mr Noah held out his hand and, after a moment, the parrot flew up and perched on it.

'It's not because I'm clever either,' Mr Noah went on. 'I'm nowhere near as clever as you with your different voices.'

'I see,' said the parrot.

'God made us all different and gave us all different gifts,' Mr Noah said. 'My family can talk to God, but we have to wear clothes as we don't have beautiful feathers like you to keep us warm. We can't fly either, although I've often wished I could.'

'Have you?' asked the parrot.

Mr Noah stroked the parrot's bright feathers and, after a moment or two, the parrot flew up to Mr Noah's shoulder.

'I'm sorry,' the parrot said. 'I've been an awful nuisance and caused a lot of trouble.'

'I don't mind you mimicking me,' Mr Noah said. 'So long as you let everyone know in advance.' He thought for a moment. 'Why don't you give us an evening's entertainment?'

The parrot brightened at the thought.

'Could I?' he asked.

'Yes,' said Mr Noah. 'You go and talk it over with your wife.'

'I haven't been very nice to her, either,' the parrot said uncomfortably.

'I know,' said Mr Noah. 'God told me.'

As the parrot was about to fly away, Mr Noah had another thought. 'If you would like to be here when I talk to God, you're very welcome to come and sit on my shoulder,' he said.

'Thank you,' the parrot said. 'I'd really like that.'

That evening the parrot and his wife entertained the animals, insects and birds in the great hall. It was a huge success and their lion and tiger impersonations caused many of the animals to cry with laughter, although the lion was not greatly amused.

The applause at the end of the show drowned out the sound of the wind and rain and echoed over the empty seas as the little ark floated on.

6

THE WOODWORM'S TALE

The cow opened her mouth and yawned, a big, wide, yawn. 'Oh dear ... I'm so ... ooo ... tired!'

'It's all this lazing about, doing nothing,' said the jackal dryly.

'I never do much anyway,' the cow replied comfortably. 'But it's not that. It's the noise. It's been keeping me awake at night.' She yawned again. 'Sorry, dears.'

'What noise?' asked the snake.

'I don't know,' the cow replied.

'Must be the rain,' said the jackal.

'It's not the rain. I'm used to the rain.'

'Well, it must have been the pigs then. They make dreadful grunting noises when they sleep.'

'It's not that either,' the cow said.

'What does it sound like?' asked the dormouse.

The cow considered. 'Like ... tapping. In the wall.'

The lion, who liked to order others around, walked

to the centre of the great hall.

'QUIET EVERYONE!' he roared.

The animals, insects and birds on board the ark all turned to look at him. The tiger opened one sleepy eye.

'What's he on about now?' he asked.

'The cow has heard a tapping noise in the walls of the ark,' said the lion. 'I want you all to be *absolutely* quiet and listen hard.'

The chatter, the grunts, the snuffles and the squeakings stopped as everyone listened hard.

'A ... A ... TISHOO ...!' The dingo sneezed loudly, then looked round apologetically. 'I'b awfully sorry everyone, bud I can't help id. I thig I'b god a cold.'

'Well, go away and sneeze somewhere else,' said the lion crossly.

'Not near me!' cried the emu in alarm. 'I don't want your nasty germs!'

The lion again called for quiet, but it was no use. The great hall was once more full of noise.

'We'll just have to listen tonight,' the lion said to the cow.

That night the lion, the tiger, the jackal, the dog and many other interested animals crowded into the cow's byre and put their ears to the wall.

'There it is!' breathed the flamingo excitedly. 'Tap, tap, tap.'

'Do you think someone's trying to get in?' asked the donkey anxiously.

'Of course not,' scoffed the jackal. 'There's only fish outside the ark and they wouldn't want to get in.'

'Wouldn't they?' said the donkey, rather surprised.

'Perhaps someone's trying to get out.' suggested the llama.

'Possibly,' said the lion after giving it much thought.

Just then a reddish-brown head popped out from inside the wall.

' 'ello,' it said. 'Can you help me? I have lost my friend. We went tunnelling together but 'e went zat way and I went zis and now I can't find 'im.'

'Who are you?' asked the lion.

'I am ze furniture beetle,' said the creature. 'Ow do you do?' The head disappeared for a moment then re-emerged. 'Sorry,' it said. 'I have to go. I think I see ze tunnel of my friend.'

And with that it disappeared for good.

The following morning, Rachel, Shem's wife, arrived in the cow's byre, carrying the milking stool and pail.

'Good morning,' she said. 'It's a lovely morning, or it would be, if it stopped raining. How are you this morning?'

'Terrible dear,' said the cow placidly. 'Didn't get a wink of sleep last night. Tap, tap, tap all night long.'

'Oh, I'm sorry,' said Rachel. She put down the stool. 'What was tapping?'

'Some beetle or other,' said the cow. 'I didn't take much notice. Most of the animals on the ark were in here and I had an awful job getting rid of them.'

'Dear, dear.' Rachel positioned the pail, sat down on the stool . . . and fell on the floor with a bump! The stool had collapsed underneath her and was now in pieces on the floor.

'Well, I never!'

'Are you all right?' asked the cow, concerned.

'I think so,' said Rachel, gingerly getting to her feet and rubbing her sore behind. She picked up the pieces of the stool and looked at them closely. 'This stool is riddled with holes! Whatever can have caused them?'

A reddish-brown head appeared out of one of the holes.

'I did,' it said brightly. ' 'Ave you seen my friend?'

High up in the great hall, the parrot was swinging on his perch practising his many different voices when there was a cracking noise. The parrot gave a shriek as the perch broke, and he flew across the hall in alarm.

'Shiver me timbers and splice me mainbrace, what hit me?'

' 'Allo,' said a reddish-brown head poking its way out of the fallen piece of wood. 'I have lost my friend. 'Ave you seen her?'

Then he turned and disappeared.

'The time has come,' said the lion, 'when we have to act!'

'Absolutely, old chap,' said the parrot, imitating the lion's voice.

'Otherwise the ark won't be safe for anyone,' the lion continued, ignoring the interruption. 'Those beetles, or whatever they call themselves, have got to be stopped!'

'Woodworm,' said the jackal.

'What?' asked the lion.

'That's what they are. Woodworm. They eat through wood.'

There was a sudden silence in the great hall as the animals, insects and birds looked at each other. The wooden structure of the ark, which had seemed so safe when they were first on board, now appeared very fragile. They could hear the rain pounding on the roof and the wind howling outside. The ark dipped and swayed in the choppy seas.

'Holes!' the emu shrieked. 'I can see thousands of holes! The ark's going to collapse!'

'I knew something like this would happen,' said the monkey in an I-told-you-so voice. 'This whole trip was doomed from the start.'

'I think we should tell Mr Noah what's happened,' said the badger in a practical voice.

'Just what I was going to suggest,' the lion said quickly. 'Tiger, shall we go?'

When the lion and tiger reached Mr Noah's cabin, they found that he already knew told about the woodworm. Rachel had shown him her broken stool. He hurried to the great hall, the lion and tiger on either side.

'What are you going to do, Mr Noah?' the jackal called to him.

'I don't know yet,' Mr Noah said, somewhat flustered. 'I shall have to think.'

'Well I wouldn't think for too long,' the monkey said sourly. 'Or the ark might fall to pieces.'

'Fleas are one thing,' said the hedgehog, busily scratching himself. 'I can put up with fleas. Wood-worm's another.'

'First we must find the woodworms,' Mr Noah said. 'And for that we need absolute quiet . . .'

In the silence that followed, everyone listened hard for the sound of tapping. But no one, not even the animals with the most sensitive hearing, could hear a thing.

'Perhaps they've gone to sleep,' suggested the badger.

'Or tunnelled their way outside and fallen into the water,' said the donkey, but no one really believed that. It was with some anxiety that everyone settled down for the night.

It was late when Mr Noah returned to his cabin and he was very tired. He threw himself on his bed and was soon fast asleep. But his sleep was disturbed by a dream that the ark was sinking. It sank lower and lower—and Mr Noah woke up in alarm.

'Help!' he called. 'What's happening?'

Then he realized. The foot of his bed had collapsed on to the floor.

'Tap ... tap ... tap ...'

'Is that you, woodworm?' Mr Noah asked crossly.

A reddish-brown head popped out of a hole in one of the wooden posts of Mr Noah's bed.

'Did someone call?'

'Have you just made my bed collapse?'

'But no!' said the woodworm. 'All I was doing was tunnelling to try and find my friend.' He shook his head sadly. 'But she is not 'ere. I go elsewhere to look.'

'Wait a minute,' said Mr Noah. 'How did you lose her?'

'We arrive on ze ark together,' said the woodworm. 'And we start tunnelling together also. We like to tunnel together. But we go tunnelling in ze wrong directions and we lose each other. It is very sad.'

'I think,' said Mr Noah, 'that the first thing to do is to find your friend. God will know where she is. We'll ask him for help.'

So he sat on the edge of his bed and asked God for help in finding the other woodworm.

There was a knock on his door. It was the dingo.

'Sorry to distub you, Bister Noah,' he said, his head full of cold. 'Bud I had by head out through the trab-door, trying to clear by doze, when I heard this tabbing . . .'

'Wait there,' Mr Noah said to the woodworm and he hurried to the roof of the ark.

'Tap . . . tap . . . tap tap . . .'

'Is that you, woodworm?' Mr Noah asked.

'It is I,' said the woodworm, poking her head out.

'Come with me,' said Mr Noah. 'I've found your friend.'

Back in his cabin, Mr Noah watched the delighted reunion of the woodworms. But he was still worried.

'What do I do with them, God?' he asked. 'If I just let them go off making more holes, what will become of the ark?'

'You don't appear to have much faith in my plans, Noah,' God said reproachfully.

'Oh I do, God,' Mr Noah protested.

'Do you think I haven't given thought to the wood-worms? They are as much my creatures as you.'

Mr Noah sat silent.

'Why not ask *them*?' God suggested.

Mr Noah turned to the woodworms. 'Now that you've found each other, would you stop tunnelling, please?' he asked.

They looked at him in surprise. 'Stop tunnelling?' one of them said. 'Oh no, that is impossible.'

'But I'm worried about the safety of the ark,' Mr Noah said.

'Did you 'ere that? 'He's worried about ze safety of ze ark!'

'That is a good joke,' said the other one.

'Well, I don't think it's very funny,' Mr Noah said.

'Oh, but it is. The wood of the ark , Mr Noah, is so hard you would need an army of us all working together

221

for a long, long time before there was any danger to ze ark.'

'That is why we chose softer wood, like ze stool and ze parrot's perch,' the other explained.

'And your bed,' added the first.

'I see,' said Mr Noah feeling much better. He picked up Rachel's broken stool. 'Would you agree to spend the rest of the voyage tunnelling through this stool? The other animals would be pleased, and it's nice soft wood. It would also mean that you wouldn't lose each other again.'

'That is a good idea,' said the first woodworm, nodding his reddish-brown head. 'We will do whatever you say.'

'Except stop tunnelling,' said the second woodworm.

'Except that, of course,' agreed the first.

Mr Noah went off to tell the animals in the great hall the good news. As he went, he could hear the distant tap, tap, tapping of the woodworms and, even more distantly, their conversation.

'No, it is this way we go ...'

'No, this is better. Follow me ...'

The sound of their talking and tapping died away until all Mr Noah could hear was the sound of the rain beating on the ark and the noise of the howling wind.

7

MRS NOAH'S TALE

Mrs Noah was not at all happy when her husband told her that God would send a flood to destroy the world, not even when he told her that she and their children and two of every creature in the world would be saved.

'It's not that I'm not grateful to God for saving us,' she said. 'Mind you, I'm not in the least surprised. You're a good man and I'm only glad to see that God recognizes the fact. He doesn't always seem to reward the good,' she added, with a disapproving sniff.

'Now, Becky, you mustn't talk like that about God,' Mr Noah said.

'I don't see why not,' said Mrs Noah. 'Anyway, that's not the point. The thing is, I don't want to go off in a boat, however well built it is—although knowing your carpentry, Noah, I doubt whether it'll stand up to much. I don't like boats and I think it's a bit unreasonable of God to plan all this without talking to us about it first.'

'He talked to me,' Mr Noah said.

'That's as may be,' Mrs Noah replied. 'But why didn't God speak to *me* as well? I could have given him some good advice.'

All Mr Noah could do was shrug his shoulders.

Mrs Noah sighed. 'God knew you'd give in to anything he said. You're soft as butter.'

'Becky, do you think I like leaving our farm like this any better than you do?' Mr Noah protested. 'But we can't go against God's will. He only wants the best for us.'

'That's as may be,' Mrs Noah said, pursing her lips.

She did not speak of it again, but she thought about it a great deal.

'It's not fair,' she thought. 'God never speaks to me, although I'm always on at him about one thing or another.' She frowned. 'Anyway, I think God should have managed better. If I'd been God, I wouldn't have let things get in such a mess in the first place. Sending a flood to destroy the world indeed! Such a waste!'

Mrs Noah was not happy on board. It was not so much the animals, or the cramped conditions, or even the rain that bothered her. It was just that she was not a good sailor and to be a sailor's wife was not what she had intended when she had married Mr Noah. So she spent a lot of time in her cabin, and although she cooked and cleaned and did all the work expected of her, she grew more and more depressed. Mr Noah became very worried and tried talking to her.

'You never smile, Becky,' he said. 'And you always used to.'

'There's nothing to smile about!' she snapped.

Mr Noah sighed. 'I know this is a lot of work and not much fun, but we should be thankful that we're alive.'

'Hmm!' Mrs Noah retorted.

Mr Noah went away and talked it over with God.

'She says that she gets seasick, but I don't think that's the real problem. I think she just doesn't trust you the way I do and that's what's making her so unhappy. Can't you talk to her?'

'She wouldn't listen if I did,' God said.

'Of course she would,' Mr Noah said eagerly. 'She's always saying that she talks to you but you never reply.'

'She doesn't talk *to* me, Noah,' God said rather sadly. 'She talks *at* me. But don't worry about her. Just leave everything to me.'

A few days later Mrs Noah found Japheth sitting by himself in a corner of the ark. Mrs Noah was very fond of all her sons and their wives, but Japheth, her youngest, was her especial favourite and she was worried when she found him in tears.

'Whatever's the matter?' she asked.

'Oh, Mum, I can't tell you. I can't tell anyone.'

'Of course you can. Now what is it?'

'Well, it's the wild animals,' Japheth confessed. 'I'm

scared of them. No, not just scared. I'm terrified. I've tried getting over it, honestly, but it doesn't get any better, it just gets worse. And I can't tell Shem or Ham because they'd only laugh and say I was being stupid. And I *am* being stupid, I know.'

Mrs Noah put her arms round him.

'The thought of being cooped up here for months, maybe longer, is just driving me crazy,' he said between sobs. 'But whenever I see that lion, my legs go all shaky. And when the tiger yawns and shows all those sharp teeth, I think about what it would be like if he began to eat me and then I feel sick all over. Oh, Mum, what can I do?'

Mrs Noah was silent for a moment. 'Have you talked to your father?' she asked at last.

'Dad?' Japheth sat up. 'Oh, I couldn't possibly tell him. He'd feel I was letting him down. I'd be so ashamed. You won't tell him, will you? Promise?'

'Not if you don't want me to,' she promised. 'Now why don't you go up on the roof and get a bit of fresh air and in the meantime I'll try and think of something.'

When he had gone Mrs Noah thought hard, but she could not think of anything, so at last she spoke to God.

'Now listen, God,' she said severely. 'You got us into this mess and it's your duty to help Japheth.'

God listened, but did not speak.

Over the next few days Japheth continued to do his

work, but some of the animals began to sense that something was wrong.

'Do you know,' said the gorilla, 'I popped up and said "boo" to him and he nearly fainted away on the spot!'

'Why did you do that?' asked the jackal. 'Seems rather a silly thing to do.'

'I just thought it would be a bit of fun,' said the gorilla. 'You know, help to pass the time.'

The tiger smiled lazily. 'It is rather fun to frighten him, I must admit,' he said. 'When I snapped my teeth the other day I thought he'd have a heart attack.'

'Little things please little minds,' said the jackal. The tiger sprang to his feet.

'Who are you calling little?' he asked in a dangerous voice.

'Oh, do lie down and be quiet,' said the jackal. 'You don't frighten me.'

'Personally, I think it's unkind to frighten the boy,' said the rhinoceros. 'He's harmless, isn't he?'

'Yes, but he's spineless,' said the wolf, baring his sharp teeth. 'I'd be ashamed of him if he was a cub of mine. He needs toughening up.'

'You won't do it by frightening him,' said the rhinoceros firmly.

'What he needs is your thick skin,' grinned the fox.

While the animals were discussing Japheth, Japheth himself was growing more and more frightened every time he had to enter the great hall. Hannah, his wife, asked if he was ill and Japheth clutched at this excuse gratefully and took to his bed. Meanwhile, Mrs Noah was busy on his behalf. Every day she spoke to God, demanding that he *do* something.

'All I'm asking, God, is that you give my poor son a bit of courage. It's not that much to ask, is it? I mean, I know you're busy flooding the world and everything, but you could take the time to give Japheth a bit of help. It wouldn't take you long. It's been a week now since I first spoke to you about it and what have you done? Nothing. I must say it's enough to shake anyone's faith!'

Just then Mr Noah came into the cabin.

'Whatever are you doing?' he asked.

'I'm giving God a piece of my mind,' Mrs Noah said firmly.

'Oh? Why?'

'Well,' Mrs Noah began, then remembered her promise to Japheth. 'Something has happened which God knows about and although I keep telling God to sort it out, I just don't think he wants to know.'

'Now Becky, you can't go *telling* God what to do. He knows better than we do what our needs are and he'll answer our prayers but in his own way and his own time.'

'That's all very well,' sniffed Mrs Noah. 'But there isn't much time and it seems to me that his way of answering is to do nothing.'

'I wouldn't be too sure about that,' Mr Noah said. 'What is the problem anyway?'

'I can't tell you. It was told to me in confidence.'

'It must be one of the boys in trouble,' Mr Noah said wisely. 'Look, why don't you try talking it over with God, instead of giving him orders? I don't like being ordered about and I don't suppose God does either.'

When he left, Mrs Noah sat alone in the cabin. At first she was cross with her husband, as cross as she was with God, but then she began to think about what he had said.

'Is he right, God?' she asked at last. 'Do I order you about?'

'Well, yes, you do,' God said.

'Is that *really* you, God?' Mrs Noah asked, surprised at being answered.

'Yes,' said God.

'Do I just give you lists of things I want done and expect you to do them?' Mrs Noah asked.

'I'm afraid so,' said God.

Mrs Noah thought about it some more.

'I'm sorry if I've been rude,' she said at last. 'It's just that I'm so worried. Nothing seems to have gone right, and you never talk to me like you talk to Noah.'

'I'm talking to you now,' said God.

'Yes,' said Mrs Noah. 'Thank you.'

She was silent for a moment, then said in a small voice. 'Please, would you help Japheth?'

'Of course,' said God. 'We'll help him together.'

Some time later, Mrs Noah went to the great hall. She walked straight through the teeming mass of animals to the lion and the tiger.

'Lion. Tiger. I need your help,' she said firmly.

'Delighted to oblige, dear lady,' said the lion graciously.

'Me too,' said the tiger, lazily scratching himself.

That evening, when most of the animals were asleep, Mrs Noah took a white and trembling Japheth by the hand into the great hall. The lion and the tiger were waiting for them.

'Now then,' she said to her son. 'There's really nothing at all to be afraid of. Look at them. They're just like big, soft cats.'

The lion winced, but the tiger only grinned and began to purr in a deep voice.

'I'm sorry I'm so stupid,' said Japheth, swallowing hard. 'But it's your teeth ... and your claws ... they make me afraid. You're both so strong.'

'Well I am the King of the Jungle,' said the lion, not displeased. 'Lord of all the Beasts. There's no harm, young man, in being afraid. It's quite sensible of you, really.'

'Really?' asked Japheth.

'Yes. Although we wouldn't hurt you.'

'Not a hair of your head,' added the tiger.

'You see, we made an agreement with Mr Noah that while we were on this voyage we wouldn't hunt other animals.'

'And certainly not eat them,' put in the tiger, a righteous expression on his face.

'So you're absolutely safe,' said the lion.

The tiger held out his paw. 'Shake on it,' he said.

Japheth looked at the sharp claws and gulped. Then he put out his hand and solemnly shook the tiger's paw, then the lion's.

'I feel better,' he said.

'You're a good lad,' said the lion. 'Don't you worry. We'll look after you.'

Japheth smiled and went to bed.

'Thank you, God,' Mrs Noah said when she was back in her cabin.

'Any time,' said God. 'Oh, and Becky ...'

'Yes?'

'Are you still unhappy about being on the ark?'

'I haven't had time to think about it,' Mrs Noah said. And she smiled.

8

THE PANDA'S TALE

When the animals, insects and birds first boarded the ark, Mr Noah had taken great pains to make them all as comfortable as possible. God had told him what food to provide and whether the animals were more at home hanging upside down from the rafters—like the bats— hiding in crevices—like the geckos—or wallowing in mud — like the hippos. Mr Noah had tried to make living and sleeping areas on the ark to suit all the different tastes. But when it came to the two pandas, Mr Noah scratched his head and was stuck. God had not told him much about them, other than that they ate bamboo shoots and did not need anywhere special to sleep.

When the pandas arrived on board they took Mr Noah to one side.

'I don't like other animals,' said the male panda gruffly. 'Never know what to say to them.'

'I see,' said Mr Noah.

'I don't like them either,' said the female panda. 'They're very loud.'

'Not all of them,' said Mr Noah.

The female panda stared at him with her big dark eyes. 'I prefer to keep myself to myself,' she said.

'Isn't that a bit lonely?' asked Mr Noah.

'I don't know,' said the female panda. 'I've never really thought about it. I've always been on my own.'

'Could you tell me,' said the male panda loudly, 'where my range is to be?'

'Your range?' repeated Mr Noah.

'Yes. My territory—the part of the ark where I can roam about quite freely and quite alone?'

Mr Noah was mystified. 'But both of you can go anywhere,' he said. 'Together or separately.'

The pandas shook their heads.

'Not together,' said the female panda firmly. 'I roam on my own.'

'So do I,' said the male panda.

'Well, if that's what you want...' Mr Noah began doubtfully.

'Oh, it is,' the male panda assured him. 'We prefer to be quite separate.'

'Very well,' said Mr Noah. 'But you'll come to the welcome meeting in the great hall tonight, won't you?'

The male panda shook his head. 'No,' he said. 'Not for me.'

'Me neither,' said the female panda, and they both turned away from Mr Noah and went off in different directions.

Mr Noah hardly ever saw them after that first day. Sometimes he or his sons caught glimpses of one or other as they made their way along a corridor or up some stairs. But usually the only signs he had that the pandas were still on the ark were the shredded remains of bamboo which he put out for their food. Whenever the other animals tried to talk to them, the pandas just walked off without saying a word.

'Don't they need friends?' marvelled the polar bear as he caught sight of a large black-and-white shape disappearing down the corridor.

'Obviously not,' said his wife comfortably.

'Well, well,' said the polar bear, shaking his head. 'I

don't know whether or not to feel sorry for them.'

Other animals were more outspoken.

'It's not natural,' sniffed the emu. 'If they don't want to mix with us that's fair enough, although I must say I do think it's rather stuck-up of them, but at least they should be together and not on their own. My husband and I are always together, aren't we, dear?'

Her husband nodded, but said, a little wistfully, 'It might be nice to be on one's own from time to time.'

'Nonsense,' said the emu briskly. 'You'd hate it. Anyway,' she continued, 'it shouldn't be allowed. Mr Noah should tell them that their behaviour might be all right in China or wherever they come from, but it's not at all the thing on the ark.'

'Oh, leave them alone,' said the jackal impatiently. 'Sometimes I think the pandas have the right idea. At least they don't have to listen to others drivelling on all the time.' The emu did not hear this for she had bustled off to speak to Mr Noah.

The animals soon found a new subject to talk about and the pandas were forgotten. Day after day they walked slowly round and round the ark, their great heads swaying from side to side. They rarely met anyone, not even one another.

But after a while, the female panda began to feel curious. Although she never entered the great hall, which was always filled with animals, insects and birds of all shapes and sizes, she sometimes stood just outside the doorway and peered in. She saw twos, threes, whole groups of animals, talking together, playing games together, eating together. She saw them squabbling and laughing and sometimes fighting. The panda was amazed.

'Whatever do they talk about?' she wondered.

Pandas do not have regular sleeping places. They sleep whenever they feel tired and wherever they happen to be at the time. Sometimes they sleep during the day and sometimes during the night.

One night the female panda crept into the great hall. She walked quietly among the sleeping animals and gazed down at them. It was all very strange, she thought. Perhaps they liked being together.

And bit by bit the panda began to be curious about the other panda on the ark. She started to follow him and they met, by accident it seemed, a couple of times. But when she tried to talk to him, he just turned and plodded away, not hurriedly, but in a very determined manner. At last, not knowing what else to do, the panda went to see Mr Noah.

'I'm very sorry to trouble you,' she said.

'It's no trouble,' said Mr Noah. 'That's what I'm here for.'

'You see, I know I said that I preferred being on my own,' said the panda. 'Well, that was true. I did like it. I didn't know anything else. But now I've seen how the animals talk together and eat together and it looks rather nice.' She stopped.

'Yes?' said Mr Noah encouragingly.

'I think,' said the female panda, 'that I'd like to meet some of the other animals. It's very lonely being on your own.'

Mr Noah introduced the female panda to some of the animals in the great hall. Although shy at first, the panda was a great success for all the animals were curious about her.

'Why are your eyes ringed with black?' asked the swallow, flying down to look at her more closely.

'I don't know,' said the panda.

'It's not because you've been in a fight, is it?' the aardvark questioned.

'No. I've never been in a fight.'

'Don't be so personal,' said the warthog disapprovingly. 'I'm sure you wouldn't be too pleased if someone came and asked about your big nose.'

'I wouldn't mind,' said the aardvark. 'It's better than being all-over ugly like you.'

The warthog grinned amiably. He didn't mind what he looked like.

But despite her new friends, the female panda did not forget about the other panda, still roaming by himself around the ark.

'I mean, we're both pandas, we must have something in common. Things we can talk about,' she explained to Mr Noah. She thought for a moment. 'Like the kind of bamboo shoots we like eating.'

'Perhaps he's shy,' said Mr Noah. 'Why don't you invite him to tea with Mrs Noah and myself?'

'I'll do that,' said the female panda. But when she went to look for the panda, she could not find him. More worrying, none of the bamboo left for him to eat had been touched for at least three days.

She hurried to find Mr Noah.

'Wherever can he be?' she asked in alarm.

'I don't know,' said Mr Noah. 'But if he's on the ark, we'll find him.'

He organized a search party and he and the animals looked everywhere.

But it was the female panda, knowing the kind of places the panda would prefer, who eventually found him, in pitch darkness, right down in the hold of the ark, at the bottom of a steep ladder.

'I slipped and hurt my leg,' he said to the female panda, 'and I couldn't climb back up again. I *am* hungry.'

The female panda tried to lift him but he was too heavy for her.

'I'll go and get help,' she promised.

She found Mr Noah and he and the animals rushed to the top of the ladder and peered down into the darkness.

'Are you badly hurt?' Mr Noah asked.

'No,' said the panda curtly. 'Just my leg. If you could give me a hand out I'd be grateful.'

The two gorillas, who were very strong, swung themselves down the ladder and formed a chain with the polar bear and the lion. Together they lifted the panda out of the hold.

After a good meal and some first aid on his leg, the panda got to his feet.

'Thanks for the rescue and everything,' he said gruffly to Mr Noah. 'Much appreciated. I must be off now.'

'Must you?' Mr Noah asked mildly.

'Oh yes.' The panda looked slowly around the great hall, which was noisy and crowded. 'I'm a loner.'

The female panda glanced at him.

'I thought I was too,' she said. 'But I've changed my mind. We all need each other. Look what happened to you. You would have died if we hadn't found you.'

'Maybe,' said the panda. 'But I'm better on my own.' He shrugged. 'I can't change my nature.'

'No,' said Mr Noah. 'But God can.' He smiled at them both and quietly walked away.

A few days later, as he was carrying the evening meal from the kitchen to the great hall, Mr Noah saw not one, but two pandas walking slowly away from him down the corridor, their great heads swaying contentedly together from side to side.

'Thank you, God,' Mr Noah said. 'I knew you would help.'

He was still smiling as he walked into the great hall.

'I don't know what there is to smile about,' said the monkey sourly. 'It's still raining, isn't it?'

'Oh yes,' said Mr Noah. 'It's still raining. But it's been a lovely day for all that.'

9

THE GIRAFFE'S TALE

It was the thirty-ninth day of the voyage. Thirty-nine days had passed since God sent the rain which had flooded the world, and on every one of those days Mr Noah or one of his sons had placed a large cross on a chart in the great hall of the ark. Each day the animals, insects and birds had crowded around—although few of them could read—to see how many days of rain were left.

'Now let me see,' said the owl, staring at the chart with unblinking eyes, 'it's been raining for thirty-nine days.'

'Is that all?' remarked the jackal gloomily. 'It seems like a lifetime.'

'And God said it would rain for forty days. That means . . .' The owl, who liked doing sums, did a hurried calculation. 'That means there's only one day of rain left,' he finished triumphantly.

'Depends whether you've counted the nights,' said the monkey.

'What do you mean?'

'Mr Noah told us that God said it would rain for forty days and forty nights,' explained the monkey. He grinned sarcastically. 'You've only counted the days.'

'Does that mean,' asked the giraffe, who was inclined to be a bit slow, 'that after tomorrow it will have rained for forty days, and then it's got to rain for forty nights before it stops?'

'Of course it doesn't,' said the gorilla, who had ambled over to see what all the fuss was about.

'Why not?' asked the giraffe.

'Because we've been asleep during the nights so we've missed it,' said the gorilla.

The giraffe shook his head. 'I don't understand,' he said, wrinkling his brow in a puzzled way.

'Never mind,' said the owl kindly. 'I wouldn't let it worry you.'

The animals, insects and birds were careful not to let things worry the giraffe as they knew that he was easily upset.

The giraffe did look anxious for a moment, then his face cleared. 'Did I ever tell you the story about the lake that wouldn't dry up?' he asked hopefully.

The animals sighed and settled down for what would be a long and not very funny story. But no one complained because everyone liked the giraffe. Only the dog remained, staring in a troubled way at the chart.

'Thirty-nine and one is...' she said to herself in a puzzled voice. 'Thirty-nine and one is...' The dog was very bad at sums.

When two of every animal, insect, reptile and bird had first entered the ark, Mr Noah had been amazed at the variety of God's creation. There were tall ones, short ones, thin ones and fat ones. Some were plain, some were ugly, some were handsome, and some, as Mr Noah afterwards said to his wife, were downright peculiar.

'But then,' he added, 'God made us all different. It would be boring if we were all alike.'

But of all the animals who entered the ark, Mr Noah found the giraffes the oddest.

'With those long necks and small heads, I wasn't sure the ark would be tall enough for them, but it is ... just,' Mr Noah said. 'I'm glad I followed God's advice in building it, and didn't try to cut any corners.'

There were not many places on the ark where the giraffes could stand and stretch their necks with any comfort but, as the giraffe's wife said placidly, 'We're a lot better off than some of the heavier animals, poor things.' She glanced at the two elephants. 'At least we don't make the ark tilt from side to side when we walk.'

The giraffe's wife was not as tall as her husband. When she walked she picked her way carefully among the teeming animals on the ark. Her husband did not find it so easy.

'Hey, mind where you're going!' squeaked the dormouse in alarm as the giraffe almost squashed him.

'Oh, sorry,' said the giraffe.

'Watch out!' cried the guinea-pig.

'Oh dear,' said the giraffe. He put his front foot down on the ground... and lifted it hurriedly as it came into contact with the hedgehog. 'Owwh!' he yelled. He bent his long neck anxiously.

'Are you all right?' he asked the hedgehog.

'Oh yes, *I'm* all right,' said the hedgehog. 'But are *you* all right? I'm terribly sorry to have got in your way.'

'Some animals just don't look where they're going,' sniffed the emu.

'It's hardly his fault,' said the ant-eater. 'It must be difficult seeing where you're going when your head's in the air. I prefer to snuffle along the ground. Better for finding ants,' he added, licking his lips.

'Thanks for nothing,' said the ant.

'It *is* difficult,' the giraffe said earnestly. 'My wife manages all right, but then you see, I'm terribly clumsy. I always have been. It makes life very hard.'

He squinted at the ground before taking a cautious step forwards. It was a mistake. A loud squealing rose above the noise in the great hall.

'Say, I'd sure be grateful if you would—uh—remove yourself out of my sty,' said the pig. 'Honey here is trying to sleep.'

His wife grunted.

'I'm awfully sorry,' said the giraffe apologetically.

He moved to one side, which was another mistake.

There was a loud splash as he fell into the tank of water which was kept for the reptiles and animals who liked bathing.

The crocodiles snapped their jaws, missing the hippopotamus by inches. The hippo heaved himself hurriedly out of the way, which caused the ark to shudder under his great weight. The two elephants began to laugh, while the poor giraffe struggled to get out.

'Help! Get me out of here! Help!'

He slipped further into the tank and fell against the water buffalo, who was knocked sideways into the rhinoceros. A great tidal wave of water spurted up, soaking all the animals, insects and birds in the great hall. Everyone floundered around making a tremendous noise and Mr and Mrs Noah came running to see what had happened.

The giraffe was soon hauled out and stood upright again, dripping wet and very unhappy.

'I'm sorry,' he kept repeating. 'I'm so terribly sorry.'

He was so upset that no one could be angry for long.

'We should be grateful to you,' said the fox, shaking drops of water from his bushy tail, 'for brightening up a boring evening. There's not been much on-board entertainment provided on the ark.'

A large tear rolled off the end of the giraffe's nose and another followed it.

'There's no need to cry,' said the swallow, circling overhead. 'No one's blaming you.'

'I'm so stupid and so clumsy,' said the giraffe. 'I really don't know why God chose me to come on the ark. I should have been left behind to d-drown!'

Another tear rolled down his cheek.

'Oh, come on,' said the jackal. 'Cheer up. Worse things happen at sea.'

'We *are* at sea,' the lion reminded him.

Nothing anyone said was of any help to the giraffe. When he accidentally trod on the dog's tail, his mind was made up. He planted himself in the centre of the great hall and closed his eyes.

'You needn't worry any more,' he said. 'Any of you. I'll just stay here and not move until the journey is over. Just pretend I'm made of wood.'

And that was where Mr Noah found him, some hours later.

'Come along old thing,' Mr Noah said. 'You really can't stay there for the rest of the trip. You'll get cramp.'

'But if I move I might tread on someone,' said the giraffe. 'I'd rather have cramp than tread on someone.' His bottom lip trembled. 'I'm so clumsy, Mr Noah And I'm such a ridiculous shape. It was all right when I was at home, but here I'm just useless and a menace to everyone.'

'No you're not,' said Mr Noah stoutly. 'Look, I'll go and talk to God. I'm sure he'll be able to help.'

'I know the ark's crowded, but he can't stand still for the rest of the voyage,' Mr Noah said, having told God the problem. 'I just don't know what the answer is.' He thought for a moment. 'What he needs is a job. Something to show him that he isn't useless.'

'That time will come,' God said. 'There will be a job for him later. Meanwhile, I suggest you speak to the animals. I'm sure they will help.'

So Mr Noah asked the animals for help. He spoke to the large animals, but it was the small ones who came up with the solution.

'If I fly beside the giraffe, I can warn him of danger,' said the swallow.

'And I can walk beside him, and call out if there's anyone in the way,' said the dormouse.

'I'll help,' offered the hedgehog.

'If the giraffe doesn't mind my sitting on his back, I can relay messages to him,' said the koala bear. 'I'm used to heights.'

The giraffe was overwhelmed by these offers of help. 'Thank you,' he said. 'Thank you all.'

The animals took up their positions.

'Make way, there, make way,' called the dog

importantly. 'The giraffe is about to move!'

'Left a bit,' said the dormouse as the giraffe took a hesitant step.

'Left a bit,' repeated the koala bear.

The giraffe moved to the left.

'Take care! There's a beetle right ahead,' called the swallow.

'Don't worry about me,' said the beetle. 'I can get out of the way. Just watch out for the centipede. He's over on your right.'

'Centipede on the right!' cried the hedgehog.

'Centipede on the right!' repeated the koala bear.

And the giraffe, with the help of his new friends, was able to move round the ark in safety.

On the fortieth day of the voyage the owl and many of the other animals watched Mr Noah make a large cross on the chart.

'Forty,' said the owl. 'It's the fortieth day.'

'Thirty-nine plus one is forty,' said the dog under her breath. 'Thirty-nine plus one is forty. I must remember that.'

The eagle suddenly swept down from the rafters.

'The rain,' he cried in a deep voice, 'has stopped!'

A great sigh went round the hall.

'God has kept his promise,' said Mr Noah.

He smiled at the hushed animals, insects and birds. When he saw the giraffe his smile suddenly grew broader.

'I've got it!' he exclaimed. 'I've just the job for you.'

'A job?' asked the giraffe. 'For me?'

'Yes,' said Mr Noah. 'Now that the rain has stopped you can act as our look-out for the first sight of land.'

'Can I?' asked the giraffe eagerly. 'Can I really?'

'Yes, please,' said Mr Noah.

So the giraffe stuck his long neck out of the trap at the top of the ark and looked for the first sight of land, while Mr Noah went to his cabin.

'Thank you, God,' he said. 'You said the rain would stop on the fortieth day and you said that there would be a job for the giraffe.'

And God looked down at the small ark floating under a cloudless sky, with the giraffe's head poking happily out of the top, and smiled.

10

THE JACKDAW'S TALE

When Mr Noah and his family arrived on the ark they brought little with them, other than the clothes they were wearing. God had told Mr Noah there would not be room for many possessions. His wife had carried a few precious pots and pans and wore her best robe, feeling that there was no point leaving it to be ruined in the flood. Her sons' wives had done the same.

But Miriam had brought some jewellery with her. A necklace of sparkling stones, which had been a present from her husband, Ham, and two brightly shining bracelets which had been given to her at her wedding.

'They don't take up any room at all,' she said to Ham, 'and it seems a shame to leave them behind.'

She wore them as she came aboard the ark, but afterwards put them at the back of a shelf in her cabin and forgot all about them. There was too much to do to think about wearing fine clothes or pretty jewellery.

But the jackdaw, who had seen Miriam wearing her

necklace and bracelets on that first day, could not forget about them. He wanted them. He wanted them very much indeed. He loved bright objects.

'It was the way they shone,' he told his wife. 'The stones of the necklace were deep blue and white, just like a cascade of water. And the bracelets... polished until you could see your beak reflected in them.'

He could not eat, he could not sleep, and he talked about them so much that at last his wife said, exasperated,

'Well, if you want to see them so much, why don't you ask Miriam if you can look at them? I'm sure she wouldn't mind.'

But the jackdaw wanted more than just one look. He wanted them for himself. So he hung around Miriam's cabin, keeping well into the shadows, and watched and waited.

One evening he was rewarded. Miriam had gone out

leaving her cupboard door open. The jackdaw saw something shining at the back of a shelf and gently pulled out the necklace and the two bracelets and laid them in a glittering heap. Then he perched on the edge of the bed and gloated. They were lovely. Perfect.

Hearing a sound, he hurriedly snatched up a handkerchief, wrapped it round the jewellery, and flew off, carrying the bundle in his beak. He flew to a spot he had already thought would make a good hiding place and hid the bundle.

During the weeks that followed, the jackdaw never went to look at the jewellery he had stolen. It was too dangerous, he thought, and besides, there was no need. It would be safe where he had hidden it and would keep until the voyage was over and he could take it away from prying eyes and enjoy it in private.

Miriam did not miss her jewellery until the evening of the party. The elephants had organized the event in order to celebrate the end of the rain and Mrs Noah, Hannah, Rachel and she dressed for the occasion in their best robes.

'I know,' she said to Ham. 'I'll wear my necklace and my bracelets. I haven't worn them for ages and they'd look nice with this robe.'

She rummaged in the drawer.

'They're not here,' she said.

She looked again.

'They've gone!'

She said nothing about it during the party, for she did not wish to spoil the fun, but afterwards she and Ham searched right through their cabin. She asked Rachel and Hannah if they seen them, and then went to Mr and Mrs Noah.

'I know God told us not to bring many possessions,' she explained, 'but they weren't large and meant a great deal to me. I'd be very sorry to lose them.'

'I should think so, too,' said Mrs Noah comfortably. 'Noah, whatever can have happened to them?'

'I don't know,' said Mr Noah. 'Perhaps the animals have seen them. I'll ask.'

But when he called the animals together, no one admitted seeing the missing bracelets or the necklace.

'Just like humans to go losing things,' croaked the raven. 'Wouldn't find one of us doing it.'

'That's because we don't wear jewellery,' said the badger.

'We don't need to,' said the peacock, eyeing his newly-grown tail with satisfaction. 'We are altogether magnificent as we are.'

'Speak for yourself,' said the warthog. 'Some of us might look a bit better with some jewellery round our necks.'

'No amount of jewellery would make you look any better, old son,' said the fox, grinning.

'Nor you, foxy-face,' said the warthog amiably.

'Anyway,' said the goose. 'Why did Mr Noah allow her to bring her jewellery in the first place? It's not as if this was a pleasure cruise. It's a life and death voyage and I strongly disapprove of her bringing trinkets on board. *We* weren't allowed to bring anything.'

'That's because we haven't got anything *to* bring,' said the buffalo. 'Don't be such a misery. She's a pretty girl and the jewellery doesn't take up any room.'

'But where's it gone? That's what I want to know,' said the lion.

'Perhaps one of the other humans stole it,' said the woodpecker. 'I wouldn't put it past Shem's wife. She could do with a bit of jewellery to brighten herself up.'

The parrot laughed at that, but the lion frowned.

'This is a serious matter which affects us all,' he said. 'I'm ashamed to think of it happening on *my* ship. And I don't for one moment think we've heard the last of it.'

He was right. Mr Noah organized a search of the ark. Everyone joined in, even the jackdaw, but the missing jewellery was not to be found.

'It's a proper mystery,' Mr Noah said as he told God about it. 'I know it must seem very unimportant to you, God,' he added humbly. 'But it's important to Miriam, and I'm fond of the child and don't like to see her upset.'

'Everything is important to me, Noah,' God replied.

'We must have a thief on board,' Mr Noah said

unhappily. 'Whatever shall I do about it?'

'Do nothing,' said God. 'I have the matter in hand. Just be patient.'

But it was hard for Mr Noah to be patient, for every day his sons and their wives pestered him about the matter.

'It's in God's hands,' he told them.

'Well if it's in God's hands, why doesn't God give it back?' bleated the goat, who overheard this. 'And I really can't think why God wants two bracelets and a necklace anyway. When would he wear them?'

'Oh, don't be so silly,' snapped the fox.

Everyone was short-tempered just then.

'It's bad enough being stuck here now the rain's stopped,' muttered the otter. 'It's worse being under suspicion of theft as well. I'm that fed up!'

'We're only stuck here because everywhere is flooded,' explained the eagle. 'Once the water has gone down we can get off.'

'It's all right for you birds,' growled the otter.

It *was* all right for the birds. Every day they left the ark, flying further and further afield to exercise their wings, and for the sheer joy of being able to fly far into the sunlit sky. The jackdaw, however, never flew too far from the ark. He watched over his hiding place, afraid that it might be discovered, anxious for a glimpse of his spoils.

'Soon,' he thought. 'Soon, I'll be able to fly away and take the jewellery with me.'

His thoughts were interrupted. The giraffe, who had been on the look-out for the first sight of land, began to shout.

'Land ahoy,' he called excitedly. 'Land!'

There was a stampede for the roof.

'Be careful now!' Mr Noah shouted. 'We don't want anyone falling off!'

He tripped over his robe in his excitement as he climbed the stairs leading to the trapdoor in the roof of the ark.

'Where is it?' he asked the giraffe.

The giraffe pointed with his long neck. 'Over there.'

Mr Noah looked, then looked again. There was a dark shape on the horizon which could have been land . . .

. . . until it did a somersault and swam away, spouting a stream of water through its blowhole.

'I'm afraid it's just a whale,' Mr Noah said regretfully.

The animals began to make their way, rather dejectedly, down the stairs.

'Stop shoving!' said the penguin crossly.

'I wasn't,' said the deer.

'Yes, you were,' said the penguin. 'You shoved me in the back with your antler!'

'I didn't!' insisted the deer.

The penguin turned. Pushed into the space behind one of the stairs was a tattered piece of cloth covering something which jutted out sharply. The vibration of the animals as they thundered up to the roof had dislodged the bundle from its hiding place.

'Mr Noah!' called the penguin. 'I think I've found something.'

Mr Noah took the bundle into the great hall. Animals, insects and birds crowded round. Slowly he unwrapped it and brought out ... one necklace and two bracelets.

But they no longer shimmered and sparkled as they had done when they had last been worn by Miriam. They were now tarnished and dull, and covered in green mould.

The jackdaw and Miriam both cried out at the same time. Mr Noah turned to the jackdaw.

'Did you take Miriam's jewellery?' he asked.

The jackdaw hung his head. 'Well, I suppose ... in a manner of speaking ...'

'Yes or no?'

'Well ... yes ...'

'Why?'

'They sparkled so much,' said the jackdaw. 'They were so beautiful. I can't resist things that sparkle.'

'Stealing is very wrong,' Mr Noah said, shaking his head.

'I don't see why,' said the jackdaw. 'She shouldn't have brought them here in the first place. Putting temptation in my way.'

'That's no excuse,' said Mr Noah sternly. 'You know how upset Miriam has been and how everyone here has been under suspicion. It was a very bad thing to do.' He looked at the faded and dull objects in front of him. 'You stole them because they sparkled. I don't suppose you'd steal them now, would you?'

'No,' muttered the jackdaw. 'They're not beautiful any more.'

'What's happened to them?' asked the guinea-pig.

'The damp air has dulled them,' sighed Mr Noah. 'It's such a shame.'

Miriam burst into tears. 'They're ruined,' she said. 'My lovely necklace and my bracelets. All ruined.'

The jackdaw looked at Miriam's tear-stained face and felt ashamed.

'I didn't mean to upset you,' he said uncomfortably. 'I only thought how much *I* wanted them. I never thought about you at all.'

'How very selfish,' said the lion.

'Yes,' said the jackdaw. 'That's true. It was very wrong and very selfish.' He turned to Miriam. 'I'll try and make amends,' he said. 'If I clean them, do you think you could forgive me?'

Miriam sniffed. 'All right,' she said.

The jackdaw set to work and cleaned them so well that the necklace and the two bracelets shone brighter than before. Miriam was delighted and she put them on. The blue stones of the necklace reflected the deep blue of the sky and the white stones the fluffy white clouds that floated past. The bracelets sparkled and gleamed in the light from the sun. And the sun sparkled and gleamed on the water of the flood—as it began to dry up.

11

THE SNAKE'S TALE

Once the rain had stopped, Mr Noah and the animals, insects and birds on the ark kept a constant watch for the first sight of land. Many of the animals took to spending at least some part of each day up on the roof, especially as the weather was fine and sunny. The birds circled overhead and Mr Noah sent the dove away to look for a sign that the flood water was subsiding. When she returned with the leaf of an olive tree in her beak there was tremendous excitement.

'This means that the tree-tops are now above the water,' said Mr Noah with a broad smile.

The doves left the ark and did not return, and the exitement grew to fever pitch, although, as Mr Noah said, 'It will take time for dry land to appear.'

The animals now jostled one another for a place on the roof. Those with the keenest sight argued with one another as to who would be the first to sight land and the birds flew out each day, travelling great distances in their search.

But it was not an animal with good eyesight who first spotted land. Neither was it a bird. It was, rather surprisingly, the snake.

No one on board the ark liked the snakes very much.

'Scheming,' said the emu whenever she saw one or other of them.

'You never know where you are with a snake,' said the bear bluntly, and the larger animals agreed with him. The smaller animals were just scared.

'My dears, I simply *shudder* every time I see that snake looking at me with those *beady* eyes,' said the shrew dramatically. 'And that nasty, slimy skin. It gives me the creeps!'

'But we do have an agreement,' said the dormouse earnestly. 'Mr Noah made a rule that none of us is to be eaten on the ark.'

'Well *you* might have agreed to it and *I* might have agreed to it, but I doubt very much whether those snakes agreed to anything of the sort,' said the shrew. 'And as for *rules* . . . I wouldn't put it past the snakes to slither their way round rules if it suited them.'

Even Mr Noah, who tried to be fair to all the animals in his charge, could not repress a slight shudder when he saw a snake slithering down one of the wooden columns in the great hall or gliding noiselessly across the floor.

'I know they're part of your creation,' he said to God.

'But I can't like them. Those snakes have nasty, slippery ways.'

The snakes knew the feeling against them. It did not worry the snake's wife, but it bothered the snake.

'It's not as if we've done anything wrong,' he said fretfully. 'We've always been civil to the other animals whenever we've met.'

'Snakes have never been liked,' his wife said comfortably. 'I heard Mr Noah talking to his wife the other day about something that happened simply ages ago that involved a snake.'

'What was it?'

'I didn't hear all of it, but it seemed to be about two humans who lived in a beautiful garden in a place called Eden. Apparently God told them they could eat anything there, apart from the fruit of one particular tree.'

'What happened?' the snake asked.

'Well, they say that some ancestor of ours dared one of the humans to eat an apple from that tree, and she did.' The snake's wife paused. 'And no good came of it.'

'I should think not,' said the snake shuddering. 'Apples indeed! I'd choke if I ate an apple—and so would you.'

'I don't know if they choked,' said the snake's wife. 'I never heard the end of the story. But it seemed a bit unfair to blame the snake,' she added thoughtfully.

'And why take it out on us now?' asked the snake.

'We're not responsible for the things that happened in the past.'

'Everyone likes to have someone else to blame,' said his wife. 'It's only natural. So what if no one likes us?' She twisted herself into a complicated knot. 'I shouldn't let it worry you.'

But the snake did worry. He tried making friends with some of the animals, and even went so far as to perform in public, shedding his skin in one complete piece at the elephants' party. Everyone applauded at the time, but no one seemed to like him or his wife any better afterwards.

Once the weather improved, the snakes spent a lot of time on the roof, coiling themselves around one of the wooden supports to make sure that they did not slide off into the water.

'Move over there,' said the aardvark crossly. 'You're always up here, hogging the best places.'

'I don't know why you come up here anyway,' said the emu with a sniff. 'You won't be the first to see land. You're too low down.'

The snakes did not reply.

'And unimportant,' added the llama with a superior stare.

'I expect,' said the lion, 'that *I* shall see land first. After all, I am assistant to Mr Noah.'

'Or I shall,' said the eagle. 'I have wonderful eyesight.'

'At all events, it won't be you snakes,' said the aardvark. 'Now shift yourselves!'

The snakes obediently slithered to one side.

As mealtime approached the animals began to leave.

'Do you want to go down for some food?' asked the snake's wife.

'No,' said the snake. 'I'm not hungry.'

So they stayed where they were, the snake's wife half-asleep in the warm, still air, the snake wondering yet again just what he had done to make the animals dislike him so.

And then he saw it.

'Look,' he said to his wife. 'Out there. Do you see it?'

His wife lifted her head.

Far away on the horizon something dark and solid poked out of the water.

The snake uncoiled himself. 'I'm going to tell Mr Noah.'

He found Mr Noah serving food in the great hall.

'Mr Noah,' he hissed, leaning over his shoulder.

Mr Noah started and dropped the dish he was holding. 'Must you frighten me like that?' he said irritably.

'I'm so sorry,' said the snake. 'But I thought you ought to know that my wife and I have seen something.'

'What?' asked Mr Noah, still annoyed.

'It could be land,' said the snake, 'or it could be a large fish. We think you should come and look.'

'Land?' exclaimed the dingo. 'Did someone say—LAND?'

That did it. The meal forgotten, the animals rushed to the roof of the ark. The birds flew out in a great cloud and winged their way over to the dark shape, clearly visible on the horizon.

The eagle was the first to return.

'It *is* land,' he said in his great voice. 'The topmost peak of a mountain.'

'There!' said the lion crossly. '*I* should have been the one to have spotted it first!'

It was exciting news, but there was little anyone could do except watch as the ark slowly drifted towards the land.

'Say, doesn't anyone have any oars around here?' asked the pig loudly. 'It would make us go a bit quicker. I mean, this is a boat after all.'

'No,' said Mr Noah, 'God never told me to make any oars.'

'Well it must have been an oversight,' said the pig. 'A boat without oars is like . . .' he thought for a moment, ' . . . is like a sty without food,' he finished.

'What the ark needs is a good strong pair of flippers,' said the penguin seriously.

As the ark drew closer to land, the animals could see a strange shape on the summit, black and twisted against the sky.

'Whatever's that?' asked the dormouse.

The eagle flew across.

'How very sad,' he said on his return. 'It's the remains of a tree.'

'What's sad about that?' asked the beaver.

'It's dead,' said the eagle.

That silenced everyone and they all sat quietly watching as the speck of land grew steadily bigger. Then a stiff wind arose, whipping the water into steep white-crested waves. The small ark was tossed from side to side.

'Look!' said the eagle suddenly. 'The wind is driving the ark away!'

It was true. The ark was slowly being forced away from the land and out to sea.

'We must stop it at once,' said the beaver.

'How?' asked the fox.

'Well...' said the beaver. 'We should put down an anchor.'

Everyone turned to Mr Noah.

'I'm sorry,' he said unhappily, 'but God never mentioned an anchor.'

'Hmm,' said the monkey sourly. 'Doesn't surprise *me* in the least.'

'If I'd know how ill-equipped this vessel was, I'd never have come,' said the goat.

'Then you'd have drowned,' snapped the fox.

The beaver was peering ahead. 'Do we have any rope?' he asked. 'If we have, we could try to throw it round the stump of that tree.'

Everyone again turned to Mr Noah, who shook his head dumbly.

'I suppose... there's nothing you can do?' the dormouse asked Mr Noah anxiously.

'I can talk to God,' Mr Noah said, and that was what he did.

'I'm sure this is all part of your plan, God,' he said, a little doubtfully. The lack of oars, anchor and even rope had slightly dented his faith. 'But is there *anything* that can be done?'

'Have a little more faith, Noah,' said God bracingly. 'There's always something that can be done.'

Just at that moment the snake uncoiled himself from the wooden support.

'Come along, dear,' he said to his wife. 'I think we're needed.'

'You?' said the emu scornfully. 'What can *you* do?'

'We have our uses,' said the snake with dignity.

He knotted the end of his tail together with the end of his wife's tail.

'Are you ready?' he asked.

She nodded and grasped the wooden support firmly.

The snake coiled himself into a neat pile, took a deep breath, and threw himself off the roof. The animals gasped.

'Whatever's he doing?' asked the beaver.

The snake uncoiled in mid-air. He touched the tree with his forked tongue, but the tug of the ark dragged him back into the water. His wife hurriedly wrapped herself around the wooden support and pulled him back on board.

For a second time the snake threw himself towards the land. This time he caught hold of the tree, but a huge wave caused the ark to roll. The snake was dragged back once again.

'Third time lucky,' he said breathlessly. This time he was successful. He sank his fangs deep into the bark and held on tightly. The wind blew, the waves tugged, but the snake slowly coiled himself round the tree, hauling the ark in to land.

There was a rasping, grinding noise and the ark

slowly came to rest. The snake released his hold and came slithering, sliding back onto the boat, assisted by many hands.

'And do you know,' the shrew said afterwards to the dormouse. 'When I touched the snake I was *amazed*! It was the strangest thing, my dear, for that snake felt *perfectly* dry and quite warm—and we all know that snakes are nasty, slimy creatures. Now whatever do you make of that?'

'That we shouldn't judge by appearances,' the dormouse said dryly.

'No, indeed,' said the shrew. '*I* never do!'

Late that night, when all the celebrations were over, and the two snakes were wearily going towards their beds, they were stopped by Mr Noah.

'I've an apology to make,' he said. 'To you and to God.'

'Think nothing of it,' said the snake.

'What you did today has taught us all a lesson,' said Mr Noah.

'It won't last,' said the snake's wife. 'This will soon be forgotten, while that unfortunate ancestor of ours in the Garden of Eden will be remembered.' She looked at him and smiled a little sourly. 'We all like to think the worst of each other.' she said.

'Well, I'll never forget,' said Mr Noah.

And he never did.

12

THE RABBIT'S TALE

The ark had come to rest on the top of a mountain called Ararat and the flood water was subsiding. Every day a little more dry land could be seen and, at last, Mr Noah told the animals, insects and birds that they could leave the ark the following day.

'About time too,' said the panther, pacing restlessly up and down the great hall.

'Well, I can't say I'll be sorry to go,' said the fox. 'Although I must admit, it's been an experience.'

'One I could have done without,' muttered the monkey.

'Oh, I don't know,' said the donkey. 'Just think of all the different animals we've met. Ones I never knew existed.'

'And hope I never meet again,' the monkey added.

'We've been saved from the flood,' said the elephant. 'And I'm sure I never thought we would be.'

'It's due to Mr Noah,' said the beaver. 'He brought us safely through all the dangers.'

The lion coughed. 'With help and guidance from others,' he said.

'You mean God?' asked the beaver.

'Oh him, of course,' said the lion. 'But I meant, help from other *animals*.'

'Like you?' said the squirrel.

'Well... yes...' the lion agreed.

'And...?' added the tiger, a dangerous sparkle in his eye.

'And the tiger, of course,' the lion went on hurriedly. 'As Mr Noah's assistants, we have helped save every animal...'

'... *two* of every animal...' the tiger put in.

'... *two* of every animal, insect and bird in creation,' the lion continued. 'I think we might congratulate ourselves.'

'No one could accuse either of you of modesty,' the fox said sweetly.

'No,' said the lion complacently. 'I don't think anyone could.'

The tiger, who knew what the word meant, laughed.

'Didn't God have a hand in it somewhere?' the donkey asked mildly.

'Oh, he made the rules, of course,' the lion agreed. 'Two of every animal to enter the ark and two of every animal to leave it. Not one more and not one less. That's what he said and that's what we've done.'

The tiger nodded. 'One must always obey the rules.'

The rabbits, who had been listening to this conversation, looked at one another and went off to their burrow rather thoughtfully.

'What are we going to do?' the rabbit asked his wife.

'About ...?'

'Yes, about ...'

They looked down at the tiny new-born baby rabbit at their feet.

'Mr Noah won't mind,' said the rabbit's wife a little doubtfully.

'Maybe not, but God might,' said the rabbit. 'After all, you heard the lion.'

'If we don't tell Mr Noah then God won't know,' the rabbit's wife suggested.

'Yes, but how do we get the baby off the ark without Mr Noah finding out?' asked the rabbit.

His wife thought about it. 'I think we should speak to the lion. After all, he is Mr Noah's assistant.'

So the rabbits went to see the lion.

'We've a bit of a problem,' said the rabbit. 'And we wondered whether you could help us.'

'Of course,' said the lion graciously.

'You told us that God wanted two of every animal to enter the ark in order to be saved. That's right, isn't it?'

'Yes,' said the lion cautiously.

'And two of every animal were to leave the ark once

the flood had gone down. That was what you said, wasn't it?'

'Yes,' the lion agreed.

'Well the problem is, there aren't two rabbits on board. There are three, and we don't know what to do about it.'

'Hmm.' The lion thought for a moment. 'Have you spoken to Mr Noah?'

'Well no, not yet. You see we don't think *he* would mind, but he would tell God, and God might not be too happy about it,' said the rabbit's wife.

'God might not like his rules being changed,' the rabbit explained.

'Hmm,' said the lion again. 'A difficult one.' He was silent for a long time. 'I think I had better consult my colleague, the tiger,' he said at last, and padded off.

The tiger had no doubts at all.

'Rules are rules,' he said definitely, 'and not to be broken. Especially ones made by God. Two of every animal, insect and bird came on to the ark and two of every animal, insect and bird are to leave the ark—on the appointed day and at the appointed time.'

The eagle objected. 'But the two doves have already left,' he said.

'That's as maybe,' said the tiger. 'But there were only two of them and not a whole flock.'

'There's not a whole flock of rabbits,' said the rabbit's

wife. 'Only three of us and he's the dearest little thing.'

'Is he now?' the elephant's wife said comfortably. 'How nice.'

'Well, I agree with the tiger,' said the scorpion. 'One or fifty, it doesn't make any difference. If it's a rule, we can't change it.'

'Rules are rules,' the tiger said again. 'When we came on board Mr Noah laid down rules about not fighting and not eating each other. And we all abided by them, didn't we?

'Yes,' said the fox sadly. 'Although it wasn't easy.'

'We kept them because if you've got rules you must obey them,' the tiger said. 'Otherwise there's just confusion.'

There was silence after he had spoken.

'Look at it this way,' the tiger went on. 'If Mr Noah hadn't laid down the rule about not eating one another, there wouldn't have been two of every animal, insect and bird left alive to leave the ark tomorrow, would there?'

'No,' shuddered the dormouse. 'There probably wouldn't have been one dormouse, let alone two.'

'That *would* have been a pity,' said the fox, licking his lips.

'There's some sense in the rule about not eating one another,' said the jackal slowly. 'And I can see the sense in saying only two of every animal were to *enter* the ark, because otherwise there wouldn't have been any room. But I can't see the sense in God saying only two can *leave* the ark.'

'Perhaps he wanted to draw a line somewhere,' suggested the donkey. 'Otherwise the world would be overrun with rabbits...'

'Or donkeys, heaven help us,' said the monkey sourly.

'Or donkeys,' agreed the donkey.

'Look, I didn't make the rules,' said the tiger. 'I only carry them out. If you've any complaint, go and see Mr Noah. But to my mind it's quite clear. Two rabbits came on the ark so only two can leave the ark.'

'I won't leave my baby behind,' said the rabbit's wife stubbornly.

'I'm sure Mr Noah or God will look after the baby if you leave him,' said the lion.

'I wouldn't let anyone else bring up *my* baby,' said the kangaroo's wife.

'And what does Mr Noah, or God for that matter, know about bringing up a baby rabbit?' the rabbit's wife retorted.

'You should have thought of that earlier,' growled the tiger.

The debate among the animals continued throughout the night, and the rabbits had an endless stream of visitors, some to give their opinions, some to offer advice, and some just to look at the baby.

The following morning Mr Noah, Mrs Noah, their sons and their sons' wives came to the great hall early. Mr Noah opened the big door to the ark that God himself had closed at the start of the journey and sunlight streamed in. Everyone cheered.

Mr Noah stood at the entrance and ticked off the animals, insects and birds from his long list.

'Iguanas... now then... H... I... Ah, here we are. I hope you enjoyed the journey. Goodbye and God bless you both.'

The kangaroos were next.

'K... Let me see... I... J... K... That's right. Goodbye to you both and God bless you.'

He looked for a moment at the suspiciously large bump inside the kangaroo's pouch, but said nothing.

The two rabbits were waiting nervously.

'Rabbits... L... M... N... O... P... Q... R... Here we are. Right down the bottom of the page. Two rabbits. Hope you enjoyed the voyage.' He looked up, smiling. 'Oh, and congratulations. What are you going to call the baby?'

The rabbits were dumbfounded.

'However did you know?' they asked.

Mr Noah's smile broadened.

'You can't fool God,' he said. 'He told me. Your baby can come out of the kangaroo's pouch now.'

The kangaroo's wife slowly brought the baby rabbit out of her pouch and handed him to his mother.

'Why ever didn't you come and talk to me?' Mr Noah asked.

'Because we knew you would tell God and we didn't want God to know that we were breaking his rule,' said the rabbit's wife. 'We were afraid he would have been angry and forbidden us to take our baby away.'

'Why should he have done that?' Mr Noah asked, mystified.

'Because the tiger said that God told you to take two of every animal on to the ark and make sure that only two were to leave it.'

'Because God doesn't want the world over-populated by donkeys,' added the donkey helpfully.

'Rabbits,' said the monkey in a long-suffering voice.

'Oh, was it?' asked the donkey.

'And it wasn't me, it was the lion,' said the tiger hurriedly. 'I never said that.'

'But you agreed to it,' said the lion sweetly.

'Well, rules are made to be kept,' said the tiger stubbornly. 'Especially God's rules.'

'Yes,' said Mr Noah. 'Rules are made to be kept, but, with God's help, we must use our judgment about how they are to be applied. God would never have forbidden you to take your baby away.' He smiled. 'Who would have looked after it—me or God?'

'Just what I said,' said the rabbit's wife.

Mr Noah turned to the lion and the tiger. 'And God

never said that only two of every animal, insect and bird were to leave the ark. He told me to bring out of the ark every living creature in order to fill the earth, and that's what I've done.'

He gazed at the animals, who were crowding the green grass in front of him, with pleasure and satisfaction.

'My dear friends,' he said. 'For you are my friends. What's important to remember is that God deals with us in all sorts of ways, but always with the kind of love he showed in saving us from the flood.'

'And that's how you've dealt with us, Mr Noah,' said the eagle, who was perched high in the branches of a tall tree. 'With love and care for our safety. We all owe *you* a debt we can never repay.'

The murmur of agreement among the animals, insects and birds grew to a roar.

Mr Noah's eyes were bright with unshed tears. 'I only did what God told me to do,' he said. 'God bless you. All of you.'

13
THE END . . .
AND THE BEGINNING

Mr Noah stared at the ark, which lay on its side on the mountain. It looked battered and worn. Its wooden hulk was water-stained and the lower part was covered with barnacles.

The animals, insects and birds had long since gone and everywhere was quiet. The only sound was that of running water.

'It's like a dream,' said Japheth.

'Or a nightmare,' said Ham.

'No,' said Mr Noah. 'Not a nightmare.'

'Did you ever doubt we'd make it, Father?' asked Shem.

Mr Noah sighed. 'Yes. Often. But I was wrong. I doubted God, and I should never have done that.'

The sky darkened and it began to rain.

'Is the flood starting all over again?' asked his wife.

'I don't know,' Mr Noah said. 'Is it, God?'

'No,' said God. 'I shall never again destroy all living things by water. Look up, Noah.'

Mr Noah looked up at the sky. The clouds parted and the sun shone out, its brilliant light reflecting against the rain. Mr Noah gasped. Red, orange, yellow, green, blue, indigo and violet, the colours flamed in the perfect arc of a rainbow.

'This rainbow is my promise to you and to all who live after you,' God said. 'Whenever you see a rainbow in the sky it will remind you that I will never again send a flood to destroy the earth. You have my promise.'

'Thank you, God,' said Mr Noah, but he did not look any happier.

'Cheer up, Noah,' God said, 'for this is a new beginning.'

'Yes,' said Mr Noah. 'I know.' He sighed again. 'It's funny, God, but now it's all over I feel rather flat. I miss the animals. Silly, isn't it? I didn't want the job in the first place and didn't really enjoy it while it was happening, but now it's over and they've all gone ...'

'But they haven't gone,' said God. 'Look around you.'

Mr Noah looked around. The trees below him were full of birds, busy making their nests. The air, fresh and clear after the shower of rain, was suddenly alive with their cries. A monkey swung from branch to branch of a tree while a squirrel raced up its trunk. Insects scurried at his feet, and he caught a glimpse of a dormouse running

across the green grass. Frogs were croaking in a nearby pool of water, while a beaver was busily building a dam across one of the many streams. A fox slunk away into the undergrowth and, in the distance, Mr Noah could see the elephants having an evening bathe. Butterflies drowsily sunned themselves on a nearby bush and a bee buzzed lazily past his nose.

'You're right, God,' Mr Noah said, feeling happier. 'They haven't gone.'

'Where are we going to sleep tonight, Father?' asked Japheth anxiously.

'And how are we going to live?' demanded Ham.

Mr Noah smiled. 'Don't worry,' he said. 'We'll sleep in the ark tonight and tomorrow we'll begin to build a new farm. We'll make a new vineyard.' He looked at his wife and smiled. 'Would you like a new vineyard, Becky?'

'Yes,' said his wife, and smiled back at him.

A large shape approached. It was the lion. Behind him were a number of other animals, insects and birds.

'Mr Noah,' the lion said, 'forgive me for troubling you. We've been holding a meeting and I—as King of the Jungle—have been given the task...'

'Oh, get on with it!' said the fox impatiently.

'... given the *pleasant* task of offering our services to help you build your new farm,' the lion went on. 'We felt...'

Mr Noah felt something rubbing against his legs and looked down to see the cat, purring softly.

'We're quite good at moving heavy objects,' the elephant's wife interrupted.

'And I'm an expert in wood,' said the beaver. 'You needn't have any fears that your new home will leak.'

'I'm good at carrying burdens,' said the donkey.

'So am I,' added the camel.

'We work tirelessly, said the ant. 'Although we can't carry much at a time,' he added.

'We'll plant your vineyards,' said the tiger.

'And I'll tell the time,' crowed the cock.

'I can tell jokes,' said the giraffe eagerly.

Mr Noah lifted up the cat and begin stroking him.

'If you like,' said the spider, 'I'll spin a few cobwebs

in the corners of your house.'

'I'll add a touch of beauty to your garden,' said the peacock graciously, unfurling his lovely tail.

'You're not much use doing anything else,' the rhinoceros said bluntly.

'We'll form a Committee,' said the tiger. 'And I'll be Works Manager.'

'Hmm . . .' The lion cleared his throat.

'Perhaps there should be *two* Works Managers,' said Mr Noah tactfully. He looked around. 'I don't know what to say. Thank you. Thank you all.'

It was late when everyone finally left. Mr Noah and his family settled themselves to sleep. It was a clear, warm night and the moon shed a soft light. An owl hooted and the bats flitted among the trees. Mr Noah looked up at the sky, which was studded with bright stars, and felt at peace.

'Thank you, God,' he said. 'With your help, everything is possible.'

Then he turned over contentedly, and went to sleep.

The Rainbow's End

& Other Tales from the Ark

CONTENTS

1
NOAH'S TALE

Mr Noah was having a bad dream. He lay tossing and turning in bed, waking his wife by his restlessness. She prodded him once or twice, but Mr Noah only tossed and turned even more. At last he flung out his arms, hit Mrs Noah squarely on the nose, and sat bolt upright in bed.

'No God!' he shouted. 'Not me! Choose someone else! I don't like animals!'

'Whatever is the matter?' asked his wife.

Mr Noah shook his head. 'I've been having a terrible dream.'

'Must have been the onions you ate last night,' said Mrs Noah, climbing out of bed in order to pick up the bedclothes that had slipped to the floor. 'They kept repeating on me, too.'

Then Mr Noah climbed out of bed and began to pace up and down. 'I dreamt that the world would be destroyed as it had become so wicked.'

'I told you not to eat so many,' said his wife calmly, tucking in the sheets.

'It would rain for forty days and forty nights until the whole earth was flooded...'

'Or perhaps it was the wine...' Mrs Noah climbed back into bed and pulled the bedclothes up around her ears. 'I said you shouldn't drink so much. Now do come back to bed. We've a busy day tomorrow.'

'But you and I and our three sons and their wives would be saved, as well as two of every animal, insect and bird...'

'I never heard anything so ridiculous,' said Mrs Noah, and she turned over and went to sleep.

But Mr Noah could not sleep, so he climbed out of bed and tiptoed out of the house.

His farm lay silent and peaceful under an inky black sky. The stars were shining and moonlight drenched his vineyard with a silver light. Mr Noah touched a bunch of grapes. They were round and fat and still warm from the sun. It would be a good harvest. A splendid harvest.

Perhaps, he thought, his dream *had* been caused by eating too many onions or drinking too much wine at dinner. The world being destroyed? What nonsense! Only his family surviving? What rubbish! Feeling a good deal calmer, Mr Noah turned back to the house.

'Noah.'

Mr Noah looked round. The voice came again.

'Noah.'

'Is... is that you, God?'

'Yes.'

'It *was* all a dream, wasn't it?' Mr Noah asked anxiously. 'I mean about destroying the world and... and everything?'

'I'm afraid not.'

'Oh dear.'

'Now listen to me carefully, Noah. You're the only good man left in the world and I'm relying on you...'

And while Mr Noah stood in the middle of his farm in the middle of the night, God told him what he wanted him to do.

The following day, Mr Noah spoke to his family.

'Build an ark?' asked his eldest son, Shem.

'Yes,' said Mr Noah.

'Large enough for all of us, as well as two of every

animal, insect and bird?' asked his middle son, Ham.

'Yes.'

'You can't be serious, Dad,' said Japheth, his youngest son.

Mr Noah sighed.

'It was the onions he ate last night,' said Mrs Noah. 'And if it wasn't that, it was too much wine. I told him, but he wouldn't believe me. And if it wasn't the food or the drink, then it has to be too much sun.'

'We've never had such a good summer,' said Ham. 'It's been the driest for years. *Too* dry, if anything.'

'That's what makes all this talk of a flood such nonsense,' said Mrs Noah as she rose to clear the table.

'And if we don't get the harvest in soon, Father, the grapes will be over-ripe,' said Shem firmly.

It was true, and in the days that followed Mr Noah was too busy to worry about any flood. The sun beat down and the family turned nut-brown as they worked in the vineyard.

At odd times though, when he was busy picking grapes, or standing upright to ease his aching back, Mr Noah did think about what God had said, but he pushed such thoughts firmly to the back of his mind.

Late one evening, when Mr Noah was looking with satisfaction at the baskets filled to overflowing with grapes, and had just popped a particularly juicy, sun-ripened one into his mouth, God spoke to him again.

'Noah.'

Mr Noah almost choked.

'Noah, what have you done about building the ark?'

'Well, God,' Mr Noah began, 'I've been very busy, and I'm really very sorry but somehow it just slipped my mind...'

'The animals will be arriving soon, Noah.'

'Will they?' asked Mr Noah anxiously, and looked around, half expecting to see them marching up the track to his front door.

'Noah, I chose you out of all the people in the world. Don't let me down.'

That made Mr Noah feel perfectly dreadful. That evening after supper he spoke to his family.

'It wasn't the onions or the wine or the sun giving me bad dreams. It was God. We must start building a big boat, so that we'll be ready to leave when the flood comes.'

For a moment there was silence. Then Mrs Noah gave a shriek.

'Leave? Leave the farm?' She threw her apron over her head, sat down in a corner and burst into tears.

'Now look what you've done, Father,' said Ham, and Mr Noah sighed.

In the days that followed, the harvest was neglected as Mr Noah and his sons began building the ark according to the plans laid down by God. Mrs Noah and his son's wives began to pack.

No one believed Mr Noah's tale.

'I mean, why should God choose to speak to Mr Noah about important matters like building an ark and saving the animals?' said Mrs Noah as she bundled up their clothes. 'He's a good man, but he's not all that special. His carpentry's a nightmare and as for animals…! He runs a mile at the sight of a spider!'

'He's either made it up, got it wrong or is as mad as a hatter,' said Ham as he knocked nails into the wooden structure of the ark. 'And I think he's got it wrong. Stands to reason. He's six hundred years old. When you get to his age you're bound to muddle things up.'

As time went on Mr Noah also began to have doubts. Perhaps everyone else was right. Perhaps he was suffering from strain and overwork. Perhaps he had only imagined that God had spoken to him. After all, why should God speak to him? The work on the ark slowed down and then stopped as the family returned to their neglected vineyard.

It was the very last day of the harvest and the family were in the kitchen eating their midday meal. Mr Noah was just congratulating himself on a good crop, Shem was saying how lucky they'd been with the weather, and Mrs Noah was planning the big feast they would have that evening, when Japheth, white-faced and shaking, ran in. Pointing a trembling finger through the open door, he managed to whisper, 'F-father… look…!'

Mr Noah turned.

The track outside the house was full of animals. There were large animals and small ones, hairy and smooth. There were animals with tails and ones without. There were wild animals and tame ones,

good-looking and ugly. And not only animals. There were reptiles and insects, beasts and birds. And not just one of each. There were two of every kind, all forming a long, long line down to the farmhouse.

A tap at the window was soon followed by a piercing

scream from Mrs Noah. Mr Noah turned. A large polar bear was looking in at them. Suddenly there was a great crash and the polar bear disappeared from view. Mr Noah picked up a stout stick, took a deep breath and went outside.

The polar bear lay stretched on the ground, while a second bear was busily fanning her with part of a broken chair.

'She can't take the heat, poor thing,' the second polar bear explained.

'That was my favourite chair!' Mr Noah groaned.

An important-looking lion with a fine golden mane strolled over. 'We've been informed by God that there's some kind of boat or ship around here. Is this the right place?'

'Yes. This is the right place. It's just that we're not quite ready...'

An emu stuck its head out from behind a tree. 'Is this the ark?' she asked in a sharp voice, peering at the farmhouse.

'No. It's just...'

'Doesn't look very watertight to me if it is.' The emu sniffed disapprovingly.

'The ark's not quite finished yet, but...'

'Well I hope the accommodation will be satisfactory. My husband and I are very fussy about where we stay.'

'It will be satisfactory,' said Mr Noah desperately. 'I assure you. Very satisfactory indeed...'

A large, hairy ape came round the corner of the

porch. 'I hope you're right,' he said in a menacing voice.

Mr Noah took a step backwards and fell into the remains of the chair, which promptly collapsed under him.

'Are you in charge here?' asked the lion in a disbelieving voice.

'Yes,' said Mr Noah, scrambling to his feet. 'That is… God's in charge really but I'm his deputy.'

'Well then, "deputy", how about some food, eh?' asked a jackal. 'We've all travelled a long way, and if we don't get something to eat, we might be tempted to eat you.' He snarled, showing a set of razor-sharp teeth, and the other animals laughed.

Mr Noah fled inside his house and shut the door. He turned to face his family, but they had run away to their rooms and locked themselves in.

'God?'

'Yes, Noah.'

'God, what shall I do?'

'You had better finish the ark.'

'Do I have to?' Mr Noah asked, watching in horror as two very black and very hairy spiders crept under the door.

'No. You don't have to.'

'Will you send the animals away then?'

God was silent for a moment.

'When I made you, Noah,' God said at last, 'I gave you freedom. The freedom to choose. You can do what I ask, or not. It is as *you* wish. I decided to save you and your family from the flood because you are a good man, the only good man in the world, but it's up to you. It's your choice. I'm offering you life, Noah, but you are free to refuse if you want.'

Mr Noah, keeping one eye firmly on the spiders, thought about what God had said. Then he went to his room, washed his face, combed his hair, put on a clean robe and called his family together.

'God and I have talked it over and I've decided to finish the ark.' He looked at his silent family. 'Now I'm just a foolish old man who isn't much good at anything, but for some reason, God's chosen me. He even asked me, very nicely, if I would do the job, and I said yes.'

'But you don't like animals…' Ham began.

'I don't, and I'm very sure the animals won't like me, and how we're all going to get along together is beyond me. But I'm sure God has it all worked out. What we've got to do now is build the ark before it's too late.'

'You mean, g-go out th-there?' Japheth asked in a small, scared voice.

'Yes,' said Mr Noah, trying to sound calm.

He walked to the door and took a deep breath.

'Please help me, God. I'm so scared, I'm shaking in my shoes.'

'Of course. You'll always have my help.'

'Thank you,' Mr Noah said, and went out alone to face the animals.

2

THE DOG'S TALE

Although Mr Noah was very grateful to God for deciding to save him and his family from the flood that would destroy the world, he did have a few worries.

'I'm not good with animals, God. Some people have a way with them, and some don't. I don't. To be honest with you, they scare me. And those that don't scare me plain terrify me. That's why I decided to grow grapes, rather than keep farm animals. Wouldn't an animal farmer suit your purpose better? Or a zoo-keeper?'

But God had every confidence in Mr Noah.

If Mr Noah was grateful to God, his family were less so.

'I don't like boats,' said Japheth gloomily. 'I get seasick.'

'It's not right God making me take a trip like this at my time of life,' grumbled Mrs Noah. 'Just when the farm was doing so nicely.'

'It seems a bit unfair on Father, too,' Ham added, 'at his great age.'

None of the animals arriving on the ark seemed grateful either. As Mr Noah welcomed them on board, complaints came thick and fast.

'Is *that* meant to be our watering-hole?' asked the hippopotamus when he was shown the small pool Mr Noah had built. 'You can't seriously expect us to wallow in that!'

'And where's the mud?' asked his wife, flopping into the water with such a splash that Mr Noah was soaked. 'Everyone knows you can't have a good wallow without mud.'

'The mud hasn't arrived yet,' Mr Noah explained. 'But Shem and Ham are down by the river digging it out right now.'

'Hmm,' said the hippopotamus, flopping into the pool after his wife and soaking Mr Noah for a second time.

The rest of the animals were just as bad.

'Say, Mr Noah!' called the pig, as Mr Noah was hurrying to his cabin to put on a dry robe. 'Honey, my wife, isn't too happy with her sty.'

'What's the matter with it?'

'The straw's smelly and my Honey has a very sensitive nose. And we would have liked to be more in the middle of the ark. Less likely to be seasick we've been told. But that's okay, we can live with that. The real problem is our neighbours. Did you *have* to put those two mean-looking scorpions right next door? It's given Honey a real fright.'

The only one who seemed at all content was Mr Noah's dog. Day after day she stayed close beside him as he welcomed the animals, insects and birds onto the ark and dealt with their complaints.

'It is very difficult for them, having to leave their homes,' Mr Noah sighed as he was getting ready for bed. 'I can understand how they feel. It's difficult for all of us.'

'They ought to be grateful to you,' said his dog. 'After all, you're giving them the chance of being saved from the flood.'

'It's not me they ought to be grateful to. It's God. He decides who's going to be saved.'

As Mr Noah's dog curled up at the foot of his bed, she thought about what Mr Noah had said. So far no other dogs had arrived on the ark. Did that mean that

God had decided to save her?

'Unlikely,' she thought. 'God will want to save two good-looking dogs, not a shabby old mongrel like me.' She sighed. It would be hard to leave Mr Noah. He was a kind, good man and she loved him very much.

'But perhaps he won't mind too much,' she reflected. 'He's got so many other animals to look after. I don't suppose he's given me a thought.'

But she was wrong. Mr Noah had thought about her. He had even spoken about her to God.

'I don't know what dogs you're thinking of saving, God, but could I put in a word for mine? I've had her for years and she's been loyal and faithful. She's a good guard dog as well, not that we need a guard dog on the ark.'

God did not answer.

'I know she's only a mongrel, but I'm very attached to her.'

God still did not answer.

'I really wouldn't bother you with such a small thing when you've so much else to do, and of course I'll accept whatever you decide, because I know it'll be all for the best, but still...'

'I need to save *two* of every living creature, Noah,' God said gently. 'And your dog doesn't have a mate.'

'I'm sure I could find another dog...'

'There's very little time. Your job is to welcome the animals onto the ark. Leave the choosing to me.'

'Oh,' said Mr Noah. 'Yes. Of course.'

The following day was hot and still, the sky black and threatening. Mr Noah's dog stood beside him as a steady stream of animals reported to Mr Noah, were ticked off his long list, and climbed on board the ark.

Late that afternoon the first spots of rain began to fall.

'It's started to rain!' called the eagle, flying into the great hall from the trapdoor set high up in the roof.

The animals fell silent. Then the emu shrieked, 'We're all going to drown!'

The ostrich tried to bury her head in the wooden floor of the hall and the elephant fainted, causing the ark to wobble violently.

'It's started to rain,' said Rachel, Shem's wife, opening the door to Mrs Noah's cabin.

'Well that's a good thing,' said Mrs Noah comfortably. 'The sooner we're afloat, the sooner the journey will be over and we can all go home.'

Mr Noah looked up at the sky. It was raining harder now and the light was fading.

'The animals will be worried,' he muttered and hurried off to the great hall.

His dog turned to follow, then stopped. In the fading light she could see two animals approaching. They looked, she thought with a sinking heart, like two dogs. Without waiting for them to come any closer, she jumped down from the ark and ran off.

It was very quiet away from the ark. The only sound was the pitter-pattering of rain on the leaves. The air felt thick and stuffy as if the world was holding its breath. Mr Noah's dog ran on into the thickening gloom.

It was pitch black by the time Mr Noah had quietened the animals. He looked round for his dog but could not see her anywhere. He ran all over the ark calling her name, then searched the entire boat twice through. She was gone. Mr Noah sat in his cabin and put his head in his hands.

'Where is she, God? Where has she gone?'

'She's all right, Noah. I'll look after her.'

Mr Noah was silent for a moment. Then he jumped off his bed.

'She's my dog and I'm going after her,' he protested. 'I'm sorry, God, but I can't leave her behind. I don't like to disobey you, but I'm afraid you'll have to find someone else to look after the animals if I don't come back in time. Shem, my eldest, is a good lad.'

And without another word he ran out of his cabin.

Mr Noah had never known such darkness. The sky was covered by thick clouds and the rain was pouring down. Mr Noah was soon soaked to the skin. His abandoned farmhouse, when he reached it, was welcome shelter and he thought he would stay there until daylight made his search easier. He pushed open the door and stepped into the kitchen.

With a loud bark, his dog flew at Mr Noah and knocked him backwards.

'It's all right,' Mr Noah said, laughing and hugging her tightly. 'It's all right. Did you think I'd go without you?'

'I couldn't bear to say goodbye,' said his dog. 'I never thought you'd come to find me.'

'Come on now, let's get back to the ark.'

'But God doesn't want me. He wants two of every animal and there's only one of me.'

'There's only one of me too,' said a tired voice, 'so we'd better go together.'

Mr Noah and his dog turned. A tired and very wet dog stood on the threshold.

He limped into the room. 'I do hope I'm not too late but it's taken me a long time to get here. I ran into a snare and hurt my leg. I was just about ready to give up when I heard your voices.'

He stopped. 'I'm very hungry and very tired but very pleased to meet you. It's Mr Noah, isn't it?'

'Yes,' said Mr Noah, bending down to pat him.

'I don't understand,' Mr Noah's dog said, as they made their way back to the ark. 'You can't want us. You've already got two dogs on the ark. I saw them. That's why I ran away.'

Mr Noah laughed. 'You must have seen the two wolves. They came soon after the rain began. In the dim light you must have mistaken them.' He hugged both the dogs. 'You're the ones God has chosen and I'm delighted. I should never have doubted.'

And as he strode towards the welcoming lights of the ark, the two dogs ran happily at his heels.

3

THE TORTOISE'S TALE

For many days now the animals had been arriving at the ark which God had told Mr Noah to build. Large ones, small ones, smooth ones, hairy ones, animals, insects and birds, they arrived two by two in order to be saved from the flood. As they walked, ran, crawled and slithered up the gangplank, Mr Noah ticked them off his long list.

By the time the two cheetahs raced up the gangplank, Mr Noah's list was almost complete and the rain had begun to fall, thick round drops out of a heavily laden sky.

'We're not too late are we?' one of them panted.

'No,' said Mr Noah. 'I've been expecting you. You're very welcome.'

Inside the ark the latest arrivals stared in amazement at the number of animals, insects and birds thronging the great hall. The noise was tremendous.

'Hello,' said the donkey, 'forgive my ignorance, but

who are you? I don't think we've met.'

'We're cheetahs.'

'Oh really,' said the donkey politely. 'How interesting. I've met so many strange and wonderful animals on this ark. Cheetahs. That's a new one to me. What do you do, if you don't mind my asking?'

'What do you mean?'

'Well, so many of the animals here seem able to *do* things. It's quite amazing. Just look at the giraffe with his wonderful long neck. So useful to see things from high up. The herons can stand on one leg and the peacock has a most beautiful tail. Everyone seems to be clever at something except me. I'm very dull and boring.'

'We run,' said the cheetah. 'Like the wind.'

'In fact,' said his mate, 'without wishing to boast, we run faster than any animal in the world.'

'Really,' said the donkey, admiringly.

A crowd of animals had gathered.

'The fastest animals in the world?' snarled the leopard. 'Prove it.'

'I always thought *we* were the fastest animals in the world,' murmured one of the gazelles.

'So did I,' said the other gazelle. She eyed the cheetahs nervously. 'Especially when there's a cheetah behind us.'

The cheetahs smiled. 'This could be a most enjoyable trip,' said the first cheetah, licking his lips.

'There's to be NO eating of other animals while on

board,' said the lion in a loud voice.

'Who said?' demanded the cheetah.

'Mr Noah. I am his deputy.'

'And I'm his other deputy,' said the tiger.

'It's one of the rules,' explained the donkey.

'It's a good rule,' squawked the chicken.

'*That's* a matter of opinion,' said the fox.

One of the kangaroos bounded up. 'While we're on the subject of speed...'

'I thought we were on the subject of food,' said the fox.

'...we're reckoned pretty fast runners,' the kangaroo said brightly.

'Why don't we have a race?' the elephant suggested. 'To find out which of the animals *is* the fastest.'

'I'll be the judge,' said the lion grandly.

'Is there a rule about holding a race?' asked the donkey, but nobody took any notice, for the birds were busy flying up to the rafters and the animals pressing themselves to the sides of the great hall in order to clear a space.

A long way away from the ark, two tortoises were sheltering from the rain under a stone.

'Don't you think we ought to be getting on?' asked the first tortoise anxiously.

'There's no rush,' said the second tortoise. She peered out. 'It's very wet out there.'

'That's because it's raining.'

'I know that,' said the first tortoise. He closed his eyes.

'You can't go to sleep now!' said the second tortoise. 'At the rate we're going, the world will be flooded before we reach the ark!'

The second tortoise opened her eyes. 'More haste, less speed,' she said, then shut her eyes again.

Safe on the ark, Mr Noah had just discovered that the tortoises were missing.

'We must search the ark. They could have slipped past without my knowing.'

'We ought to close the doors, Father,' Shem objected. 'Otherwise the ark will be flooded.'

'This might just be a shower,' said Mr Noah hopefully. 'And we can't leave the tortoises behind.'

'If it's a choice between saving the tortoises and drowning, I know which I'd choose,' muttered Shem.

Inside the great hall, the animals who were entering the race were lining up.

'Three times round, and no pushing, biting or scratching,' said the lion.

'Are those more rules?' asked the donkey.

'On your marks… get set… go!'

Everyone cheered and the race was on.

'Stop!' shouted the lion. 'Stop!' He walked up to the ostrich.

'You are not an animal, you are a bird. Therefore you are disqualified from this race.'

The ostrich's eyes filled with tears. 'Oh please let me join in!' she begged.

The lion shook his great head and the ostrich slunk away, sniffing.

'Mean, I call it,' squawked the parrot. 'What harm would there have been in letting the ostrich race?'

'My dear parrot,' said the lion in his grandest manner. 'This race is to find the fastest land animal. Therefore only animals can take part. Rules are rules.'

'I thought there would be a rule somewhere,' said the donkey, satisfied, and the race began again.

Inside his cabin, Mr Noah was talking to God.

'It would be terrible if tortoises were to die out because they didn't arrive in time to travel on the ark. But what can I do? They could be anywhere.'

'Trust me,' said God. 'I haven't forgotten the tortoises. But they may need some help.'

'From me?'

'From you and the animals.'

Just then, Mr Noah's three sons burst into his cabin.

315

'The tortoises aren't anywhere on the ark,' said Shem.

'The water's coming right up the gangplank!' Ham exclaimed.

'You'll never believe what the animals are doing!' Japheth shouted. 'They're having a race!'

Mr Noah looked up. 'A race...?' he said. 'Now I wonder...'

In the hall the race had just ended.

'You cheated!' said the kangaroo crossly.

'Are you calling me a cheat?' asked the cheetah.

'Cheat by name and cheat by nature.'

The cheetah circled the kangaroo, snarling.

'Now, now,' said the elephant. 'No fighting on the ark.'

'Another of Mr Noah's rules,' explained the donkey to anyone who was listening.

'We'll have one deciding round between the cheetah and the kangaroo,' said the lion.

Mr Noah entered the hall. 'Animals!'

'On your marks... get set...'

'I need your help!'

'What do you want our help for?' asked the panther bluntly. 'I thought you and God had it all sewn up between you.'

'The tortoises are missing.'

'That's their problem,' said the panther. 'They shouldn't be so slow.'

'*We* got here on time,' said one of the snails. 'And no

one could call us fast animals.'

'You're not animals at all,' said the fox. 'You're...
you're...'

'Food,' said the eagle.

The snails went into their shells.

'On your marks... get set...' said the lion once more.

'Wait!' said Mr Noah. 'I have an idea.'

Far away from the ark, the two tortoises plodded on.
They were wet, cold and miserable.

'Why don't we hibernate?' asked the second
tortoise. 'Find some nice dry shelter somewhere and go
to sleep until it's all over.'

'There aren't any nice dry shelters,' said the first
tortoise. 'Or there won't be, soon. Come on slowcoach.'

The second tortoise sighed. 'You know, you're the
nearest thing to a speedy tortoise I've ever met.'

Heads down, feet slipping and sliding, the tortoises
slowly struggled on and did not notice the eagle, flying
high above them. The eagle paused in mid-flight, circled
once, twice, then turned on his wing and flew away.

'I've found them, Mr Noah,' he called, flying in
through the trapdoor high up in the roof of the ark.

Mr Noah and the animals left the great hall and
crowded round the entrance.

'Are you ready?' asked Mr Noah.

The cheetah and the kangaroo nodded their heads.

'Then...' said Mr Noah, 'on your marks... get
set... go!'

To cheers from the animals, the eagle flew off,

showing the way to the cheetah and the kangaroo.

The cheetah reached the tortoises first.

'Hello,' said the first tortoise. 'If you're looking for the ark, you're going in the wrong direction.'

'I'm looking for you,' said the cheetah. 'You'll have to hurry or you'll be too late. The water is rising.'

'We're coming as fast as we can.'

'Could you climb on my back?' asked the cheetah. 'I run like the wind.'

The tortoises looked up at the cheetah, considered for a moment, then shook their heads. And they were still all standing there when the kangaroo arrived.

'All right,' said the kangaroo. 'You win. You *are* the fastest animal.'

'I might be able to run fast,' said the cheetah. 'But how do I get the tortoises safely to the ark? They can't climb on my back.'

The kangaroo looked at the tortoises and smiled. 'Leave it to me,' she said.

Back on the ark, Mr Noah was staring at the rising level of the water.

'You'll have to close the doors, Father!' said Shem urgently.

'Not until the tortoises arrive,' Mr Noah said stubbornly.

There was a stirring in the air. The eagle flew down and landed at Mr Noah's feet.

'Phew, it's wet out there,' he said, shaking his dripping feathers.

'Are they coming?' Mr Noah asked anxiously.

'Oh yes,' said the eagle. 'They're coming all right, although why God made wingless animals in the first place, I'll never know. Now if the tortoises each had a decent pair of wings, there wouldn't have been all this fuss in the first place.'

The cheetah came first, walking slowly and wearily. As he entered the ark, the animals cheered.

'I award you, cheetah, land speed record,' said the lion.

'I might be the fastest,' said the cheetah, 'but we all have our uses.'

'Where are the tortoises?' Mr Noah asked as the kangaroo bounded onto the ark.

A head popped out of the kangaroo's pouch.

'Here,' said the first tortoise.

'Here,' said the second tortoise. She turned to the kangaroo. 'Thank you for a very comfortable journey.'

God himself closed the great doors of the ark just as the water began to lap at the entrance. The ark rocked and the wooden frame creaked. Animals, insects, humans and birds fell silent. Then the eagle flew into the great hall.

'The ark,' he called in a loud voice, 'is afloat.'

4

THE GORILLA'S TALE

Once the ark was afloat, everyone began to settle down for the voyage.

'After all,' said the cow placidly, 'we're all in the same boat, so we'd better learn how to muck in together.'

'I've no wish to "muck in" with anyone,' said the goose, holding up her nose. 'In my opinion this entire venture has been badly managed from the start.'

'I couldn't agree more,' said the peacock. 'I asked for first-class accommodation but apparently there isn't any. Mr Noah said that God hadn't told him to provide it. Quite shocking!'

'In my opinion, Mr Noah is a bit too fond of blaming God,' said the goose.

'No one asked for your opinion,' muttered the cockroach.

The goose ignored this. 'Didn't Mr Noah have *any* say in building the ark? Let's face it, God can't have much experience in boat-building.'

'Neither has Mr Noah,' said the peacock. 'When I arrived he was putting the door in upside down.'

The goose sniggered. 'Well in *my* opinion...' she began, but at that moment the goat ran bleating into the hall.

'Save me! Oh save me! It's after me!'

'Who's after you?' asked the cow.

'The... the... monster!'

'I didn't know there were any monsters on board,' said the donkey in an interested voice.

The goat was trembling violently and uttering little bleating cries.

'Now just calm down, dear, and tell us all about it,' said the cow.

'It... it was black... and... and hairy,' the goat began.

'Are you referring to me?' asked the spider spinning down on a fine thread from the rafters.

'Of course not,' bleated the goat. 'This was enormous... and it walked on two great legs and had two long arms and a horrible face.'

The fox grinned. 'Are you sure you're not referring to our host, Mr Noah?' he asked. 'He walks on two legs and has two arms.' He thought for a moment. 'I wouldn't consider his face *horrible* exactly, not as human faces go, but there's no accounting for tastes.'

'No it wasn't Mr Noah!' said the goat. 'It was a monster!'

'I'd like to see a monster,' said the donkey.

Just then there was a footfall behind him and he

turned round. The goat bleated loudly, the emu had hysterics, the ostrich fainted, the goose flew up and down in a panic, while the cause of all the fuss stared at the animals with black, unblinking eyes, then shambled off.

'Wh-what was it?' asked the goose breathlessly.

'Enough to give one nightmares,' said the peacock, fanning himself vigorously with his tail.

'Was that the monster?' asked the donkey.

'No,' said the chimpanzee, swinging down from a beam. 'That's the gorilla.'

'Oh. One of *your* relations is it?' snapped the emu.

'Only distantly,' said the chimpanzee.

'I don't care what his name is,' said the goat. 'If I'd known creatures like that were going to be on this trip, I wouldn't have come.'

'You'd rather have drowned, I suppose,' the fox murmured drily.

'Well I think it's quite horrible and should never have been allowed on the ark,' said the peacock firmly.

And that was the opinion of most of the animals, insects and birds.

It was not that the two gorillas did anything to upset the animals, it was just that they were always there: dark menacing shapes disappearing round corners, large flat faces staring from the back of the great hall, hairy black bodies turning up in unexpected places before shambling slowly away.

'It makes life very uncomfortable,' said the emu. 'I really think someone should complain to Mr Noah.'

'I agree,' said the goose.

'Me too,' quacked the duck, who did not really know what was being discussed but liked to agree with the goose as it made him feel important.

But when Mr Noah heard the animals' complaints, he shook his head.

'I'm sorry, but God told me to take two of every living creature—other than fish—onto the ark and we must all learn to get along with one another.'

'*They* should learn to get along with *us*,' said the goat firmly.

'Have you tried talking to the gorillas?' Mr Noah asked mildly.

'Talking to them?' said the peacock. 'Me? You must be joking!'

'May I suggest that if there's any talking to be done, then you should do it, Mr Noah,' said the lion. 'God saw fit to make you our captain, our fearless leader, and it's your duty to protect us weak animals from danger.' He smiled as he said this, showing a mouth full of strong, well-sharpened teeth.

'I thought you'd say that,' muttered Mr Noah and retreated to the safety of his cabin.

'You see, God,' Mr Noah said, 'I'm scared of the gorillas too, as I expect you know. They are so very big and so very strong and so very hairy.' He shuddered. 'They might be angry if I speak to them, and an angry gorilla doesn't bear thinking about.' He closed his eyes. '*Two* angry gorillas would be even worse.'

With that he climbed into bed, but it was a long time before he went to sleep. He was woken by a loud noise. The ark shuddered violently and Mr Noah found himself thrown out of bed and across the room.

The noise had woken most of the animals in the great hall. As Mr Noah entered, the ark shuddered again, then started to tilt. Animals began sliding to the far end and the birds rose from their perches and flew up to the rafters.

'Hey... whoa...!' called the horse, sliding past the giraffe.

'Have we reached land?' squealed the rat, its claws skittering on the floor.

'As your deputy, Mr Noah,' said the lion, clinging tightly to a wooden beam, 'I think I ought to be informed when the boat behaves in this irregular manner. It's very… very… undignified…'

The ark shuddered once more, the lion lost his grip and crashed into the tiger.

'I don't know what's going on,' said Mr Noah, 'but I'll try and find out.'

'Well I blame it on those gorillas,' said the goat. 'They're probably jumping up and down at the other end of the ark to make it tip up.'

Mr Noah climbed the steps that led to the trapdoor in the roof and peered out. What he saw made him turn pale and he climbed back inside.

'The ark,' he said, 'seems to have run aground.'

'Does that mean that it's all over?' asked the pig, hopefully. 'Say, Mr Noah, have we reached land?'

'No,' said Mr Noah. 'I'm afraid we've hit something.'

'I knew it!' shrieked the emu. 'We've hit an iceberg! We're all going to drown!'

'Nonsense,' said the polar bear. 'There's no ice around here. It's far too warm.' And he fanned himself with his great paw.

'I think the ark has become trapped between the peaks of two mountains,' said Mr Noah.

'How long before it's smashed to pieces?' the monkey asked gloomily.

'We *are* going to drown!' cried the emu. 'We're trapped and we're all going to drown!'

The ostrich gave a great sob and tried to bury his head in the wooden floor.

'Nonsense,' said Mr Noah, with a certainty he was far from feeling. 'God won't let us drown.'

'Then why did he let us get stuck on these rocks?' asked the jackal in a smooth voice.

The ark shuddered once more.

'I'm going to try and push us off,' said Mr Noah.

'Have you any oars?' asked the beaver.

'Well, no,' said Mr Noah. 'God never said anything about oars.'

'You see?' said the goose to whoever was listening. 'Blaming God *all* the time.'

Mr Noah again climbed out onto the roof of the ark. The wind was blowing furiously, the rain lashing down. The roof was very slippery. Mr Noah made his way tc the end that was wedged and pushed against the rock. Nothing happened. He pushed harder. Then he called his three sons and their wives and they all pushed but it was no use. The ark was stuck fast.

Inside the hall several of the animals were beginning to feel seasick.

'This is a terrible way to travel,' said the camel. 'Give me the desert any time.'

'I always said it would end in tears,' said the monkey in an I-told-you-so voice.

Up on the roof, an exhausted Mr Noah was talking

to God. 'You can't mean it to end like this, God,' he said. 'Not after all the trouble you've taken to save us. Please tell me what to do.'

The trapdoor opened.

'Uh, sorry to bother you, Mr Noah,' said a hesitant voice, 'but perhaps we could help?'

Mr Noah turned and almost fell off the roof, for right behind him stood two very large, very black and very hairy gorillas.

'We don't like to interfere,' said the gorilla's wife in a quiet, earnest voice, 'we're not animals who put ourselves forward you know. Do feel free to tell us to go away.'

'No,' said Mr Noah, 'no, please don't go. I think you could be the answer to a prayer. Could you... would you... push us off the rocks?'

'We can try,' said the gorilla. 'What do you think, petal?'

His wife nodded her head vigorously. 'Yes indeed. We can certainly try.'

So taking a firm grip of the floor with their massive feet, the two gorillas pressed their great arms against the rocks and grunted.

The ark creaked and groaned. Then, with a loud sucking sound, it floated free. The movement was so sudden that the gorillas almost overbalanced.

They came down from the roof to loud applause.

'Three cheers for the gorillas!' the elephant trumpeted.

'No... no... it was nothing,' said the gorilla, trying to hide behind Mr Noah.

'Hip, hip...!'

'Please don't... it's all very embarrassing,' said the gorilla's wife.

'We are... hmm... very sorry if we've given you any cause to think we didn't... um...' the lion began.

'No, not at all,' the gorilla assured him.

'You see, it's just because you look like monsters,' said the donkey. 'At least, that's what the goat said, but as I've never seen a monster, I can't tell if she's right.'

'We knew how you felt,' said the gorilla's wife. 'That's why we tried not to bother you. We're really very peace-loving animals you know. We wouldn't hurt a fly.'

'Thanks,' said the fly.

'Thank you,' said Mr Noah. 'You saved the ark from sinking.'

'Nonsense,' said the eagle, from his perch high up in the roof.

'What do you mean?'

'If you had only waited until the water had risen some more, the ark would have floated off the rocks without any other help at all.'

'Why didn't you say so?' demanded Mr Noah.

'You didn't ask,' said the eagle, and closed his eyes.

'But if the gorillas hadn't come to the rescue, we'd all still have been scared of them,' said the donkey.

'That's very true,' said Mr Noah. 'Perhaps it's taught us all a lesson.' He went over to the gorilla and took his hand. 'Not to judge by appearances.'

Later that night, as Mr Noah was about to go to sleep, he suddenly had a thought.

'You knew that the ark would float off the rocks if we did nothing about it, didn't you God?' he demanded.

'I don't tell you everything, Noah,' said God.

5

THE FOX'S TALE

The first faint streaks of daylight showed a grey, wet world as the rain, which God had sent, poured down from overcast skies. Floating in the sea of rainwater was the ark, bobbing up and down at the mercy of the wind and waves.

Inside the ark most of the animals were still fast asleep. But as dawn broke, the cock got to his feet, filled his lungs with air, and crowed.

'Cock-a-doodle-doo! Wakey-wakey!'

He turned to his wife.

'Don't you think my voice sounds rather fine this morning?'

His wife, the hen, nodded.

The cock puffed out his chest. 'Cock-a-doodle-doo! Time to get up you sleepy heads!'

There was a stirring among the animals in the great hall.

'Can't you pipe down?' muttered the tiger.

331

'Cock-a-doodle-doo!'

'Cock-a-doodle-doo yourself,' snapped the fox. 'Stop that noise or I'll stop it for you!'

He bared his teeth and jumped at the cock, who gave a loud squawk and leaped out of the way. The fox laughed.

'Did you see that?' said the cock. 'Violence! I've been threatened with violence.'

'It's your fault for crowing,' said the tiger unsympathetically. 'It's all very well on a farm, but this is the ark and I don't see any need to get up early.'

'Neither do I,' said the crocodile. 'Sleeping helps pass the time.'

'It's not even day yet,' grumbled the goat.

'Yes it is,' said the cock. 'It's a fine day.'

'It's not a fine day,' said the skylark from high up in the roof. 'It's another wet one.'

'Cock-a-doodle-doo!' crowed the cock.

'Well I'm going back to sleep,' said the goat,

'and if you start crowing again, I'll, I'll…'

'Eat you?' suggested the fox.

'I don't eat animals. I only eat grass and leaves.'

'But I don't,' said the fox, licking his lips. 'I'd be happy to take care of the cock for you. Very happy indeed. And the hen. Especially the hen, who's a nice, plump little bird. Just as I like them.'

He pounced at the hen who squawked loudly.

'Here, you leave my wife alone!' shouted the cock. 'Bully!'

'If you're calling names,' said the fox, 'then your crowing makes you sound like a… like a strangulated duck!'

'Quack,' said the duck. 'Did someone mention my name?'

The cock bristled. 'I've never been so insulted in my life!'

He puffed up his chest and crowed as loudly as he could. 'Cock-a-doodle-doo! Cock-a-doodle-doo!'

His crowing brought Mr Noah, half-dressed and only half-awake, into the hall.

'Is anything the matter?' he asked.

'Yes there is,' said the cock. 'That fox attacked me and my wife.'

'It was only a joke,' said the fox.

'Funny sort of joke. He said he would eat us.'

The tiger opened one eye. 'It was only because the cock *would* insist on crowing in the middle of the night.'

'It's not the middle of the night,' snapped the cock.

'It's early morning. Cocks always welcome the dawn by crowing.'

'If I was the dawn,' said the fox, 'I'd do without your welcome.'

'Now fox,' said Mr Noah, 'You know the rules of the ark. No eating one another on the voyage.'

'Rules are made to be broken,' murmured the fox.

Mr Noah eyed him sternly. 'These rules are for the good of everyone on board.'

'But it's *such* a temptation, Mr Noah,' the fox said, casting longing looks at the cock and the hen. 'Just imagine having your favourite food walking in front of you when you're starving.'

'But you're not starving,' said Mr Noah.

'No, but it's not the same eating the food you give us,' said the fox. He grinned. 'I like my food live. Gets my taste buds working and the hunt adds to the pleasure of eating.' He licked his lips. 'It's really very difficult seeing two such delicious morsels of food strutting around. And it's very dangerous,' he added, 'the cock waking me up by crowing. I mean, I might eat him without realizing it, while I'm still half-asleep.'

'Then you'd best go and sleep on the other side of the hall, far away from temptation,' said Mr Noah.

The fox sighed and slunk away.

But the following morning he was up well before the cock. He crept round the edge of the hall until he was right outside the hen-coop.

The cock woke up, looked at the thin shaft of

daylight filtering in through the trapdoor high up in the roof, got to his feet and filled his lungs.

The fox leaped forwards, snapping his teeth. The cock jumped high in the air and gave a loud shriek.

'Just like a strangulated duck,' said the fox laughing, and slunk back to his lair on the far side of the hall.

The cock was furious. 'Something ought to be done!' he shouted.

His shouting woke the tiger, who roared, 'Can't you let a poor old animal sleep in peace?'

'You're one of Mr Noah's deputies,' said the cock, 'so get off your lazy backside and do something!'

'All right.' The tiger got to his feet. 'Anything for a quiet life.'

The fox protested, 'But I only meant it as a joke!'

'I know that. In fact between you and me, I wouldn't be too sorry if something did happen to that cock.'

'Well then.'

'But the thing is that it's just not on. It's letting Mr Noah down.'

The fox shrugged. 'What's Mr Noah got to do with it?'

'He saved us from being drowned in the flood.'

'He didn't do that. God did.'

'All right,' said the tiger patiently. 'It's letting God down.'

The following day, when Mr Noah was cleaning the lower deck of the ark, he found a single white feather lying on the ground. A little way on he found another feather. A trail of feathers led right round the ark.

He went to the great hall.

'What does all this mean?' he asked sternly.

'Oh Mr Noah,' squawked the hen. 'Mr Noah, it was the fox!'

The fox blinked. 'Me?'

'He chased me right round the ark and tore out those feathers. I nearly had heart failure I was so scared!'

'But I didn't,' the fox protested. 'I didn't do anything.'

'He said he'd eat me next time he caught me.'

Mr Noah turned to the fox. 'Well?'

'She's lying,' said the fox.

'Why should she lie? Someone's torn out her feathers and she's obviously upset. I'm going to move the cock and the hen to a different part of the ark so they'll be well out of harm's way.'

For a few days there was peace. The cock and the hen were in such a remote part of the ark that the cock's crowing did not wake the animals, and no further complaints were made about the fox.

Then one evening, both the cock and the hen went to find Mr Noah.

'He's at it again,' said the cock.

'Why, what's happened?'

'Go on,' said the cock. 'Tell him.'

'I was just having a scratch around for some seed when that fox popped his head over the edge of my coop and leered. "That's it," he said, "fatten yourself up. All the tastier for me." ' The hen sniffed. 'I'm so upset, it's stopped me from laying.'

'You should lock him up,' said the cock. 'He's a public menace.'

'All right,' said Mr Noah. 'Leave it with me.'

But the cock and the hen had plenty more to say before they could be persuaded to go back to their coop, leaving Mr Noah free to speak to God.

'What shall I do, God?' he asked. 'For if the fox does eat the hen, then all the other animals will start eating each other. By the time the floods go down and the ark finds land there'll be no animals left to repopulate the world. I don't like the idea of locking up the fox, but what else can I do?'

God was silent for a moment.

'It's not as simple as it appears,' he said at last.

'Isn't it?'

'Do nothing for the moment, Noah. Just keep your eyes and your ears open and then you will find out the truth.'

'Yes, God. And I'll watch that fox and make sure he doesn't get near the chickens.'

'Watch the chickens, too.'

'Yes, of course I will. To make sure they're safe.'

It was while Mr Noah was on his way to pay a visit to the cock and the hen that he heard them talking.

'So the next time I say that the fox grabbed hold of my wing, is that it?' asked the hen.

'Yes, but say that he let it go when I rushed up,' said the cock.

'He let it go when you rushed up,' repeated the hen.

'That'll fix him!' said the cock and crowed loudly.

Mr Noah stepped forwards. 'I heard what you both said. You've been lying, haven't you?'

The cock and the hen hung their heads. 'Well, yes,' they admitted.

'Why?'

'It was too much of a temptation,' the hen explained. 'It gave us a chance to get our own back. After all, he *would* eat us if he could.'

'A lot of animals on the ark would eat each other. But as I've explained, you've all been specially chosen by God and you've agreed not to eat each other while you remain here.'

The cock and the hen looked at one another.

'That wasn't the only reason, was it?'

'Well, no,' said the cock. 'That fox was very rude about my crowing. He said... he said that I sounded like a strangulated duck.'

'It was a very rude and unkind thing to say,' said the hen.

'So you thought you would teach the fox a lesson, is that it?'

'Yes.'

'Come along,' said Mr Noah. 'I think you owe the fox an apology, don't you? And—if I might make a suggestion—why don't you stop crowing first thing in the morning?'

'I can't do that,' said the cock. 'I must crow. It's in my nature.'

'It's in the fox's nature to hunt for food,' said Mr Noah gently. 'And he's agreed not to on this voyage.'

The cock said nothing.

'How would you feel about crowing at some time other than first thing in the morning? Perhaps when it's time for food? I can't see that the animals would mind that.'

'All right,' said the cock.

The animals agreed and, for the rest of the voyage, the cock only crowed at mealtimes and everyone was happy.

6

THE CAMEL'S TALE

When Mr Noah was building the ark, God told him to pay special attention to the living quarters of the animals, insects and birds.

'I want the creatures I save from the flood to be as comfortable as possible during the voyage,' said God.

Mr Noah had given the matter a lot of thought and was rather pleased with the plans he had worked out, especially as he had no idea what most of the animals looked like.

So when one of the two camels arrived on board the ark, Mr Noah welcomed him and showed him to his quarters.

'I think you will like it,' he said as he led the way to the lower deck. 'It is a bit cramped I'm afraid—not like your home in the desert—but you should both be fairly comfortable.'

'Both?' queried the camel. 'What do you mean, both?'

'Well, your wife, the other camel,' Mr Noah said, surprised. 'I assume she'll be here very soon.'

'I don't know what you are talking about,' said the camel haughtily.

'But God has arranged for there to be two of every animal on the ark.'

'No one said anything to me about it, and I'm not at all sure I like the idea.'

A short while later, Mr Noah was welcoming a second camel onto the ark.

'Your husband is already here. I've shown him to his quarters.'

'Husband? I didn't know I had one.'

'Well,' Mr Noah began rather uncomfortably, 'most of the animals arrived here in twos. In fact I was a bit surprised when your husband arrived by himself because God insists that there are two of every animal, insect and bird on board the ark.'

'Hmm,' said the second camel, drily.

'I'm also a bit surprised because... Well, you'll see for yourself.'

He led the way to the first camel's sleeping quarters.

'There you are.'

The two camels stared at one another.

'Who,' asked the first camel, 'is this?'

'It's the second camel,' said Mr Noah.

'That creature is not a camel.'

'I could say the same about you,' said the second camel.

'How dare you say I'm not a camel! I am, as it happens, a dromedary, which is a highly superior camel, I'll have you know.'

'Well, if it comes to that, I'm also a superior camel. I am a Bactrian.'

'Never heard of them!'

Mr Noah looked nervously from one camel to the other. 'But you are both camels. I mean, you've both got humps.'

'That,' said the dromedary, 'is a matter of opinion.'

'Indeed,' said the Bactrian. 'If it comes to humps, I think you'll agree that I have the advantage. I, after all, have *two* humps. You only have the *one*.'

'Better to have one perfect hump than two inferior ones.'

The two camels glared at one another.

'Well,' said Mr Noah nervously, 'I'll just leave you two to... er... make friends with one another.' With that, he fled.

'Has there been some mistake, God?' he asked.

'No,' said God. 'There's been no mistake.'

'But I don't think they like each other very much.'

'They will, in time.'

But as time went on, the two camels appeared to dislike each other more and more.

'It's very common to have two humps,' said the dromedary. 'One is far more elegant.'

The Bactrian looked at him pityingly. 'I really don't know how you manage with only one hump. I wouldn't feel complete without my two.'

Both went, separately, to Mr Noah and demanded that they be given quarters at opposite ends of the ark.

'I'm sorry but there's just no room,' said Mr Noah. 'Do please try to get on together.'

'Get on? With that... that misshapen beast?' asked the dromedary.

'You must be joking!' said the Bactrian.

The two camels only spoke to each other when they thought of fresh insults, and at night-time they bit and kicked each other in their sleeping quarters. It was a nightmare for the animals who slept near them and they soon complained.

'It's bad enough having to sleep near animals who grunt, snort, squeak and snore, let alone those who fight all night,' the lion grumbled. 'There's a lot of unrest, Mr Noah, and I suggest you do something about it pretty quickly.'

'Oh dear. I did think that the camels might have learned to get on with each other by now.'

Mr Noah spoke to the camels, but it wasn't much use.

'Well, I'm sorry,' said the Bactrian, 'but I didn't start it. It's that one-humped monstrosity you should be talking to, not me.'

'No one mentioned sharing my quarters with a shaggy-haired, two-humped freak!' retorted the dromedary.

'When God created camels, he must have experimented with you and discovered that two humps were best!' the Bactrian shouted.

'*You* were the experiment. *I* was the finished product!'

Mr Noah hurried away.

'I shall have to separate them, shan't I, God?'

'You must do what you think best, Noah.'

'They do seem to hate each other so.'

'Hate? Do you think it's hate?'

'Well it's certainly not love,' Mr Noah retorted, and went to find some other living quarters for the Bactrian.

Although separating the two camels meant that everyone slept more peacefully at night, it did nothing to improve the atmosphere on the ark during the day, for both camels carried on their war. The animals, insects and birds on the ark grew sick of their constant fighting.

'You're both camels, aren't you?' asked the fox. 'So why can't you get on? I could understand the hyena and myself not getting on well, but surely you two have a lot more in common than the hyena and I.'

'But I do get on with you, fox,' said the hyena. 'I find you a very witty and amusing animal.'

'Do you really? Thank you very much. I find you quite pleasant too.'

The dromedary glared at the fox. 'First, I am not a hyena and have no wish to be. Second, I am not a fox and have even less wish in that direction, for I find you a very frivolous sort of animal. Third...' he broke off. 'I've forgotten what the third is.'

The Bactrian laughed nastily. 'Going soft in the head. It's the one hump you know.'

'I know that both you camels give me the hump,' said the monkey sourly.

'A hump is a very odd thing to have,' the jackdaw said thoughtfully. 'What do you keep in it?'

'I have a hump,' said the snail. 'But it's my shell. It's very useful because I can squeeze myself under it if it rains.'

'Then why aren't you squeezed under it now?' asked the jackdaw. 'It's raining, isn't it?'

'Not in here it's not.'

The jackdaw turned to the camels. 'Do you squeeze yourselves into your humps when it rains?'

'Of course not,' said the dromedary. 'I store food in my hump.'

The Bactrian smiled sweetly. 'I can store twice as much food as him, for I've two humps for storage.'

The dromedary kicked the Bactrian, who turned and bit the dromedary. Order was only restored when Mr Noah sent both animals to their sleeping quarters.

'What am I going to do with them, God?'

'Stop worrying, Noah.'

'That's all very well, but they're upsetting the other animals.'

For a few days neither camel was heard or seen in the great hall of the ark, much to everyone's relief.

'Perhaps Mr Noah's locked them up,' said the fox hopefully.

'Perhaps they're plotting how to kill each other,' said the yak.

'Perhaps they've already done it, which is why they're so quiet,' said the rat.

Just then the dromedary entered the hall and the animals gasped. For his hump, which had always been quite large, was now enormous, and the dromedary had to walk quite slowly and carefully in order not to overbalance.

The rat sniggered, the yak snorted, the fox guffawed, then all the animals, insects and birds inside the great hall burst out laughing. The dromedary took

one disdainful look at them, turned around—with great difficulty—and walked off.

'What on earth does he think he's doing?' asked the jackdaw.

'Whatever it is, he looks quite ridiculous,' said the fox.

Some days later, Ham, who was giving the larger animals their food, came running.

'Father, Father, you must come at once!'

Mr Noah hurried after Ham to the Bactrian's sleeping quarters. He looked down at the camel, lying on her bed of straw and was shocked. Her two humps had shrunk away and the flesh hung loosely on her back. Beside her was her untouched food.

'Are you ill?' Mr Noah asked.

The Bactrian looked at him weakly. 'No, not ill,' she said, and burst into tears.

Mr Noah had a long talk with God, then went in search of the dromedary.

'The Bactrian is dying. She won't eat.'

'More fool her. What do you expect me to do about it?'

'I don't know that I want you to *do* anything. I just thought you ought to know.'

'Oh,' said the dromedary.

Late that afternoon one end of the ark began to shake violently. Mr Noah went to investigate, but found his way barred. The dromedary's hump was firmly wedged in the doorway which led to the Bactrian's sleeping quarters.

'I'm stuck! Help me! Please help!'

In the end it took the combined efforts of Mr Noah, Ham, Shem, Japheth, both rhinoceros and one hippopotamus to push the dromedary through the door into the Bactrian's sleeping quarters.

The Bactrian tried to get to her feet but could only look up as the dromedary towered over her, his ungainly hump bruised and sore.

'I'm sorry,' he said. 'I've been very silly. I was jealous of your two humps, you see, and thought that if I ate a lot, I might grow another hump to store the surplus food. But I've only given myself a sore hump and made myself a laughing stock on the ark.'

'And I stopped eating as I was jealous of you,' said the Bactrian. 'I thought that if I stopped eating, one of my humps might disappear.'

They both turned to Mr Noah.

'Could I stay here with my friend?' asked the dromedary. 'Just until she's strong enough to walk?'

'And until *my* friend's hump has gone down, so that he can go through the doorway easily?' added the Bactrian.

They looked at one another and smiled. And Mr Noah, leaving the two camels together, made his way contentedly back towards his cabin.

7

THE SQUIRREL'S TALE

The great revolt of the animals began over a small pile of nuts taken by the squirrel. It was not as if the squirrel had *stolen* the nuts, for he had asked Ham, Mr Noah's middle son, if he could take them.

'You see my wife and I are planning to have a long sleep, which seems a sensible thing to do while we're on the ark. And when we hibernate we like to have a small stock of nuts in case we wake up and feel peckish.'

But Ham had forbidden it. 'We can't have animals hoarding food. There's only just enough to go round as it is.'

So the squirrel had gone to the food store and helped himself.

'It's not stealing,' he explained to his wife. 'For we won't be eating at all unless we wake up. We're actually doing Mr Noah a favour.'

Unfortunately Ham had not seen it that way. He had given the squirrel a telling-off, and moved the entire stock of nuts to his cabin. 'So that they'll be safe from thieves like you.'

The squirrel was very upset.

'He had no right to take my nuts away! No right at all! And I wasn't stealing. I asked him nice and politely if I could have some and what did I get in return? Rudeness!'

'Why don't you complain?' asked the peacock, fanning his beautiful tail. 'I'm always complaining. Not that anyone takes the slightest notice.'

'That's a good idea,' said the squirrel. 'I'll complain to the lion. Or the tiger. They're Mr Noah's deputies. They ought to know how I've been treated!'

'I wouldn't do that,' hissed the snake, uncoiling himself from a beam high up in the roof. 'I wouldn't go to either of them.'

'Why not?'

'Because they're on Mr Noah's side,' he hissed and coiled himself up again.

'I didn't know there were "sides",' said the racoon, who was busy washing his food.

The jackal, who had been pacing restlessly up and down the hall, stopped and stared in amazement.

'What on earth are you doing?'

The racoon looked up. 'I always wash my food before eating it. Don't you? You never know where it's been.'

'In the hands of that Ham,' said the squirrel bitterly. '*And* he's taken away the entire store of nuts so I can't get any more.'

'Typical,' said the weasel sympathetically. 'But that's

humans for you. Taking our nuts, laying down the law, not listening, it's all part and parcel of the same thing.'

'That's why we're in this pickle,' said the jackal, who had resumed pacing up and down. 'Stuck on the ark with the world flooded and no sign of the rain stopping.'

'I don't understand,' said the giraffe with a puzzled expression. 'What has the rain got to do with the squirrel's nuts?'

The jackal sighed. 'Humans have made such a mess of the world that God had to destroy it,' he said slowly. 'Do you understand that?'

The giraffe nodded his long neck.

'But when God sent the rain to flood the world, he decided to save two of every creature, so that when the rain does stop and the flood goes down we can all begin again. Got it?'

'Yes.'

'But, and this is the bit I just don't understand, God put Mr Noah in charge of the ark.'

'What's wrong with that?'

'Mr Noah is a human,' said the jackal.
The giraffe looked puzzled.

The jackal sighed. 'Why didn't God put *animals* in charge?' he asked.

'I don't know,' said the giraffe, quite pleased at being able to answer the question.

'Perhaps he never thought about it,' said the penguin. 'God can't think of everything.'

'He should have thought about it,' said the snake from his ledge high above them. 'He *is* God after all. Wiser and cleverer than all of us put together—or so we're led to believe.'

'How wise or clever was it to put Mr Noah in charge?' asked the jackal.

'I don't think Mr Noah would have taken away my nuts,' said the squirrel, after much thought.

'This,' said the jackal impatiently, 'is far more important than nuts.'

'*Nothing* is more important than nuts,' said the squirrel firmly.

'I didn't mean that it's not important…'

'I think we should support you,' said the weasel

firmly. 'This issue of the squirrel's nuts is one that should unite us all!'

'That's very true,' said the jackal. 'We must act now!'

'You'll be saying next that we should take over the ark,' the monkey said, sarcastically.

'That's exactly what we should do!'

'But I don't want to take over the ark,' protested the squirrel. My wife and I only want to hibernate with a small store of nuts in case we get hungry.'

The jackal wasn't listening.

'A committee,' he said briskly. 'We must form a committee to plan the revolt.'

'It won't work,' said the monkey drily. 'You mark my words, humans will win every time. Haven't they got God on their side?'

'Once God sees what a fine job we're making of things, he'll soon come over to our way of thinking.' He turned to the squirrel. 'You must be our leader.'

'No, really...' the squirrel protested.

'If it hadn't been for you, none of this would have started.'

'And I wish it hadn't,' the squirrel said to his wife that night.

'Don't worry,' she replied, 'it won't last. They'll soon find something else to think about. Anyway, if you're the leader you can always put a stop to it.'

But the squirrel soon found that that was easier said than done.

News of the revolt spread quickly among the animals.

Some of them agreed with it, some disagreed, but all were interested.

'We must have a simple message,' said the jackal. 'One that the less intelligent among us can understand.'

'What about "Tail good, no tail bad"?' asked the peacock, spreading out his beautiful tail.

'What's that meant to mean?' asked the guinea-pig.

'It means that you're on our side if you've got a tail and not if you haven't,' explained the peacock. 'Humans don't have tails.'

'Neither have I,' said the guinea-pig.

'Or I,' said the chimpanzee.

'And I lose my tail from time to time,' said the gecko.

The monkey grinned. 'That means you're sitting on the fence. You're not on one side or the other.'

'I think we ought to be supporting Mr Noah rather than going against him,' said the elephant. 'God's given him a hard enough job as it is.'

'Hear, hear,' said the beaver, thumping her tail on the floor.

Heated arguments continued on all sides and, from time to time, fights broke out.

Mr Noah soon realized that something was wrong. But he could not find out what it was. He asked the lion and the tiger.

'Nothing is wrong, Mr Noah,' said the lion, firmly. 'Nothing at all. I would be the first to know and I can tell you, without a shadow of a doubt, that everything is just as usual.'

The tiger nodded agreement and Mr Noah went away.

But the lion and the tiger did know about the planned revolt and had decided not to tell.

'After all,' said the tiger, 'although we are Mr Noah's deputies, he is a human and we are animals. One does have one's loyalties.'

'Yes,' agreed the lion. 'And if there had been any justice at all in the world, God would have put me in charge. I am, after all, King of the Jungle and Lord of All Beasts.'

'And big-headed too,' added the tiger sourly.

As the day of the revolt drew near, the atmosphere in the great hall grew more and more tense. Despite the assurances of the lion and the tiger, Mr Noah was convinced that something was very wrong.

'I know the animals are planning something,' he said to God 'I just wish I knew what it was. There are arguments and fights breaking out all over the place, but whenever I try to find out what's wrong, no one will tell me. Is it my fault? Have I done something wrong?'

God sighed. 'No, Noah, you have done nothing wrong. But because you are human, you are being blamed for the wickedness of the world.'

'Can I do anything to put it right?'

'You *can* put right the wrongs on the ark.'

'Tell me.'

So God told Mr Noah about the squirrel.

'I'll go and see the squirrel at once,' said Mr Noah, getting off his bed.

'No,' said God. 'Wait.'

Now while Mr Noah was talking to God, the squirrel was talking to his wife.

'I don't know what to do for the best. After all, if God had wanted to put squirrels in charge, or jackals, or weasels, he'd have done it, wouldn't he? He must have had a good reason for putting Mr Noah in charge. If only I knew what to do.'

'Perhaps you should go and see Mr Noah.'

'That's sneaking.'

'Would you like *me* to go and see Mr Noah?'

'No,' said the squirrel. 'That's not right either. Oh what shall I do? All I wanted was a small supply of nuts so we could go to sleep without worrying and now look what's happened!'

All night long he ran up and down outside his nest, worrying about what he should do. Just before morning he had come to a decision.

Head down, so that the other animals wouldn't see him, he crept along to Mr Noah's cabin and knocked on the door.

'I felt I had to tell you, Mr Noah,' he said, when he had reached the end of his story. 'Although I don't like telling tales. But it was my fault in a way that it all started, so I should be the one to try and stop it.'

'It wasn't only your fault,' Mr Noah said. 'I have already spoken to Ham, and he'll apologise and give

you some nuts so that you can go to sleep without worry. It was very brave of you to tell me. It can't have been easy.'

Mr Noah called a meeting in the great hall.

'Look,' he said, 'I'm sure that some of you would be much better at being in charge on the ark. But God gave me the job. I don't know why he did, and I didn't want to do it, but I agreed to it and now I'm trying to make the best of it for the sake of us all. So can I appeal to you to give up this idea of a revolt? If there's anything you're unhappy about, come and tell me and we'll try and work out a solution.'

The animals muttered among themselves. Then the jackal spoke.

'How did you know about the revolt?' he asked

suspiciously, glaring at the squirrel.

'God told me,' said Mr Noah.

'Oh,' said the jackal, 'well if *God* told you...'

And he slunk away to his corner of the hall. The great revolt of the animals on the ark was at an end.

8

THE CATERPILLAR'S TALE

The rain fell day after day. Inside the ark the animals, insects and birds could hear it spattering against the wooden sides and drumming on the roof. It seemed as if it would never stop.

'It's never going to end,' said the monkey. 'We'll spend the rest of our lives in this dark, leaking tub...'

'It's not leaking,' said one of the termites, who had just finished mending some holes made by the woodpeckers. 'Our work is watertight.'

'The food will run out and we'll die of hunger,' the monkey continued.

'But we have Mr Noah's promise that the rain will stop after forty days and forty nights,' the dormouse said.

'If you believe that, you'll believe anything.'

'The clouds will roll away, the sun will shine and the water will dry up.'

'Yes, and pigs might fly,' added the monkey sarcastically.

'We must have hope,' said the dormouse, 'and faith in Mr Noah.'

'I've no hope and as for faith in Mr Noah…!' The monkey turned away in disgust.

A hairy green caterpillar had been listening to this conversation as she slowly munched a tasty leaf which Shem had just provided. She looked at her friend, a white caterpillar with brown stripes.

'I didn't think pigs could fly,' she said.

'They can't,' said her friend, who was busy chewing the leaf from the other end.

The green caterpillar raised her head. 'Excuse me, pig, but can you fly?'

'Hey, is that some kind of a joke?' asked the pig. He turned to his wife. 'Honey, that caterpillar's just asked if we can fly!'

Both pigs burst out laughing.

'Told you so,' said the striped caterpillar. 'Mmm. This leaf is *good*.'

'I wish *I* could fly,' said the green caterpillar.

A bumblebee flew past her head. The caterpillar watched him.

'How do you do that?'

'What—buzz?'

'No. Fly.'

'I've got wings. That's how.'

'But I've heard,' said the caterpillar, who liked collecting bits of information, 'I've heard that bumblebees are so heavy they shouldn't be able to fly at all.'

'Are you calling me fat?'

The caterpillar looked at the bumblebee's round, striped brown and gold body.

'Oh no. Not at all. I think you're very handsome. Very handsome indeed.'

'Well then.'

'But I *have* heard that you shouldn't be able to fly.'

'Oh really?'

'Yes,' said the caterpillar earnestly. 'It's really quite impossible for you to fly.'

'No one's told me that,' said the bumblebee. He laughed and flew away.

The caterpillar watched him go. 'I do wish I could fly.'

'You're always wanting the impossible, said the striped caterpillar, starting on another leaf. 'Why can't you just be happy as you are? It's warm and it's dry and

there's a non-stop supply of leaves. A bit of sun would be nice, but you can't have everything.'

The bumblebee went into his nest. 'Do you know what I've just been told? I've been told that bumblebees can't fly!'

The other bee burst out laughing. 'No one's told *me* that!'

Both bees flew round the great hall, buzzing up and down. 'See how well we can't fly!' they shouted to the caterpillar. 'Aren't we clever!'

The caterpillar watched as she nibbled a corner of a leaf. 'There's no need to laugh. I must have got it wrong, that's all.'

The bees flew away and the caterpillar carried on eating.

'Have you ever thought how boring it is, being a caterpillar?' the caterpillar said to the bumblebee when he returned.

'I can't say I've lost any sleep over it.'

'You can fly, but I've got to walk wherever I want to go.'

'That's true, but you do have an awful lot of legs.'

'I suppose so,' sighed the caterpillar, 'but it still takes a long time to get from one end of a leaf to the other.'

'It wouldn't if you didn't stop to eat all the time.'

'But I'm always hungry.'

'That's your problem,' said the bumblebee, about to fly away.

'I've been thinking,' said the caterpillar. 'If bumblebees

can fly, even though they're not built for flying, perhaps I can fly, even though I haven't any wings.'

'Perhaps,' said the bumblebee doubtfully.

'It's worth a try anyway.'

The bumblebee watched as the caterpillar wriggled her way to the very edge of the ledge on which she was lying, bunched her legs under her and jumped...

She landed on top of the baboon.

'I didn't think it was raining caterpillars,' said the baboon, who was not very bright.

'I'm sorry,' said the caterpillar. 'I was trying to fly.'

The baboon scratched his head. 'I didn't know caterpillars could fly. Whatever next?'

The caterpillar looked at the ledge far above her and sighed. It was going to be a long, long crawl before she reached her food again.

'I could have told you that caterpillars can't fly,' said the bumblebee. 'You call *me* large, but just look at *your* funny shape! It would take a miracle to make you fly and I don't believe in miracles!'

'What's a miracle?'

'Something wonderful and amazing that doesn't normally happen.'

'Well, it's pretty wonderful and amazing that *you* can fly, seeing as you're so fat,' retorted the caterpillar crossly as she began the long crawl back.

It was late when she reached the ledge and she was tired. She nibbled part of a leaf and went to sleep. When she woke the next morning she had another idea.

'I've been thinking.'

'Again?' said the striped caterpillar through a mouthful of food. 'I wish you wouldn't. It makes my head ache.'

The caterpillar called to the bumblebee. 'I think you can fly because you have wings which you wave up and down.'

The bumblebee thought for a moment. 'That's right.'

'Well, I haven't any wings, but I do have legs. Lots of legs. If I waved them up and down, perhaps they'd do the same job as your wings and I could fly.'

'Do you really think so?'

'I don't see why not.'

'I do,' said the striped caterpillar, pausing before attacking another leaf.

But the first caterpillar was already taking a deep breath and did not listen. She closed her eyes and jumped. But this time, instead of bunching her legs under her, she waved them wildly in the air.

She landed upside down on the floor.

'Are you all right?' asked the bumblebee, flying down to join her.

'No,' said the caterpillar, trying to roll over onto her front.

'It didn't work, did it?'

'No. It didn't.'

'Told you so,' the striped caterpillar called down.

The caterpillar looked up at the ledge, high above her, and sighed at the thought of the long crawl back.

Mr Noah, walking through the great hall, only just missed stepping on her.

'Fallen off, have you?' he asked, picking her up and replacing her carefully on the ledge.

'I was trying to fly,' said the caterpillar. 'If it's a miracle that the bumblebee can fly, because he's so fat, I thought that maybe I could have a miracle too, as I do want to fly so much.'

Mr Noah smiled.

'It's a miracle we're all alive and safe on this ark when the rest of the world is flooded. Perhaps you should be content with that.'

'That's what my friend says. And it's not that I'm not grateful, but I would like a little miracle of my own. How do I make one, Mr Noah?'

'Miracles come from God. And nothing is impossible for God. You just have to hope.'

The days passed. The caterpillars ate and ate and grew to their full size, while the bees flew up and down.

'Oh, if only I could fly,' the caterpillar said, but by now she had grown so large and lazy with all the food she had eaten, she was too weary even to try. No one answered her, for the bees had gone back into their nest and the other animals in the hall were resting.

'I don't suppose I'll ever fly now,' she thought sadly and carried on eating.

A few days later the caterpillars found that they were no longer hungry, just very tired. They spun fine threads of silk around themselves until they were completely covered, then fell fast asleep.

The caterpillar woke with a start. She felt weak and cold and a bit light-headed. With some difficulty she struggled out of her cocoon and sat on the edge of the ledge. Her friend was still sleeping, snugly tucked up in her silken cocoon.

'Perhaps I overate,' thought the caterpillar. 'Or I've woken up too quickly. I think I'll just sit here quietly for a while.'

Slowly she began to feel stronger. She also felt happy. Happier than she had felt for a long, long time. She looked up, and although there was only the roof of the ark above her, and although the rain was still pouring down, the caterpillar thought that it was going to be a very fine day.

The bumblebee flew past.

'Hello, good morning!' called the caterpillar. 'What a lovely day it is!'

'Is it?'

'If I could only fly,' the caterpillar continued, 'life would be perfect, even though it's raining.'

'There's nothing to stop you,' said the bumblebee, buzzing round her head.

'Of course there is! You remember, I tried to fly but I can't. I haven't any wings.'

'Haven't any…? Is that some sort of a joke?'

'Joke?'

'You have the most beautiful wings I've ever seen,'

said the bumblebee. 'And if you can't fly with those wings, then I'm sure I can't fly with mine.'

'What do you mean?'

'Try it and you'll see!'

So the caterpillar, who was no longer a caterpillar but a beautiful butterfly, arched her back. She felt her wings begin to stir. She rose into the air and, as if she had been doing it all her life, she began to fly.

'Who said miracles don't happen?' she called to the bumblebee as she flew lightly up into the roof of the ark.

9

THE BISON'S TALE

Thud, thud, thud, thud! Mr Noah shuddered as the heavy footsteps went past his cabin.

'Left, right, left, right!' Thud! Thud…! The ark shook from side to side.

'You'll really have to do something about those bison,' said Mrs Noah the following day. 'They make such a noise and shake the ark so much, I'm sure it could capsize.'

Thud! Thud!

'Mr Noah, can't you stop those bison?' complained the ostrich. 'The noise they make has given me a dreadful headache.'

'Me too,' agreed the goat. 'And they never stop. Day and night, night and day…'

'It's bad enough being on the ark in the first place, without having two great hairy bison thundering round the place,' the peacock grumbled.

'All right,' said Mr Noah. 'I'll speak to them.'

He did not have to search very far, for they could be heard all over the ark.

Thud! Thud!

'Left, right, left, right, halt!' said the first bison. Both bison stopped.

'Mr Noah! Sir!'

They pawed the ground with their hooves.

'Two bison, present and correct...'

'...if a bit cramped,' the second bison finished.

'Not that we're complaining,' said the first bison. 'We bison were brought up to make the best of things. It's a hard life out there on the prairie.'

'We're not blaming you, Mr Noah,' said the second bison.

'Orders are orders and must be obeyed, and you've had your orders from the very top.'

'But it is a bit difficult, you must admit.'

'What is?' asked Mr Noah.

'It's just so very small.'

'Small?'

'We're used to the wide open prairies, Mr Noah,' the first bison explained. 'How I miss the great plains we used to roam across.'

'Of course, we're very grateful to be saved from the flood, and we try to make the best of it, but it is very boring roaming round and round the ark,' said the second bison.

'That's what I came to see you about,' Mr Noah said, thankful to get a word in. 'I'm afraid your roaming

has upset some of the animals.'

'Upset the animals?' said the first bison. 'Rot! Just because they won't take any exercise themselves, they shouldn't complain about those of us who like to keep fit. Do some of them good to walk around the ark a bit more.'

'Possibly,' said Mr Noah.

'Of course it would. I tell you, Mr Noah, some of those animals won't be able to walk off the ark when the flood goes down—they'll be too fat. Why, they don't even have to hunt for their food.'

'I never thought of that,' said Mr Noah, thoughtfully.

'Tell you what. We'll organize some keep-fit classes.'

The second bison nodded enthusiastically. 'That's a good idea.'

'Need a good shaking up, some of those idle good-for-nothings,' the first bison continued.

'I've had complaints about the noise you make,' said Mr Noah.

'Noise? What do you mean—noise? We just trot round the decks, that's all.'

'We can't help being rather heavy, you know,' added the second bison.

'Of course not. But could you try to trot a bit more quietly...? Not thud about, if you see what I mean...? And perhaps not *all* the time?'

'We'll do the best we can, but really, Mr Noah, we can't stop roaming.' He turned to the second bison. 'Ready?'

'Ready.'

'Forward march! Left, right, left, right...'

Mr Noah explained the situation to the rest of the animals and told them of the bison's suggestion.

'Keep-fit?' sniffed the ostrich. '*Keep-fit? How insulting!*'

The crocodile laughed so much he almost choked. 'Bison giving keep-fit lessons?'

'Say, now I've heard everything!' said the wallaby, his eyes streaming.

'What I don't like is the suggestion that we're fat and lazy,' said the pig.

'But you are,' said the crocodile. 'Very fat and very lazy.'

'That's as may be,' said the pig. 'All I said was that I don't like a loud-mouthed, heavy-footed bison telling me so.'

'I get all the exercise I need,' said the heron. 'I stand first on one leg... and then the other. It's very exhausting.'

'But is it such a bad idea?' Mr Noah looked round the assembled animals, most of whom were lying half-asleep in the great hall. 'We'll need to be fit to face all the challenges when we get off the ark.'

'Oh, I don't think you should worry too much,' said the fox. 'Show me a couple of chickens and I'll soon get fit chasing them.'

'I regard this cruise as a rest,' said the tiger, lazily flicking his tail to and fro. 'A small oasis of calm in the middle of a busy and stressful life.'

The lion snorted. 'Your life has never been busy! Everyone knows that tigers are the laziest of creatures!'

'Is that so?' asked the tiger, a dangerous glint in his eye. 'Then perhaps we should have a little warm-up exercise right now and I'll show you just how fit I am! Put your paws up!'

They circled each other, snarling.

'Tiger, lion,' said Mr Noah hurriedly. 'Please. You're my deputies and shouldn't fight.'

From then on the bison tried to walk quietly. But for some reason, the noise was a lot worse than before and the animals were soon complaining again.

'Right, left, right, left!'

Mr Noah waited for them to arrive.

'Halt!'

'I'm sorry bison, but the animals are still complaining about you.'

'You can't have a good bracing walk if you're going about on tiptoe,' said the first bison.

'We are trying to move quietly,' said the second bison.

'Perhaps if you tried moving more slowly?' Mr Noah suggested.

'Where's the exercise in that?' the first bison snapped and they set off once more.

'Did I get the measurements wrong, God?' Mr Noah asked anxiously. 'Should I have built a bigger ark?'

'No, Noah. It's just the right size. But you must realize that the ark would seem as small to large animals as it would seem large to small ones.'

Mr Noah thought about it.

'Is there anything I can do to help?'

'They will have help very soon,' God promised.

The following day the bison were stopped in the middle of their morning trot.

'Mind where you're putting your great hooves!' called a small, frightened voice at their feet.

'What's that?'

'I said, "MIND WHERE YOU'RE PUTTING YOUR GREAT FEET!" ' squeaked the ant in her loudest voice. 'YOU NEARLY SQUASHED US!'

'Terribly sorry,' said the first bison. 'I didn't see you.'

'It's very worrying, you roaming round like that. We never know when you might be coming.'

'I never thought of that.'

'We're used to roaming the wide open prairies and not used to being cramped up on a small ark,' explained the second bison.

'What do you mean, a *small* ark?' squeaked the ant. 'This place is enormous!'

'It's so enormous, we can't even imagine its size,' her husband added.

'It's tiny compared with what we're used to,' said the second bison.

The ant sighed. 'Everyone tells us that we're floating on an ark and lucky to be here and safe from the flood. But for us it's just like being on land. We've been running around, trying to see as much as we can, but even if we spent our entire lives on the ark, we'd never see more than a fraction of it.'

'And it's such an experience,' added her husband. 'One we'd love to tell the grandchildren.'

The bison looked at his wife. 'I think we've been rather selfish, don't you?'

'But it's never too late to put things right,' his wife agreed.

Soon afterwards the animals in the great hall were amazed at the sight of the two bison walking very slowly and very carefully.

'This,' the first bison was saying, 'is the great hall. It's where most of the animals, insects and birds spend their time. Am I going slowly enough for you?'

'Oh yes, thank you,' said the ant who was clinging to his back.

They walked out.

'Well I never,' said the mandrill, scratching his pink and red bottom.

'You could knock me down with a baboon,' agreed the wallaby.

'This,' the second bison was explaining, 'is the lower

deck. And here are the great doors which God himself closed when all of us were safely inside.'

'Can we stop for a moment? It's all so big, it's a bit hard to take it in.'

'Of course. Take as much time as you like.'

Both bison stopped and waited patiently.

'It's really very kind of you to give us this guided tour,' said the ant shyly. 'You must have far more important things to do.'

'We're enjoying it,' said the bison. 'It's made me look at the ark in quite a different way. I'll never complain of it being too small again.'

Mr Noah, on his way to the great hall, smiled to see the bison and the ants.

'Thank you, God,' he said. 'I knew you would sort things out.'

'I care for the small as well as the large, Noah,' God replied.

Inside the hall the animals were quiet and rather thoughtful.

'Say, Mr Noah,' said the wallaby. 'I've been thinking. Perhaps this keep-fit thing isn't such a bad idea after all. Would you speak to the bison about it?'

'Of course,' said Mr Noah.

10
THE FLEA'S TALE

When God told Mr Noah that he was going to flood the world but that two of every animal, insect and bird should be taken onto the ark to be saved, the two fleas nearly got left behind. It was only when Mr Noah caught sight of the chimpanzees scratching themselves that he thought about the fleas and asked God whether or not they should be saved from the flood.

'Two of *every* creature must be saved,' God said.

Mr Noah scratched his head. 'If you say so, God. But the animals won't like it.'

The animals did not like it, not only because the fleas made them itch. From the moment they boarded the ark—on the backs of the two monkeys—the fleas annoyed the animals.

'I say, I say, I say, have you heard the one about the dog that visited the flea-circus and stole the show?' one of them said, jumping onto the dog's back.

The dog sighed.

The other flea joined him.

'Why did the fly fly?'

'I don't know,' said the first flea. 'Why did the fly fly?'

'Because the spider spied her!'

'I don't wish to know that. Kindly leave the dog.' Both fleas rocked with laughter.

'If you must tell jokes, would you mind not doing it on my back?' asked the dog patiently.

'Whoops, there we go again,' said the first flea. 'Upsetting the natives!'

'Where shall we go now?' asked the second flea.

'How about... the horse? He looks as if he needs cheering up.'

'Why couldn't the pony talk?'

'I don't know the answer to that one. Why couldn't the pony talk?'

'Because he was a little horse! A little hoarse. Get it?'

The fleas laughed even more.

'Now watch this, everyone!' the first flea called in a loud voice. 'My friend and I will perform our latest, death-defying leap from the back of the dog, right across the great hall, and onto the back of the horse.'

'Must you?' asked the horse.

'We will do this,' continued the first flea, 'in one mighty spring, with two back somersaults and a forward flip! Never, in the entire history of the ark, has anything so daring been attempted before!'

'That's not much of a claim, as the ark's brand new,'

said the mongoose. 'But I don't mind what you do, so long as you don't land on me.'

'Allez-oup!' called the fleas and the mongoose began to scratch herself.

'I think you don't entirely understand,' said the first flea, 'just how lucky you are to have my friend and me. We're not your average common-or-garden fleas. Oh no. We are Fleance and Fleaty, your world-famous performing fleas. We come from a long, long line of theatrical fleas...'

'...whose ancestors had Adam and Eve roaring with laughter in the Garden of Eden,' added the second flea.

'...now alas the sole surviving members.'

'Don't count your chickens before they're hatched,' advised the fox. 'You might not survive very long.'

'Why did the fox cross the road?' asked Fleance.

'Because he saw a couple of chickens!' The fleas laughed.

'My turn now,' said Fleaty. 'On which side do chickens have the most feathers?'

'I don't know, Fleaty, on which side do chickens have the most feathers?'

'On the outside of course!'

Both fleas laughed so much they had to clutch tightly onto the mongoose to prevent themselves from falling off.

'We don't care for jokes about us,' said one of the chickens.

'We don't care for your jokes at all,' said the fox.

'But we're here to entertain you,' said Fleance. 'We'll perform amazing acrobatic feats on and off the backs of your good selves. Just watch this…!'

'What?' asked the donkey.

'Ouch!' said the yak, beginning to scratch himself.

'Didn't you see how we somersaulted off the back of the mongoose, did a triple turn in the air and landed on the yak's back?'

'How many yaks does it take to…' Fleance began.

'Oh get off my back!' said the yak crossly.

'I didn't see anything,' said the donkey.

'That's because you weren't watching,' said Fleaty. 'Let me ask you a question.'

'I'm not very clever with questions,' said the donkey cautiously.

'You'll get this one. Now listen carefully.'

The donkey pricked back his ears.

'Is it raining *outside*?'

The donkey looked pleased. 'I know the answer to that,' he said proudly. 'Yes. It is raining outside.'

'Does it ever rain *inside*?' said Fleaty and both fleas burst out laughing.

The donkey looked puzzled. 'I don't think I quite understand...' he began.

'Ask you another. When do you see cows with eight feet?'

The donkey shook his head. 'I don't know.'

'When two cows are side by side!'

'Is this sort of vulgar humour going to continue for the entire voyage?' asked the emu.

'Probably,' said Fleance.

'In that case, I shall definitely complain to Mr Noah!'

'Is he "The Management?" ' asked Fleance.

'Yes,' said the emu.

'Under God,' the dormouse added. 'God's really in charge.'

'Time to move on,' said Fleance. 'Now watch this, everyone!'

The animals watched, but it was only when the

jaguar began to scratch that they realized that the fleas had jumped.

'I didn't see anything,' said the donkey.

'Then you missed the performance of a lifetime,' said Fleance sadly. 'I think I surpassed myself there. I've never managed a triple somersault at the same time as a triple back-flip. I don't suppose I'll ever do it again.'

'Well I think it's a load of nonsense,' snapped the jaguar.

'No it's not. It's a triple somersault at the same time as a triple back-flip.'

'Rubbish! It's an illusion!'

'I thought it was Fleance the flea, not an illusion,' said the donkey. 'What is an illusion? Is it another animal?'

'An illusion is when you're tricked into thinking you've seen something that didn't happen,' said the eagle swooping down from his usual perch high up in the rafters.

The donkey shook his head. 'I don't understand.'

'I'm not surprised,' said Fleance.

'I feel a headache coming on,' complained the ostrich.

'To put it another way,' said the lion grandly, '—and as King of the Jungle, I know about these things—it's when you believe in something that you can't see and doesn't exist.'

'But if you can't see it and it doesn't exist, why should you believe in it?' asked the llama.

'Why indeed?' said the lion, who had no idea of the answer but didn't want anyone else to know.

'You mean, like God?' asked the donkey, after much thought.

'No,' said the eagle. 'Not like God. You can't see God but he does exist so he's not an illusion.'

'Which brings us back to my triple somersault and triple back-flip,' said Fleance brightly.

'If you pesky fleas don't stop squirming around and making me scratch, I'm going to get very angry indeed!' said the jaguar crossly.

'Do you know what animal eats the least?' asked Fleance.

'No, what animal eats the least?' Fleaty replied.

'A moth. It just eats holes!'

Mr Noah soon found himself surrounded by angry animals, insects and birds.

'It's very wearing, having to listen to all those jokes,' said the goose.

'They're such bad jokes as well,' said the mongoose.

'Do you think so?' asked the donkey. 'I think they're rather good myself. At least, I don't really understand them, but I'm sure they're very funny.'

'They give me a headache,' said the ostrich.

'And those fleas jump from one animal to another without so much as a "Do you mind?" or "Will it trouble you if I sit on your back for a while?",' said the yak. 'It's very rude of them.'

'They make me itch,' said the rat.

'All right, all right!' said Mr Noah. 'I'll go and talk to them.'

But the fleas, seeing Mr Noah approach, decided to play hide-and-seek with him. After an hour spent running all over the ark, Mr Noah was very cross and quite worn out.

'I'll have to speak to God about you two,' he said. 'So I hope you're listening, wherever you are.'

'We're here,' said Fleance.

Mr Noah scratched his hand. 'Where?'

'On your hand,' said Fleaty.

'This behaviour has got to stop,' said Mr Noah severely. The fleas sighed.

'It's very sad,' said Fleance. 'We only want to be friends.'

'That's why we keep hopping from one animal to another,' said Fleaty. 'Just hoping that someone will like us enough to let us stay with them.'

'You must stop annoying the animals.'

'All right,' said Fleance.

'If you say so,' agreed Fleaty.

Two days later Mr Noah was visited by Mrs Noah.

'Mr Noah, you must do something about those fleas,' said Mrs Noah.

'What have they done now?'

'If they're not jumping on to me, they're jumping onto Rachel and Miriam. We've all been scratching. You must speak to God.'

So Mr Noah spoke to God.

'There doesn't seem to be an answer, God. I really don't know what to do about them.'

'There's always an answer.'

'I can only think of drowning them.'

'You'd have to catch them first,' God said, with a smile in his voice.

'It's no laughing matter!' Mr Noah said severely.

'I'm sorry, Noah, but think of it from the fleas' point of view. They want to be accepted, they want to be friends, yet everyone rejects them.'

There was a knock on the door of the cabin. It was the two hedgehogs.

'Excuse us, Mr Noah, if we're interrupting anything, but we've a suggestion to make about the fleas.'

'Come in. Any suggestion would be most welcome.'

'The thing is, we're used to providing homes for fleas. We've got thick skins and don't mind them...'

'So long as they behave themselves,' added the other hedgehog.

'We don't even mind their jokes, so long as they tell them to each other and don't bother us with them.'

Mr Noah got to his feet.

'You're an answer to a prayer,' he said simply.

So the fleas found a home on the backs of the hedgehogs and, by agreement, limited their jokes to three a day. And the fleas performed feats of daring at the party organized by the elephants and everyone applauded, although no one could actually see their amazing acrobatic moves—not even the donkey who tried very hard.

'It must have been that thing they called an illusion,' he told his wife later that night. 'But a very clever one. It had all of us fooled.'

His wife looked at him with affection. 'I expect you're right,' she said gently.

11
THE SPARROW'S TALE

After forty days and forty nights of rain, a great wind began to blow, sending the clouds scudding this way and that across the sky. The eagle was the first to bring the news to the ark, flying in through the trapdoor in the roof and crying in his loudest voice, 'The rain has stopped!'

Mr Noah poked his head out into the air and felt the fresh wind on his face. The animals and insects all cheered while the birds streamed out of the ark and soared into the air. There were larks and linnets, swallows and chaffinches, owls, blackbirds, thrushes, wrens and many, many more besides. All the birds of God's creation rose into the air and flew round and round, swooping and diving, singing, warbling, glad to feel the wind under their wings once more.

Everyone was happy that day, except for Hannah, wife of Mr Noah's youngest son Japheth. This was strange, for during the forty days and forty nights of rain when everyone on the ark had, at times, felt sad,

Hannah had always remained happy and smiling. She had a smile for everyone, and she was always singing, whether she was taking food to the animals, cleaning their quarters or tending those who were hurt. She was kind and she was gentle.

'Hannah is the sunshine on the ark,' Mr Noah had said to his wife many times.

But on the day the rain finally stopped Hannah, after opening the trapdoor in the roof and looking out on the world for the first time, burst into tears.

'Whatever is the matter?' Japheth asked anxiously.

Hannah shook her head.

'Hannah, what's wrong?' asked Mr Noah.

'I never realized it before,' she sobbed.

'Realized what?'

'I never really believed that the whole world would be flooded.'

Mr Noah was silent.

'You see, I thought that when the rain stopped, we'd all go back to the farm and that the lovely garden I made would still be there, filled with flowers and birds. I never really thought that we would never go back.'

'I see,' said Mr Noah sadly. 'I'm very sorry.'

So while the sun grew daily stronger in the sky and the flood waters slowly subsided, Hannah stayed in her cabin. She grew pale and thin and everyone worried about her.

'When we find land, we will plant a new garden,' Mr Noah promised.

'It won't be the same,' Hannah said.

'No. But with God's help it will be as beautiful.'

The animals, insects and birds all tried to help, for everyone loved Hannah. The cow gave her fresh milk, the giraffe told her a long and not very funny story, the spiders spun her a gossamer scarf, the peacock gave her one of his precious tail feathers. Even the lion and the tiger paid her a visit. And as for the birds! They flew in and out of her cabin singing all her favourite songs, but Hannah grew weaker day by day.

It was some time before the sparrow heard about Hannah. Small and brown and timid, he was scared of the other birds on the ark. He tried to keep out of their way, for they had not been kind to him.

'How dare you!' the hawk had said when the sparrow had taken a small crumb from the bird table. 'Just who do you think you are to take the last, the best, the choicest crumb?'

'Only a sparrow,' said the sparrow humbly.

'A sparrow,' said the hawk. 'An ordinary sparrow.'

'Very ordinary,' said the peacock, looking down his long nose. 'Not beautiful like me.'

'No. I'm not beautiful.'

'And not accomplished either,' said the nightingale. 'I don't suppose for a moment that you can sing.'

'I *can* sing, but not as well as you.'

'Are you wise?' asked the owl, blinking rapidly. 'I am. I can tell you the exact position of the ark in relation to the sun.'

'A fat lot of use that is,' retorted the hawk. He looked at the sparrow. 'You're common,' he said. 'The most common of all the wild birds. In fact you're so common, I wouldn't even bother to eat you unless I was absolutely starving.'

The sparrow had flown away to a dark corner of the ark high up in the roof.

'The other birds called me common,' he said to his wife.

'They don't really mean it,' she replied.

'They said I was ordinary, not beautiful like the peacock.'

'Who would want to be like that stuck-up bird?'

'I'm not wise like the owl.'

'I think you're very clever.'

'But what they said was true,' said the sparrow. 'I am small and brown and ordinary and it makes me very sad.'

'Take no notice,' said his wife, but the sparrow grew more and more unhappy. He stopped eating and would have died if Hannah had not seen him one day, sitting hunched up in a dark corner. She had taken him in her hands, stroked his wings and spoken to him kindly. She fed him herself until he was strong. So when he heard how sick Hannah was, he flew into her cabin early one morning, perched on her pillow and gazed sadly at her pale, thin face.

'Is there anything I can do to help?' he asked. 'I can't sing like the nightingale, and I haven't any beautiful tail feathers to give you like the peacock. I'm not clever like the owl, but if there is anything, please tell me.'

Hannah turned to watch him. 'A leaf from a tree in my garden,' she said in a faint voice. 'So I'd know it hadn't all been destroyed.'

'But that's impossible.'

'That's all I want.'

The sparrow went away sadly.

'Are you all right?' Mr Noah asked, seeing him flying past. The sparrow told him and Mr Noah shook his head.

'I have no idea where in the world we are. We could be miles and miles from Hannah's garden. And even if we are floating above it, there would be nothing left now.' He looked at the sparrow. 'Besides, you're not strong enough to go on such a journey and anyway it isn't necessary. The dove has gone looking for land. Why don't you go back to Hannah and sing to her instead? I know she likes your company.'

The sparrow thanked Mr Noah for his advice and flew away.

'I did do right, didn't I God?' Mr Noah asked, once the sparrow had gone.

'You did what you thought best,' God replied.

The sparrow, meanwhile, had gone back to his nest, eaten a large meal, kissed his wife and flown out of the trapdoor in the roof. He had a task to perform. All that day he flew over the sea, his small bright eyes looking for signs of land. He flew towards the sun and when the sun sank and it grew dark, he flew by the light of the full moon.

He was hungry and thirsty and his wings felt so tired it became an effort to keep himself up in the air. As the sun rose the following morning, the sparrow could scarcely fly. His throat was dry, his eyes kept misting over and his wings hurt every time he flapped them feebly up and down.

'Mr Noah was right,' he thought. 'I'm not strong enough.'

And on that thought his wings failed him and he began to fall.

But instead of plunging into the cold sea, his fall was broken by one single branch, sticking out from above the water. On it was a handful of leaves.

The sparrow weakly plucked at one and it came away in his beak.

'It's too late,' he thought sadly. 'I'll never have the strength to fly back to the ark.' And he closed his eyes as he felt himself slipping from the branch.

But at that moment a wind arose. The sparrow's feathers began to ruffle. Feebly he flapped, once, twice. The wind caught under his wings, bore him up from the branch and took him high over the sea.

Inside the ark Mr Noah was talking to God about the missing sparrow.

'I'm so worried about him, for he's very small.'

'He has a big heart,' God said.

'I know, but he's not strong. I'm afraid he might have drowned.'

While Mr Noah was talking to God, the wind died down and the sparrow, still with the leaf held tightly in his beak, fell in through the trapdoor in the roof and onto the floor of the ark. No one saw him arrive. With his last ounce of strength he made his way to Hannah's cabin and laid the leaf on the pillow beside her bed.

Hannah looked at it with wondering eyes. She touched it gently. Then she looked at the sparrow and saw how thin and tired he was.

'You fetched that, for me?'

'Yes.'

'From a tree from my garden?'

The sparrow sighed. 'I don't know. It might have been.'

Slowly she sat up in bed and picked up the sparrow gently in her hands.

'I'm sure it was.' She smiled at the sparrow and stroked his small head. 'Thank you. Thank you so very much. Now we must find some food and water for you and then we'll look for land and a place where I can plant a new garden. Will you come and live there?'

'Oh yes. Please,' said the sparrow.

A short time later Mr Noah knocked on the door of Hannah's cabin and was surprised to find it empty.

'You'll find Hannah and the sparrow on the roof,' God told him.

Mr Noah picked up the single green leaf, still lying on Hannah's pillow, and stared at it in amazement.

'Don't ask,' said God, gently.

12

THE DOLPHIN'S TALE

The ark, which God had told Mr Noah to build in order to save his family and two of every animal, insect and bird from the flood, drifted on the wide open sea. The rain had stopped and a bright sun shone from a cloudless sky. The animals, pleased to get into the fresh air, took turns to sit on the roof, laze in the sun and search for land.

'Although I don't know how we head for land even if we find it,' said the monkey, 'considering that the ark can't be steered.'

The beaver shook his head. 'Pity there are no oars on board,' he said. 'Big mistake.'

'We'll just have to wait until the flood has gone down,' said the tiger. 'I don't mind.' He stretched himself lazily. 'This is the life. I could get quite used to sea cruises.'

'Speak for yourself,' said one of the reindeer. 'It's a bit too warm for me.'

'We'll see land soon,' said the dove in her gentle voice. 'It's some days since I found the olive branch, and the heat of the sun must be drying up the flood waters.'

The eagle, who was flying high above them, looked at the empty seas around the ark, sighed and shook his head.

'It's very sad to think that we are the only creatures left alive.'

But the eagle was wrong. There were plenty of other creatures still alive in the world, for the seas were teeming with fish, and when the ark first began to float, they swam around it with interest.

'Funny old vessel, when all's said and done,' sniffed a shark.

'Not like anything I've ever seen,' said a flounder. He dived underneath. 'I'm surprised it floats,' he said,

when he had finished his inspection.

'Do you see all those animals?' asked a sardine.

'There'll be rich pickings when it sinks,' the shark grinned, showing razor-sharp teeth. The smaller fish swam hurriedly away.

'Do you think it'll sink?' asked a whale.

'Bound to.'

'Well I've never seen anything like it,' said a dolphin. 'What do you think it is?'

'A flash in the pan,' said an electric eel.

'Come away, children! You might get hurt,' said a large porpoise, guiding a school of smaller porpoises well out of range.

As the days passed and the ark did not sink, most of the fish lost interest and swam off. But the dolphin stayed, wondering what such a strange vessel was doing there.

'Where do you think it's going?' she asked a sea urchin.

'Search me.'

'It's very peculiar. There's no sail and no one's rowing.'

And as the rain fell and water covered the earth, the dolphin remained with the ark.

'I'd love to be on that boat,' she said to a passing halibut.

'Well I wouldn't,' the halibut replied. 'Not with all those fish-eating animals on board. You mark my words,' he continued, severely. 'No good ever came of mixing with animals.'

But the dolphin wasn't listening and the halibut swam away.

For forty days and forty nights, while the world was covered with grey skies and driving rain, the dolphin swam beside the ark. When the rain stopped and the sun came out, the birds streamed out into the brilliant blue sky and the animals and insects crowded onto the roof. The dolphin swam closer and wished and wished she could join them until at last she could bear it no longer. She waited for a big wave and, as it bore her upwards, she leaped high into the air.

She landed on the deck, right on top of the tiger.

'Oouf!' said the tiger. 'What hit me?'

'Is God throwing thunderbolts?' asked the lizard.

'I'm sorry,' said the dolphin. 'I didn't mean to squash you.'

'Hello,' said Mr Noah. 'Where have you sprung from?'

'The sea.'

A group of interested animals had gathered by this time and were circling the dolphin warily.

'Just look at that!' said the donkey, in amazement. 'This voyage has been full of surprises. No sooner have I met all the wonderful animals, insects and birds on the ark, than a fish drops in!'

'I'm not a fish,' said the dolphin. 'I'm a mammal.'

'You're a stowaway,' said the goose in a sharp voice, 'and you shouldn't be on this ark at all!' She stretched her long neck and began to hiss.

'You mustn't do that,' said Mr Noah. 'The dolphin is our guest.'

'Uninvited,' said the mongoose.

'Have you paid your passage?' demanded the aardvark.

'No.'

'Neither have you,' the lizard retorted to the aardvark, 'so pipe down.'

'We're God's chosen,' said the goose, self-righteously. 'God didn't choose you, so I think you should leave.'

'I'm sorry, but I'm not sure I can.'

'What made you come aboard in the first place?' asked Mr Noah. 'Was it an accident?'

'Well, no,' said the dolphin. 'Not really. I've followed you the whole of the voyage. It's been very boring since the world was flooded, for there haven't been any bays for me to explore and I like doing that.' She sighed.

'It looked such fun on the ark.'

'Fun!' said the monkey sourly. 'That's the last thing I'd call it.'

'I think it's very nice to meet a dolphin,' said the elephant. 'Not the kind of creature one gets to meet in the normal course of things. I'm pleased to make your acquaintance.'

The dolphin was a source of great interest to the animals, insects and birds on the ark and a steady stream of them visited her. But as the day wore on and the hot sun beat down on the dolphin's back, she began to get tired.

'It's been very nice meeting you all, but I think I'd like to go home now,' she said at last in a faint voice. 'I'm not feeling at all well.'

Mr Noah touched her. Her skin felt dry and rough.

'Water,' she said in a thread of a voice. 'I need water. My skin mustn't dry out.'

'I'll see what I can do.'

Mr Noah went to his cabin to talk to God.

'Speak to the elephants,' God said. 'They'll help.'

So Mr Noah spoke to the elephants.

'Leave it to us,' they said and leaned over the side of the ark. They drew water up into their long trunks then turned and sprayed it over the dolphin. The dolphin began to revive.

'I've been very silly,' she told Mr Noah. 'If I was in the sea now, I'd be riding on the waves and playing with the other dolphins. Why did I ever think it would

be more fun on the ark?' She gazed longingly at the sea.
'I wish I could go back.'

Mr Noah again talked with God.

'How can I return her to the sea, God? She's so
heavy and slippery as well. I'm afraid of hurting her.
But I don't think she'll survive for long on the ark.'

'No,' said God. 'She must go back. Why not talk to
the largest animals on the ark? They might help.'

So Mr Noah called a meeting of the biggest and
heaviest animals on the ark. The rhinoceros, the
hippopotamus, the bison, the oxen and all the other
large animals joined the elephants beside the dolphin.

'What's this all about?' asked the rhinoceros.

But no one answered, for the ark was beginning to tilt under the weight of the heavy animals crowded to one side. And as more heavy animals came, the ark tilted further. Slowly the dolphin began to move. Faster and faster she slid towards the edge of the deck until, with a splash that caused a wave of water to soak all the large animals, the dolphin slid into the sea.

'Quickly!' Mr Noah called to the heaviest animals. 'Half of you hurry to the other side of the ark, or we'll capsize!'

And with a noise like thunder, the bison and the rhinoceros stampeded round to the other side and the ark righted itself.

'I feel seasick,' groaned the emu.

'Thank you!' called the dolphin, ducking and diving. 'Thank you, Mr Noah! Thank you, elephants and animals! Is there anything I can do in return?'

'If you see land, come and tell us!' Mr Noah called back, and the dolphin raced away.

'So that's that little excitement over,' said the tiger, resuming his perch on top of the roof the following day.

'It was very upsetting,' said the emu. 'I was sure we were going to capsize.'

'But it made a change,' said the aardvark. 'Added a bit of fun to an otherwise dull and boring life.' He looked out to sea. 'No sign of land.'

'No sign of anything,' said the goose.

'But land can't be far away,' insisted the dove in her

gentle voice. 'I did find a leaf and a twig, remember.'

The emu sniffed. '*And* you've never let us forget it.'

'You're only jealous because you didn't find it,' said the aardvark.

There was a sudden commotion on deck. The dolphin had returned and was swimming up and down.

'Land!' she called. 'Tell Mr Noah I've found land!'

Mr Noah came running. 'Where? Is it far?'

'Not far,' said the dolphin, turning and swimming off. 'Follow me!'

'We can't! We can't steer the ark.'

The beaver shook his head. 'What did I say?' he asked of no one in particular. 'Big mistake not having oars.'

The dolphin swam back. 'Can't steer the ark?'

'No,' said Mr Noah. 'We've no sail and no oars.'

The dolphin swam off.

'I know that there must have been a good reason for not bringing a sail or oars,' said Mr Noah that night as he sat in his cabin and talked to God. 'Otherwise you would have told me to take them. So please don't think I'm doubting you, for you've brought us all this way in safety. But it is a bit hard to know that land is so near and we can't get to it.'

'Now Noah,' said God, 'have a little more faith.'

'Yes,' said Noah. 'I'll try.'

Early the following morning, when Mr Noah was on the roof of the ark watching the sun come up and flood the world, he saw a disturbance in the water. It looked at first like huge waves, but as it grew lighter, Mr Noah could see that the waves were caused by shoals and shoals of fish who were following the dolphin.

'We've come to guide you to land,' called the dolphin. 'Now then everyone, surround the ark!'

Four dolphins, two sharks, a killer whale and a whole school of porpoises surrounded the ark.

'All right?' called the dolphin. 'Now SWIM!'

And together the fish began swimming, with the ark in their midst.

'Thank you!' Mr Noah shouted.

'Thank you, thank you!' shouted the animals and insects, while the birds flew high up into the air.

Swiftly the ark was carried along and soon Mr Noah could see land.

'The current will take you, now,' said the dolphin. 'Goodbye, Mr Noah. Goodbye elephants. Thank you for saving my life. Goodbye animals. It's been fun meeting you all.'

With a last wave of her fin, she and all the fish veered off and swam away.

'Thank you, God,' said Mr Noah as the ark finally began to head towards land.

13

THE RAINBOW'S END

The ark came to rest with a bump on the top of a mountain called Ararat.

'We've landed!' called the giraffe, who was up on the roof at the time. In his excitement, he tumbled down the steps and fell into the great hall.

'Are you sure?' asked the panther.

'Ouch!' said the giraffe, rubbing his long neck. 'Of course I'm sure!'

'Hooray!' shouted the elephant, lifting up her trunk.

'At last!' exclaimed the cheetah. 'A really good, fast run in the fresh air!'

'A gallop across the wide open prairies!' the bison shouted.

'A wallow in a first-rate watering-hole!' thundered the rhinoceros.

'A stream or two to dam,' said the beaver in a quieter, more uncertain voice.

The animals looked at one another, then fell silent.

'And yet...' the beaver began.

'Exactly,' said the cheetah.

'Just what I was thinking,' said the elephant.

'What do you think it's like out there?' asked the ostrich. 'Is it—well—safe?'

'Being on the ark might have its drawbacks, but at least it's safe,' said the emu thoughtfully.

The tiger looked at her in astonishment. 'I thought you hated it here. You've moaned about it often enough.'

'Well, I know,' the emu agreed. 'But that's just me—always moaning. You shouldn't have taken any notice.'

'We didn't,' said the tiger.

'Quiet!' called the eagle. 'The great moment has arrived!'

'I should have said that,' complained the lion. 'After all, I am Mr Noah's deputy.'

'*One* of Mr Noah's deputies,' added the tiger.

Mr Noah, his wife, his three sons and their wives entered the big hall.

'Strange that,' said the fox. 'Something I've never thought of before.'

'What?' buzzed one of the wasps.

'Why do you think God allowed Mr Noah to bring his entire family on the ark? After all, there's only two of each of us.'

'Favouritism,' said the monkey sourly. 'God likes humans better than he likes us.'

'Oh, I don't think so,' said the beaver. 'I think we've all been very privileged and shouldn't complain.'

'Hear, hear,' said the emu, and everyone turned to stare at her in astonishment.

'Eight,' said the owl suddenly.

'Eight what?' asked the beaver.

'Eight humans. Mr Noah, Mrs Noah—that makes two. Their sons, Shem, Ham and Japheth—that's three more, making...' he thought for a moment, 'five. And their three wives—that makes eight.'

'Wonderful!' said the monkey sarcastically.

'It is, isn't it,' said the donkey sincerely. 'I couldn't do sums like that in my head.'

'I am rather good at sums,' said the owl, blinking his eyelids rapidly.

'I think God let Mr Noah bring all his family because there was far too much work just for two of them,' the dormouse said thoughtfully. 'Looking after us can't have been easy.'

'If it hadn't been for Mr Noah, we would never have been saved from the flood,' added the beaver.

'If it hadn't been for humans, God wouldn't have had to flood the world in the first place,' muttered the jackal quietly, but no one was listening, for at that moment Mr Noah opened the great doors of the ark.

Sunlight streamed in. The animals made a rush for the exit.

'Line up there!' snarled the tiger, suddenly remembering his position as one of Mr Noah's deputies. 'Two by two, that's right. No pushing or shoving. Let's show God that we know how to behave.'

The animals lined up and Mr Noah led them off the ark and onto dry land.

'It feels... kinda funny,' said the pig, trotting uncertainly on the thick green grass. 'Don't you feel it should be rolling from side to side?'

'Oh, how good to stretch my legs!' said the bison. He looked down at the ants, scurrying beside him. 'Can we give you a lift anywhere?'

The ants stopped scurrying. 'No,' said one of them

uncertainly, 'for I don't know where we're going.'

And indeed all the animals and insects were stopping, looking round them almost fearfully.

'It's just a bit… well, frightening to start again,' said the mole. 'We could start digging, I suppose, but somehow…' her voice trailed off.

Even the birds had alighted on the ground, as if afraid to fly away.

'It's all so… so *big*,' said the bison. 'Silly, really, when I've been complaining about the ark being so small.'

'We've grown used to being on the ark,' said the leopard.

'*Too* used to it,' said the rat drily. 'Like prisoners being scared when they're given their freedom.'

'And *you'd* know all about prisons,' said the peacock. He unfurled his bright tail then shivered. 'The wind feels strange on my tail,' he said and closed it with a snap.

Everyone fell silent and turned to Mr Noah, and Mr Noah, who had spent the morning preparing a long farewell speech, looked at the animals, insects and birds and forgot every single word. He felt just as anxious as they did.

'I could almost wish we were still on board the ark,' he thought.

Suddenly a cloud passed in front of the sun. The fox looked up.

'Don't look now, but I think it's going to rain,' he said. 'Here we go again, everyone back on the ark!' There was even a note of relief in his voice.

The animals began to move towards the ark as the first drops of rain fell.

'Is it true, Mr Noah?' bleated the goat. 'Is the flood starting again?'

'Hey, wait a minute,' said the pig, stopping suddenly. 'I thought we'd gotten through most of the food. How are we going to survive?'

The animals stopped and stared at Mr Noah.

'Is it all starting again, God?' Mr Noah asked.

'Look up, Noah,' said God.

Mr Noah looked up. Although it was still raining, the sun had come out from behind the cloud. Clear against the sky, Mr Noah could see a shimmering light. Red, orange, yellow, green, blue, indigo and violet, the glowing rainbow formed an archway which stretched across the sky.

'This rainbow is a sign of my promise to you,' God said. 'Never again will I send a flood to destroy the earth. Whenever you see a rainbow in the sky, you will be reminded of this promise. Now speak to the animals, Noah. Give them hope for the future and strength to meet the challenges that lie ahead.'

'But I'm frightened, too, God,' said Mr Noah. 'And I've forgotten the speech I'd prepared.'

'Just speak from your heart,' said God. 'And leave the rest to me.'

So, for the last time, Mr Noah stepped forward and held up his hand. The animals fell silent.

'Animals,' Mr Noah said in a loud voice. 'Insects and

birds. My friends. I've only ever tried to do what God wanted, and sometimes I didn't do very well. But it's God who's really been in charge and always will be. Just trust in God and you'll be all right.'

'Will we ever see you again?' asked the dormouse.

'You know where to find me,' said Mr Noah. 'You're welcome at any time.' He looked at the fleas. '*All* of you.'

With that he held up his hands and blessed them, then called goodbye as the animals went their separate ways.

'So now it's all over, God,' Mr Noah said, a little sadly, when the last animal had gone.

'No, Noah,' said God. 'Look around you. It's a new beginning.'

As Mr Noah looked around him, the rain stopped, the clouds rolled away and the sun shone in a brilliant blue sky. Raindrops glittered and sparkled like gems on the fresh green grass and hung dripping from the leaves of the trees.

And as Mr Noah stared closer at the round droplets of water, he suddenly caught his breath. For there, reflected deep in the heart of each tiny drop of rain, was the image of a rainbow.

'Thank you, God,' said Mr Noah contentedly. 'It's good to be home.'

All Lion books are available from your local bookshop,
or can be ordered via our website or from Marston
Book Services. For a free catalogue, showing the
complete list of titles available, please contact:

Customer Services
Marston Book Services
PO Box 269
Abingdon
Oxon
OX14 4YN

Tel: 01235 465500
Fax: 01235 465555

Our website can be found at:
www.lion-publishing.co.uk